Non

Jonas Lane

Best wishes
Jonas Lane

First edition. October 26th 2017
This revised edition. November 5th 2024

Copyright © 2017.2024 JONAS LANE

Written by JONAS LANE

Published by Jonas Lane Publishing

First published 2017.
This revised edition published 2024.

©2017.2024 Jonas Lane.

Publisher's Note: This is a work of fiction. Certain characters and their actions may have been inspired by historical individuals and events. The characters in the novel, however, represent the work of the author's imagination. Any resemblance to actual persons, living or dead, is entirely coincidental.

The moral rights of Jonas Lane to be identified as the author of this work has been asserted by him in accordance with the Copyrights, Designs and Patents Act, 1988.

All rights reserved. No part of this publication may be reproduced, stored in a retrieval system, or transmitted in any form or by any means, electronic, mechanical, photocopying, recording or otherwise, without the prior written permission of the author and publisher.

Cover Design by James, GoOnWrite.com

Nona's Ark

Jonas Lane

First edition. October 26th 2017
This revised edition. November 5th 2024

Copyright © 2017.2024 JONAS LANE

Written by JONAS LANE

Published by Jonas Lane Publishing

This is a work of fiction. Similarities to people, places or events are entirely coincidental.

Nona's Ark

About the author

Jonas Lane is an acclaimed author and educator who is never happier than when he's telling a tall tale, whether it's to his readers or the children he teaches daily. He has written several books across a number of different genres, including the hugely popular Lord Thyme-Slipp series, regularly fusing historical fact with hysterical fiction.

Although predominantly classified as a children's and YA author, Jonas Lane's books appeal to all ages, his reading audience being those that are still young at heart. Every novel Jonas has had published so far has been rated as 5-star by those who have reviewed them, young and old.

In addition to writing novels, Jonas Lane is also a published poet and has written articles both locally and nationally, as well as being a former television and music critic for the Bedfordshire Times newspaper.
Jonas lives in a North Bedfordshire village over the hills and far away…

Visit Jonas at his website
www.jonaslaneauthor.com

For Meris,

*The angel who helps me
fight the demons away.*

JL x

Chapter 1 – Kingston

"To put it bluntly, the bottom line is…you're running out of money. There's not much more that I can do for you I'm afraid…" Roger Kingston looked all his seventy-five years as his accountant gave him the news, news he'd expected but dreaded. His rheumy blue eyes teared up as his worse fears were realised as Kingston took off his glasses and gave them a cursory wipe with his handkerchief whilst trying to regain his composure.

"Are you absolutely sure, John?" Kingston quietly asked, stroking his thick white moustache as his accountant, John Stafford, gathered up the paperwork which covered the desk in his office. Stafford nodded sadly as Kingston looked towards his grandson Lewis, who was stood by the window, looking out across the zoo grounds which were bathed in the bright, early evening sunshine caused by the clocks having sprung forward the weekend before.

"I've checked every invoice, every credit and debit, in and out, twice, Mr Kingston. The zoo is no longer able to support itself, and…" Stafford gently laid a hand on Kingston's forearm, "your own personal fortune has diminished considerably over the past year. The pot's almost dry, Mr Kingston. It's time to give up on the Kingdom, you can't continue to bail it out any longer. You have to let it go."

Lewis Kingston frowned as he watched the accountant smile reassuringly at his grandfather before Stafford continued.

"Shut the zoo down, then sell the land off to the highest bidder. I promise you there'll be plenty of interest in redeveloping it."

"Never!" Kingston snapped, violently pushing his chair out from under the desk.

However, old age was steadily catching him up as he shakily stood and rested his hands on the desktop to steady himself.

"Property developers are soulless vultures," Kingston growled, "they'll raze this place to the ground and then turn it into a theme park, shopping centre, housing estate or the like."

John Stafford thought Kingston's head was going to explode as it turned an angry shade of red as though preparing to volcanically erupt. He watched nervously as Lewis turned to look at his grandfather, his skinny body almost twisting around in his over-sized and ill-fitting cheap designer suit.

"I think you might be over-exaggerating just a tiny little bit there, Grandad," he said quietly.
"Oh, I am, am I?" Kingston barked.
Lewis ran his hand through his greasy, slicked backed hair. "Yes, Grandad and you're working yourself up whilst you're at it," Lewis replied, concern etched across his face. "Remember what your doctor's told you - you have to remain calm and not get stressed or upset, OK?"
Kingston sighed and nodded, quietly proud of the fact that his grandson was actually thinking of someone other than himself for once. It was true, even though - in his head - he still felt like a young man, his heart and general health were not what they once were, causing enough of a concern for his doctor to repeatedly warn him to avoid anything that might raise his sky-high blood pressure any further than it already was.
"I appreciate that you're just looking out for me, Lewis, but this place is my life," Kingston replied, continuing, "I'll never willingly sell Kingston's Kingdom, not whilst I have an ounce of breath or fight left in me!
"Then retire instead, Grandad, let me take full control and run the zoo for you," Lewis smiled.
"You, run Kingston's Kingdom? You couldn't run a bath, let alone a business!" Kingston scoffed, "No, the zoo belongs to me and me alone and it'll stay that way until the day I die. Good night, gentlemen."
Stafford took that as his cue to leave as he closed his briefcase and smiled sadly.
"Well, whilst I admire your determination, Mr Kingston, there's only so much I can do," the accountant sighed, "unless there's a major change and upturn in the zoo's fortunes, we'll have no option but to close the gates of the kingdom for the very last time come the end of the year."
"Thank you for your honest, professional advice as always, Mr Stafford," Lewis firmly replied, "but you heard my grandfather - the zoo is not for sale anytime soon. Now, let me walk you to your car. Night, Grandad."
Kingston, having sat again spun his chair around to gaze out of the office window himself, raised his hand and waved.
"Night kiddo, see you tomorrow," he said without once turning to look at his grandson or accountant.

Lewis opened the door and held it for the accountant to leave the room first, pausing to look at the shock of white hair which protruded over the back of his grandfather's chair. He smiled and shook his head before walking out after Stafford, closing the door behind them.

The two men slowly walked down the metal stairs which led away from Kingston's office, before turning to where their two cars sat side by side in the car park directly behind it. Stafford stood his briefcase on the ground as he fumbled around in his suit pocket for his car keys as Lewis Kingston stood watching him, a cigarette now stuck between his crooked yellow teeth as he cupped his hand around his lighter to shield the flame from the soft evening breeze as he tried to light the cigarette.

"I've done all I can, Lewis, I've bled the old beggar dry," Stafford shrugged as he pointed his key fob in the direction of the car, "your grandfather has got no other option but to close the zoo and sell up."

Lewis drew long and hard against the now lit cigarette before exhaling again, a large plume of acrid, grey smoke rapidly filling the face of the bald accountant, causing him to cough heavily.

"Well, it still ain't enough, is it?" Lewis sneered, making himself look even more weasily than he usually did, "We're against the clock here, John. We can't hang about for too long or the deal will be off!"

"But you heard what he said, he's not going to close Kingston's Kingdom," Stafford replied as he climbed into the front of his old, battered estate car.

Lewis leant down and peered through the open car window, his nicotine-stained teeth now clenched tightly together.

"Then, we'll just have to find another way to persuade him to change his mind and sell the zoo then, won't we?" he grinned.

From his office window, Roger Kingston watched as the two cars below it followed one another out through the electronic gates to join London's busy rush hour traffic.

Safe in the knowledge that he was now alone with his thoughts, Kingston got up from his chair, drew the blinds and finally left his office, locking the door behind him. He gingerly made his way down the stairs before turning to walk through the one place that he always felt at peace in, especially after the zoo was closed for the evening.

Once his nightly walks were something he looked forward to, passing the many different enclosures where the animals he'd rescued or saved from extinction were settling down for the night. But recently, he took no pleasure in looking at the rare or endangered species he'd sworn to always protect, time, fortune and circumstance now catching up with him.

"Night, Mr Kingston," came a voice from behind a shutter at one of the kiosks dotted around the various paths which wove through the zoo grounds. Kingston raised a hand in acknowledgement to the unknown and unnamed worker as he silently continued on his way whilst lost deep in his thoughts.

Soon, he'd reached his destination, climbing a steep incline which led to a railing overlooking the largest enclosure, deliberately designed and built to be the central point of the zoo. Kingston leant on the top of the railing, the exertion of the climb causing him to cough and wheeze as he tried to regain his breath. He rubbed his chest, as though trying to wipe away the dull and uncomfortable ache he now felt there.

To the right of him, Kingston noticed a tall, lean man, much younger than himself, slowly approaching him. The zoo owner smiled at the sight of the dark-haired man pushing the wheelbarrow, now recognising the unmistakable figure of Kingston's Kingdom's head zookeeper who was dressed from head to foot in black, his heavily tattooed arms rippling from the effort.

"Owaya, Mr Kingston?" the man said, his thick Irish accent curling around every vowel and consonant he spoke, "And what a fine night it is an' all!"

Kingston turned his head and smiled slightly.

"Good evening, Doyley, still here? I thought you'd have handed over to the night shift by now," he replied.

Doyley swept his long, black fringe back over his head, leaving the two shaven sides of it jealous by the gesture.

"Dat Oi have, but Oi had a little time to kill before Oi goes on me date tonight, so Oi tought dat Oid give meself a head starts for der morning," the zookeeper winked.

"Who's tonight's lucky lady then?" Kingston asked, trying hard to make polite conversion.

"Her names Dana," Doyley smiled, "Oi connected with her via

the dating site *Geek2Geek."*

"What will this be then, Doyley? Blind date number 51?" Kingston smiled. He'd had the dubious pleasure of listening to all the dating misfortunes Doyley had encountered in his long and desperate search for *Mrs Right*.

"The seventy-terd," Doyley replied matter of factly before continuing, "Oi tink dat dis one might be der one dough. We've a lot in common, more shared interests."

"That's promising. So where are you taking her tonight? Dinner?" Kingston asked, adding, Chinese? Indian? Italian?"

Doyley shook his head, quickly sweeping back the hair that had fallen out of place again.

"St. Martin's Hall. Her local UFO society is holding their annual meeting dere. Well, it's more of a reunion party really," the Irishman replied, "Dana's an abductee, yer know. Yep, she's not seen some of her friends for quite a while, at least not since der mothership left. Dey've lost touch a bit with one another..."

Kingston laughed at the welcome bit of light relief on an otherwise depressing day.

"I suppose it's hard to FaceTime with someone in Alpha Centauri!" he quipped.

But the irony was lost on Doyley.

"Dey have no need for dat," he replied seriously, "been given telepathic abilities dey have, though dey it's about as reliable as der feckin' mobile signal around here dis time of night…"

Doyley paused for a moment and glanced down at his watch before continuing,

"Well, Oid best be off - don't want to be keeping der future Mrs Doyle waiting now, do Oi?" he winked, "Night den, Mr Kingston."

"Night Doyley," Kingston replied as he watched the lanky Irishman swagger down the path behind him, whistling a tune which sounded pretty similar to the theme of the classic 90's sci-fi show, *The X Files*.

Kingston reached into his inside jacket pocket as he turned back to the railing, pulling a vape from his pocket before putting it in his mouth.

As he pressed the button to activate the battery, he glanced at the sign which was mounted on the wall to the far left of the railing which introduced the public to Elsie, Kingston's Kingdom's most beloved and longest staying resident…

ELSIE - QUEEN OF THE KINGDOM.
Kingston's Kingdom has been a sanctuary for the Borneo Pygmy Elephant since the zoo first opened its gates to the public over fifty years ago. She was the first of these rare and endangered elephants to ever be born in captivity and has been loved and cared for here ever since.
Elsie has watched over us all from her vantage point here - at the very centre of the Kingdom – every single day since then. But don't be alarmed if you don't see her in her enclosure when you first arrive here – Elsie might be on one of her daily walks she likes to freely take around the Kingdom!'

Kingston smiled ruefully before his wracking cough returned, the sound of it attracting Elsie to come out of her shelter and lumber toward the side of her enclosure.

The old elephant raised a trunk to the railing and pointed the tip of it up towards where her owner and friend now stood. Kingston gingerly stepped up onto one of the crossbars that ran across the railings, again rubbing his chest with one hand as he waved the vape he held at Elsie with the other.

"Like this do you girl?" he whispered, "Liquorice flavour. Doc says I've got to pack up smoking. He's right mind – it's a filthy, disgusting, habit, a dying relic of the past, a bit like the two us, eh Elsie? Says that this vape might help-"

But before he could continue, Kingston turned to where he thought he'd heard a rustling sound coming from some nearby bushes. He paused momentarily, looking closely at the thick, green foliage. However, seeing nothing untoward there, he slowly turned to continue to chat with the old, brown elephant.

"They want to take the zoo away from us, old girl," Kingston sighed sadly.

Somehow Elsie seemed to understand the sadness in his friend's voice and trumpeted gently as though to comfort him. She turned and began to slowly lumber away from Kingston, sweeping the floor with her trunk, as though looking for something lost.

"What you searching for, Elsie?" Kingston asked, "Don't you go fretting now, I promise that I won't let anyth-"

But Kingston stopped again, turning his head slightly, now almost certain he'd heard yet more movement in the undergrowth behind him.

Nervously, he ran his hand across his sweat-covered forehead, as he felt a tightness rapidly building in his chest before breathlessly saying, "Hello? Is anyone there…?"

Elsie had eventually walked back into her shelter in her attempt to find a gift to cheer up her friend and master. At last, she found one - a large stuffed toy she'd been given years before by Kingston himself.

Normally elephants like to play with tyres or balls to either fight boredom or to keep themselves occupied, but Elsie had always been a little bit different to others of her kind. She'd loved playing with her cuddly toys and snuggle blankets ever since she was a calf. Now she happily turned with the giant, battered old teddy bear and slowly made her way back to the enclosure wall, raising her trunk back up to the railing with the toy animal wrapped in it. But Elsie stopped in her tracks upon seeing that her friend was no longer stood there, the empty black railing now silhouetted against the evening sky.

Elsie dropped her eyes in disappointment, back towards the bottom of the wall where they immediately fell upon the white-haired figure who now lay there, motionless. The old elephant cautiously walked over to it and nudged it gently with her trunk, which was still wrapped around the bear, hoping to wake the figure from its apparent slumber.

Nothing…

She nudged again, but still there was no response.

Carefully laying the bear down beside the figure, Elsie slowly made her way back into her shelter and picked up her favourite pink blanket. Dragging the blanket along the ground behind her as she walked, Elsie returned to the figure, lifted the blanket up and laid it over the figure's back and legs, pushing the sides of it in against the still motionless form, as though she was tucking her baby in for the night.

There Elsie stood guard and watched over the lifeless figure, long after the zoo lights had dimmed, and darkness had silently claimed the night…

13

Chapter 2 – Nona

Life don't get any better than this, Nona Lancaster thought to herself as she made her way home from after-school football practice that day. Even though the Easter holidays were due to start in just a couple of days, Nona found that for once she wasn't wishing her school life away.

As she walked the final couple of narrow streets towards her house, Nona felt as happy as she'd ever been, finally feeling like she was accepted and that she belonged somewhere else other than the safety of her own home.

Feeling wanted is all that anyone ever truly wants but it was especially important to this particular elfin-like twelve-year-old. Growing up as an only child to a single mother was commonplace for many on the numerous housing estates in Ventham, near Woolwich, in the south-east of London and, in the main, it didn't bother Nona.

No, her only real problems had stemmed from being caught slap-bang in the middle of two totally different school systems which failed to meet her needs, gifts and talents.

Nona had been due to attend the infamous Walter Raleigh Secondary School when she'd finished primary school along with many of her closest friends. However, the prospect of going to a school with such a notorious and fearsome reputation for poor behaviour and ill-discipline had filled many a child and parent with both dread and horror, all the other alternative schools close to it having been closed in the years before due to official government inspections deeming that they all required improvement…improvements which were never funded, so never occurred, hence their enforced closures.

The only other alternative nearby was one of the new grammar-centric schools that had been created by a right-wing government obsessed with academic brilliance and league tables. But these blue-tinged *'super-schools'* only accepted pupils if their grades were sky-high and they managed to pass the entrance examination set them, an entrance exam designed to be passed by those who were naturally academic or were financially blessed to be tutored to succeed. Unfortunately, Nona was neither.

That's not to say that she wasn't smart, on the contrary - she was bright in a very different way, meaning that Nona was never going to excel in traditional subjects such as English, maths or science.

However, when it came to physical activities, well, that was a different matter altogether…

Nona was a natural athlete, easily and comfortably turning her hand to any game or sport, her lack of size and physique compensated by a fierce and determined competitive streak as well as a passionate will to win instead.

No matter which sport she played or took part in, both in and out of school, Nona could hold her own against anyone, no matter their age, size or gender. But it was when playing football that Nona's star shone brightest…

Named by her mother after one of three Roman goddesses who legend states helped to control a life's destiny, Nona had, at first hated, then reluctantly got used to being teased with various nicknames created by using random words which rhymed with her unique and highly unusual first name.

Nona the loner was the first moniker ever given to her at school, mainly due to her initial shyness when first meeting people. This then changed to *Nona the moaner* which soon fizzled out too as, generally, Nona seldom complained, even when she had very good reason to.

Other nicknames soon followed, some random, some nonsensical but all rhyming with words made up by the poor young poets on the primary playground. However, the nickname which had eventually stuck stemmed from the first time Nona ever had a football at her feet.

It was in year 4, when one of the free community coaches that the local FA used to send into schools to promote the sport took Nona's class for the very first time during PE one afternoon.

Although naturally sporty, Nona had never really played the game properly before, having only kicked a football around a few times on the street near her house with one of the neighbourhood latchkey kids. But Nona was always keen to take part in any physical activity, her thirst to play, learn and improve the driving factor in anything she did.

At first, Nona had stayed close to the other girls in her class, dribbling the ball back and forth across the pitch, gently tapping the ball between her feet, easily managing to keep it under control as though it was attached to her foot with a short piece of invisible string. Of course, the over-confident boys who dominated both her class and year group had moved well away from the girls and were busy showing off the skills, tricks and bad habits they'd learned from watching overpaid and undertalented footballers on the television, paying little to no attention to any of the commands the FA coach was giving them.

But Nona listened intently, hanging on every word the coach said, using different parts of her foot to guide and caress the ball across the uneven surface of the school field. Eventually, Robbo, as the community coach preferred to be called, gathered all the children together.

"Right, kids, today was just a taster session for me to get to see what you all can or can't do," Robbo smiled, his face creased and tanned from hours spent coaching out in all weathers, "so, to finish off we'll play a game of *Cops and Robbers*. I need a volunteer to be a cop and go stand in the centre of the pitch."

A host of excited hands went up, along with numerous cries of *'Pick me...pick me...'*

Finally, Robbo settled on the largest boy and loudest boy in Nona's class – Brian Blunt.

Typical, Nona thought as she looked at the smug face of the boy who now stood in the middle of the marked-out field, hands on his hips as though he owned the place which was typical of him as Brian Blunt arrogantly thought he was better than everyone else at everything he did.

However, it wasn't all his fault though, his friends, family and teachers all going out of their way to tell him how brilliant he was and couldn't believe he could be anything less than perfect in all that he did or attempted, which he often wasn't in both his attitude and behaviour towards others he deemed to be lesser than him.

"OK, so, I want everyone else to line up on the side of the pitch with a ball. You are going to be the *robbers,*" Robbo began to explain before continuing, "All you have to do is dribble the ball from one side of the pitch to the other, past Brian who's the *cop...*"

"That sounds easy enough!" Luca, one of Nona's best friends, cheerily piped up.

Famous last words, Luca-baby, Nona thought, smiling as she shook her head at her friend's misplaced optimism.

"It should be if you use all of the skills I've shown you today," Robbo smiled back at Luca, adding, "However, be warned - if you lose control of your ball, Brian can kick it away to *arrest* you and put you in *jail* at the side of the pitch!"

The colour immediately drained out of the little Italian's face at Robbo's revelation.

"He can kick the ball away from me?" Luca gulped.

"Not quite so easy now, eh?" Robbo laughed as the same look of despair filled most of the other children's faces - all except Nona's, whose face was now fixed in a grimace of fierce determination instead.

"Ready, steady, go!" the coach shouted, dropping his raised arm to indicate that the game had started.

Suddenly, the field became a hive of fevered activity as almost thirty children of various shapes and sizes, with a variety of different coloured balls moving before them, sped towards the large boy who was standing opposite, waiting for them to approach. Brian Blunt began to move forward at first looking like King Cnut trying to hold back the sea.

However, the adult-sized schoolboy was far more successful at stemming the tide of children who threatened to wash over him, quickly kicking errant balls away, easily weeding out the weak from the strong.

At the end of their first pass across the pitch, only around twenty or so children remained.

"And now back again! Robbo shouted, encouraging the children to run across the pitch once more, back to where they'd all originally started the game from.

Nona kept at the far end of the line, cleverly keeping out of trouble, easily moving the ball ahead of her as Brian ploughed through the rest of the class, balls and children haphazardly flying in every direction.

Soon, the remaining twenty children were whittled down to just eleven by the end of the second game with most of the girls now sitting down beside the pitch with an occasional boy glumly sat and interspersed between them.

"Again!" Robbo bellowed, waving his arms in front of him as though conducting the school orchestra rather than a football session in PE.

Brian cut a huge swathe through the remaining children once more, kicking the footballs away with great relish as he successfully reduced the numbers of active players even further, a total of seven children left with still a chance of winning, Nona included - the last girl standing…

"Come on Blunty!" one of the boys who'd quickly fallen by the wayside shouted from the side of the pitch, "you can't let a girl beat you!"

As she looked down the line of the children who were left, ready for the next dash, Nona suddenly realised that she was now standing alongside the best footballers in her class - possibly the year group - all of whom had played for the school team at one time or another. However, she quickly brushed away the thought from her mind as she waited for Robbo to drop his hand to signal the start of the next relentless attack.

"Come on Nona!" Luca cheered as he watched his friend spring from the goal line, like a 100-metre sprinter in an Olympic athletic final. This seemed to catch Brian Blunt completely unawares as Nona easily darted with the ball towards the opposite side, Brian having to content himself with claiming four balls off the boys who had all unwisely and unsuccessfully decided to charge directly at him, foolishly believing that there was safety in numbers when doing so..

Nona was now in the final three children who remained unbowed and undefeated. That in itself should have been a moral victory for her but now she'd got this far, Nona's eyes were firmly fixed on the prize….

Brian Blunt deliberately seemed to ignore her as she next made her way across the pitch, his focus and attention centering on one boy who he scythed through when claiming the ball, leaving the unfortunate child theatrically rolling around, clutching his ankle.

"Not so hard in the tackle, Brian," Robbo said firmly, helping the unfortunate boy off the pitch, the pupil's ego seemingly more bruised than his ankle by the way that he quickly managed to recover and jogged off, none the worse for wear from his encounter with Brian Blunt.

In truth, Nona was relieved at the enforced break in play to have a much-needed rest, her lungs having only just about recovered by the time the football coach ordered them to go once more.

But, yet again, Brian Blunt totally ignored Nona, instead chasing around the pitch like a rampaging bull seemingly determined to steal the football away from Deano, his best friend who was an equally obnoxious and arrogant boy from her class.

Finally, after several failed attempts to pass Brian, Deano lost control of the ball, allowing his jubilant opponent to ferociously kick the football away in triumph, thrusting both fists in the air to celebrate his hard-fought victory.

"The final then – Brian versus Nona!" Robbo declared, adding, "if Brian wins, then the boys will all earn ten praise points. If it's Nona, it's ten each to the girls!"

Suddenly, with such an important and valuable school reward at stake, the noise from the children looking on dramatically increased as they began to chant their support for their champion, the girls for Nona, the boys - except Luca of course – raucously cheering for Brian Blunt.

"You're going down, Lancaster," Brian sneered, trying to psych out his much smaller and slighter opponent, "they'll be calling you *Nona the groaner* when I'm finally done with you!"

Nona, as was her way, didn't respond. Instead, she quietly waited for the off, tapping the ball back from one foot to the other as she looked at the brute of a boy who stood a little way in front of her. Although Nona appeared cool, calm and composed outwardly, inside her stomach was turning somersaults and flipping cartwheels.

Robbo raised his hand and paused for a moment before swiftly dropping it and shouting "Go!"

Nona flew towards Brian Blunt like a greyhound let loose from its trap, her agile and nimble body diagonally racing across the pitch, hoping to catch her opponent off balance and off-guard. But Brian was far too sharp and had already anticipated what she would do and was now rapidly closing the distance between them. *I won't make it past him - for such a big guy he's so damned quick!* Nona thought, her eyes focused on the line ahead of her, all too aware that Brian had now leapt towards her, lunging two-footedly in her direction, *unless...*

Brian Blunt thought that he'd timed his leap to perfection with both of his feet landing squarely on the football, sending it hurtling off in one direction, with Nona violently flying off in the other.

Ball and man, his brute of a football coaching father had taught him, *fairly or unfairly - it's all the same in the grand scheme of things, son, as long as you don't get caught...*

What Brian Blunt hadn't counted on though was the fact that as he was just about to land his illegal tackle, Nona had already stopped - dead in her tracks - and placed the sole of her left foot on top of her football.

She smiled as she watched Brian's smug, toothy grin suddenly turned into a look of utter anguish as Nona quickly dragged the ball back just before he made contact with it. This caused Brian Blunt to toboggan past her across the pitch on his bottom, skidding haphazardly away from her whilst Nona casually dribbled the ball forwards to stop it on the touchline to claim victory and the prize offered by Robbo for the girls.

Having eventually come to an unceremonious stop, Brian Blunt rolled over and lay there, his shorts having ridden up to expose his bare, grass-stained butt-cheeks, angrily thumping the ground in frustration as he watched Robbo enthusiastically applaud Nona's efforts whilst warmly shaking her hand.

"Well done, you really owned him there, Nona," the coach grinned.

That's the nickname that Nona liked most and the one that had stuck with her - *Nona the Owner*...

After that, Nona's football career had gone from strength to strength the more she trained and developed her skills, both in and out of school.

From being the only girl playing in the now mixed school football team – much to the disgust of the likes of Deano and Brian Blunt - to being selected for the FA Girls Development Centre, thanks to Robbo's personal and professional recommendation. She'd then received invitations to join a couple of the Women's Premier League teams in southeast London, but had turned them both down, saying that she was quite happy playing for Ventham Girls FC, this after her school had sent the club's flyer home one night. Nona had begged her mother to go to the open trials they'd had at the end of the season before last. Of course, Nona's mother had agreed, as usual, always wanting the very best for her only child. No sooner had the trial with Ventham Girls FC ended than Nona was quickly signed up, soon becoming their star player as the side reached the local cup final last year, narrowly losing it despite Nona's best efforts.

However, Nona's brilliant individual performance in the cup final wasn't completely in vain as the medals that day were handed out by Lindy Smith, one of Ventham's most famous daughters, who'd captained the England Women's Football team on many occasions.

At the end of the presentations to the winning team, Lindy had set out to find Nona and her mother to ask them which school Nona attended as it was obvious to the former international player that Nona had a very bright future ahead of her. When Nona's mother had explained that Walter Raleigh Secondary was to be her daughter's next school, Lindy had looked absolutely horrified at the prospect.

"Leave it with me, I can't promise anything, but there may be another and much better option for her," Lindy had said.

Nona and her mother left the tournament in a state of stunned disbelief whilst excited at the slight glimmer of hope of a better education that they'd been dangled in front of them.

However, after their initial optimism and excitement, Nona and her mother had begun to think that it was all just false hope, another pipedream when, true to her word, Lindy Smith rang them a couple of days later.

"I'm phoning on behalf of the Trinity Free School," the former footballer had said, "we'd like to offer Nona a place in Year 7 this coming September…"

Lindy had then gone on to tell Nona's mother that as Ventham had always had a strong history and reputation of producing many talented performers and sports people for such a small and disadvantaged area over the years, a group of powerful and influential people had set out to create an all-through free school for children aged from five to eighteen to attend to help nurture future generations of natural, untapped talent.

Nona's mother had continued to listen intently as Lindy explained how she had helped to lend her name and support the original application for funding which had been made backed by a petition raised by parents, teachers, businesses and community groups, helped along by a couple of local MPs hoping to win favour at any forthcoming election.

It was felt by all those involved in the proposal that there was a real need and desire for a performance-based school in Ventham, solely based upon its children's unique talents and abilities, along with its famous and illustrious past - a school where pupils were to be judged on their individual skills and talents rather than just on an academic basis.

Keen to avoid any more controversies for their deeply unpopular government, the Department of Education had swiftly agreed the application. However, they did so by attaching a key condition to it - the new school was to use the numerous empty school buildings which were already available on a privately owned and disused site in Ventham. These had been left vacant by the sudden closure of its only private and government-backed super-school, which had been failing miserably for years, despite numerous interventions, bailouts and backhanders...

Those behind the new bid quickly agreed to these conditions and Trinity received the green light to open at the start of the next academic school year.

By the end of their conversation, Nona's mother was also convinced of Trinity's potential and, after fully explaining everything to her daughter, so too was Nona.

Although reluctant to leave all the friends she'd made at her primary school behind when they eventually went to the secondary schools allocated to them, the prospect of attending a specialist school with a curriculum totally themed and planned around sport and the creative arts was just too good to be true for Nona.

However, her fears at having to leave her school friends were quickly dispelled the following day when, upon confiding to her two oldest and closest friends, Nona found out that they too had applied for - and been accepted - Trinity Free School themselves. Luca, who'd appeared in a couple of well-known and highly popular nappy advertisements as a baby and Keeley, an extremely talented singer and dancer, had explained to Nona that they'd each applied for and been given a place at Trinity some weeks before, but hadn't known how to break the news of their acceptance to Nona, let alone each other. But on discovering Nona's news, they could both hardly contain their happiness and delight.

"That's so freakin' awesome!" Luca had said, smiling broadly.

"Looks like we're stuck with each other for another four years at least!" laughed Keeley, hugging her two best friends to her...

Now, as she happily replayed the moment her life had so dramatically changed for the better in her head, Nona slowly turned the corner and happily began to walk past the sprawling, maze-like estate which her home sat on the fringes of, wearing a calm and contented smile on her face.

It's been an incredible year so far, Nona thought as she walked up the tiled path which led to the small, end-terraced house she shared with her mother, Mel, and her great-grandmother.

Turning her key in the lock, Nona smiled at the thought of all the exciting things she could now look forward to for the rest of her school days at Trinity. Little did she know then that, soon, life was never, ever, going to be the same again...

Chapter 3 – Bad News

"Hi Mum, I'm home!" Nona yelled as she stepped through the door into the narrow little hallway of the terraced house, accidentally slamming the front door behind her. She tightly screwed her eyes up, ready for her mother to shout and tell her off yet again for waking her great-grandmother, but for once the firm rebuke never came.

"Mum?" Nona loudly repeated, throwing her school sports bag down against the foot of the stairs before walking into the kitchen which was directly at the back of the house.

There she found her mother sat at the table, a copy of the local paper – the Ventham Gazette - open before her on the tabletop.

"Hi hun," her mother, Mel, said, looking up from the paper. Where normally a huge smile often filled her face at the sight of her daughter, now a fixed and forced grin sat in its place.

"Sit down, sweetheart, there's something that I need to talk to you about..." her mother said quietly.

Nona immediately knew that something was wrong.

Normally, her mother was so bright, bubbly and chatty, unable to sit still for more than five minutes, Nona often wondering if she had ADHD as she wasn't entirely sure where her mother always got her boundless energy and enthusiasm from.

Today was different, however...

"Mum, what's the matter?" Nona asked anxiously.

"Sit down Nona," her mother said, patting the chair beside her, "it's your grandfather, he's..."

But before she'd even managed to finish the sentence, Nona's eyes had wandered onto the page of the newspaper which was sat open in front of her mother, a big and bold headline instantly jumping off the page at her, with a grainy, captioned photograph of her grandfather directly beneath it...

KING OF THE KINGDOM DEAD!
End of an era as London zoo legend dies aged 75.

"No, it's some sort of mistake...that's not real..." Nona gasped, collapsing onto the wooden chair beside her mum, "It's not true – it can't be..."

Nona could feel the tears push at the back of her eyes, ready to come flooding out and cascade down her face as her mother placed a reassuring hand on her knee, rubbing the top of it gently with her thumb as she nodded.

"Nona, I'm so sorry, baby," she whispered.

The initial horror and shock Nona had angrily felt now gave well to full-blown and abject sorrow and grief as Nona flung her arms around her mother's neck as she began to sob uncontrollably, her chest and shoulders heaving up and down as her despair poured out of her.

"It's OK, let it go, let it all out," her mother said quietly, stroking Nona's back gently, her heart almost breaking in two from seeing her precious daughter so distraught without being able to help her or take any of her terrible pain away.

After a while, when her sobbing had slowly started to subside, Nona began to loosen her grip on her mother and slowly slumped back into her chair, her breathing still interspersed with fitful sobs. Her mother stretched a sleeve down over her hand and, lightly gripping it between her fingers, used the base of her palm to wipe away Nona's snot and tears. Mel stood and looked down into her daughter's blood-shot, blue eyes.

"Cuppa?" she smiled.

"Yes, please - three sugars," Nona replied numbly.

Mel Lancaster came from a long list of Lancaster women who firmly believed that tea was the remedy to all evils. She smiled and flicked the switch on the rapid boil kettle which sat on the counter behind the two of them.

"How, Mum?" Nona asked, not wanting to read any more of the article, her grandfather's kindly face, now permanently frozen in time, smiling back at her.

Mel sat down again and stretched a hand across the table towards Nona, who clutched it gratefully.

"They're not exactly sure, sweetheart," she replied, "all they do know is that one of the night shift staff found him lying on the floor of the elephant enclosure."

"Elsie's enclosure?" Nona asked, a confused look now filling her tear-streaked face, "Why was Grandpa in there?"

The shrill beep of the kettle caused her mother to pause momentarily before replying.

"Again, no one knows for sure," Nona's mother said, adding, "but

they do think it may have been his heart and that he might have fallen over the railings. It's too early to say for definite though."
Nona nodded sadly as her mother stood once more, opening the cupboard to take out two large but chipped mugs, as well as a couple of tea bags which she put into them before pouring the boiling water onto them. She poured some milk into the mugs and began to dunk the teabags up and down as Nona looked at the photograph again and tried to remember the very last time she'd seen her grandfather.
Last Christmas, Nona wondered, *and the time before that...?*
Her quiet thoughts were broken as her mother slid the steaming mug of tea in front of her. Nona took a huge mouthful from it, the tea causing the bits where your top and bottom jaws meet to ache just a little at its bitter sweetness.
"You all right, hun?" her mother asked as she took a huge gulp of the brew herself.
Nona, looking over the top of her mug as she drank from it again, nodded slowly, surprised to find that, despite her initial shock at the news, she now felt quite calm. She was sad, of course, but the pain at the sudden loss of her grandfather loss was somewhat lessened due to the extremely the very complicated nature of Nona's strained relationship with her father's family...

Nona had never actually met her real father - he was out of the Lancaster family picture long before Nona had screamed her lungs out for the very first time at Ventham General Hospital over twelve years before. Her mother, Mel, had met Ben Kingston a little over a year prior to her birth whilst working as a waitress in a cocktail bar, trying to earn some extra money whilst she completed her teaching degree.
At first, Mel had thought Ben far too old for her, she having just turned twenty-two, Ben being nine years older. But eventually, after he'd relentlessly worn her defences done with his smooth-talking cheekiness and easy-going charm, they'd begun to see one another three or four times a week.
Eventually, after completing her teacher training, Mel had managed to get a job covering a teacher on maternity leave at a primary school in the autumn that year and was staying at her grandmother's house nearby in Ventham whilst she tried to save for a deposit for a flat of her own closer to the school, who'd

promised to take her on when the next full-time vacancy arose, so impressed was the headteacher with Mel's teaching ability.

Everything was going swimmingly both personally and professionally for Mel - new man, new job, with a new home planned.

Then, just after the last of the New Year fireworks had fizzled out and been long forgotten, Mel discovered that she was pregnant with Nona. Initially, Mel was stunned as she hadn't planned on becoming a mother at such a young age. But it wasn't too long before the shocked surprise had changed to turned to joy and delight, Mel excitedly ringing Ben to tell him their good news...

Except Ben didn't share her happiness – on the contrary, he calmly and callously told Mel that it was all over between the two of them as he didn't want or need *another* baby.

Unsurprisingly, Mel was both hurt and confused by the rejection. "What do you mean, *another baby*?" she'd screamed down the phone at him once her pain had turned into anger.

It was then that Mel learned that Ben was already married and, to make matters even worse, already had a nine-year-old son of his own.

After several minutes of arguing with one another, followed by Mel's tears and desperate pleas, Ben curtly and coldly told her to '*never call this number again,*' before the mobile phone line went dead. That was the last time Mel ever spoke to Nona's father...

Initially Mel felt a numbed state of shock at the fact Ben had been lying to her all the time they were together and that her *'soulmate'*, as he always referred to himself whenever they were alone together, was nothing more than a liar and a cheat.

Naturally, her grandmother had tried to console her as best she could, telling her that *'no man is worth your pain, cariad,'* but Mel was in pieces, unable to eat, sleep or work, much to the frustration of her school and its headteacher.

After a week of moping about and feeling sorry for herself, as well as a few more tough-talking pep talks from her grandmother, the fiery Lancaster gene kicked in once more, Mel deciding to phone Ben's mobile number again, determined to let rip and to give him a real piece of her mind. Having steeled herself to hear his voice once more, Mel was completely taken aback to hear the icy clipped, tones of a much-older woman answer on the other end of the line instead.

"Er, can I talk to Ben please?" Mel stuttered.

"He's not here at the moment," came the cool, emotionless response, "can I take a message for him?"

Thrown and now totally caught off guard, at first Mel was unsure as to how best to respond.

However, the woman's next seven words soon made the decision for her...

"Is that Mel Lancaster by any chance?"

"You know who I am?" Mel answered.

The woman laughed, not the type of laugh which naturally comes out when something tickles or amuses you. No, this was a taunting sound, one of distain and disgust, the sound that someone makes when laughing *at* you...

"Oh yes, my husband Ben has told me all about you and your wicked and deceitful ways, Miss Lancaster," she sneered as she continued, "I believe he has politely asked you not to bother him ever again, so I strongly suggest you take his advice - we don't take too kindly to money-grabbing, gold-diggers around here. Goodbye."

And with that, the line suddenly went dead. Stunned, Mel stared open-mouthed at the phone.

"Well, if she thinks she's going to get away with talking to me like that, then she's got another thing coming..." Mel muttered angrily as she jabbed the redial button on her mobile phone.

She stood waiting for the call to connect, tapping her foot impatiently, only to be met with a monotonous and repeating three-note tone, followed by an automated message which said, *'Sorry, but the number you have dialled has not been recognised- please try later...'*

Mel never did call back. She decided there and then she and her baby would be better off without the lying, cheating presence of Ben Kingston in their lives. Of course, it helped massively that Mel's grandmother had also told her that she could live with her for as long as Mel wanted after the baby was born as her widowed grandmother would be glad of the company.

However, when Mel finally plucked up the courage to tell her school that she was pregnant, her headteacher was less sympathetic, telling her that the next full-time position, which she'd been promised was hers when it became available, Mel would now have to apply for if she wanted to stay with the school after her temporary contract had ended.

Therefore, it came as no great surprise to Mel when she wasn't even shortlisted for a teaching post which was advertised to start the following September, so she left at the end of that academic school year, much to the distress of the pupils and staff she'd made such a positive impact on.

When Nona was born in the following October, it left Mel having to juggle being a new mum with whilst working various part-time jobs leaving Nona with her grandmother as she tried to make ends meet. Not once did she ever see or hear from Ben nor did Mel ever receive a single penny of child support from him, despite repeated attempts and requests by various agencies on her behalf. For the first five years of Nona's life, her family consisted of Mel, Mel's grandmother and Clive, Mel's childhood best friend. And that was more than enough for the little girl. Although money was tight, and times could sometimes be a little tough Nona was blessed to be bathed in love by all those closest to her.

The first real contact Nona ever had with her father's family was shortly after her fifth birthday. She was at home, in the front room after finishing school, watching one of those TV shows which seem to think that kids need to be spoken to in baby terms as they aren't intelligent enough to be spoken to properly, when there was a loud knock on the front door.

"You wait here a moment, sweetheart," Mel had said as she got up from the sofa beside her to go answer the door. In truth, Nona didn't notice her mother leave the room as she stared intently at the weirdly coloured creatures that were singing and dancing on the TV screen in front of.

Mel quickly turned to check back on her daughter and smiled to herself before answering the door. On the doorstep stood a smartly dressed, slightly portly and elderly man, a large black car parked across the road behind him, its driver still sat with his hands firmly gripping the steering wheel in his gloved hands.

"Oh, good afternoon," the man said, nervously, playing with a small package he held in his hands, "does Miss Melanie Lancaster live here?"

"She does," Mel replied suspiciously.

"May I speak with her please?" the man nervously asked before sweeping a hand through his thinning but neatly parted coarse, white hair.

"You are," Mel replied, crossing her arms in a slightly defiant manner as she leant against the doorframe.

"Who is it, Mummy?" Nona's curiosity had, by now, got the better of her as she stood, both arms curled around her mother's leg as she looked up into the face of the kindly looking man.

"Hello - are you Santa?" Nona asked innocently.

The man smiled sadly, his eyes beginning to well up with tears. "No, my dear, sadly not," he replied quietly before continuing, "however, I do believe that I am your grandfather. May I please come in?"

Although initially taken aback by the man's revelation, at seeing the excitement on her daughter's face, Mel nodded and grudgingly gestured for the man to come in. Instantly, Nona took the man's hand and led him to the sofa, patting where he should sit as she climbed up beside him, Mel perching on the edge of the armchair which sat in the opposite corner of the room. The old man placed the package he held down on the floor beside the sofa, before turning back to look at Nona.

"So, I take it that you're Ben Kingston's father then?" Mel finally asked after watching the man sit and chat to Nona for a few moments about the TV show she was watching.

The man nodded, a sudden wave of sadness immediately wiping the smile off his age-worn face.

"Sorry, yes, I'm Roger Kingston," Kingston stroked a hand across the back of Nona's head as she popped a sweet into her mouth. "she looks so much like my Ben did when he was a little boy..."

"Why now, after so long?" Mel said, trying hard to contain the anger which was beginning to boil up inside her.

Kingston stopped stroking Nona's hair and clasped his hands together in front of his bushy, white moustache, as though praying as he took a deep breath as though composing himself.

"Believe me, it was not by choice," he replied sadly.

"Really? So, what's stopped you contacting us before? Was my daughter not good enough for you to want to ever want to see or know?"

By now, Mel was struggling to contain herself, the pain, bitterness and rage she'd fought to keep so tightly under control for the over five years now violently threatening to erupt from her.

Roger Kingston shook his head repeatedly.

"Far from it - she's adorable," he smiled gently, "No, the sad truth of the matter is that I had absolutely no idea of my granddaughter's existence until quite recently…"

Mel quietly listened as Roger Kingston explained that as far as he'd ever been led to believe, Ben's son, Lewis was his one and only grandchild.

"I totally blame that damned wife of his," Kingston continued, "Ben and I were once extremely close, especially after his mother and I divorced and she returned to South Africa, leaving me to raise him alone. But when he hooked up with that witch of a woman, Ben changed, and not for the better, I might add."

Despite her initial misgivings, Mel was now beginning to feel slightly sorry for the old man who was sat opposite her, an arm wrapped protectively around Nona.

"Like I said, why now?" Mel again asked, her mood and tone now softening.

"Ben died in a car crash a little over a year ago." Kingston sighed wearily.

"Oh my god - I'm so sorry, I had no idea," Mel replied, now feeling incredibly guilty for how she'd acted despite being taken aback by the news herself.

"It's OK, as I've already said, we'd grown apart over the years but the pain of his death is still hard to bear…" said Kingston, adding, "So, I've taken it on myself to try and spend more time with my grandson, Lewis, and repair a few family bridges before it was too late. He's just turned fourteen and is a bit of an odd bird to be honest with you, too much of his mother in him for my liking…However, I wanted to do the right thing by his father as he was my only grandchild - or, at least, so I originally thought…"

Kingston looked down at Nona, who looked back up at him, thrusting a love heart shaped jelly sweet into his face.

"Want one?" she asked innocently.

Kingston laughed loudly, a not unpleasant sound, as he gently took the sweet from her hand with his teeth.

"It'll play havoc with my dentures, but it'll be so worth it! Now, where was I…?" he asked.

"You were about to tell me why you're here?" Mel reminded.

"Yes…yes…" Kingston nodded, "well, you see, Lewis and I were going through his father's personal belongings a few weeks ago. His mother wanted Ben's study cleared out as she wants to turn it into a day room to entertain her cronies…"

Roger Kingston tutted as he continued to speak, trying to lick the sticky remains of the jelly off his false teeth.

"I offered to help as I thought it might be difficult for Lewis to do all of it on his own," he continued, "it was while I was going through Ben's desk that I found these..."

Mel watched as Kingston reached into his pocket and pulled out several official-looking letters, each addressed to his son, asking Ben to make child support payments to both Mel and Nona.

"I never asked for a damned penny - it was one of those government departmental officials who didn't want to help me when Nona was born who insisted we contact him," Mel said defiantly. "I've scrimped, scraped and paid my own way with no help from anyone and I don't want no help now!"

"That's not why I'm here," Kingston softly answered, "I must admit that, at first, it came as a complete shock to me to find out I had another grandchild. Did Catherine - Ben's wife - know anything about you and the baby?"

Mel nodded angrily. "Oh yes!"

"Doesn't surprise me, she's a cold and callous heart that one," Kingston replied, "Lewis, on the other hand, he still has no idea. When we've been alone together, I've discreetly asked him in passing if he knows anyone names Nona. I can tell you that he doesn't as he just looked at me as though I've got a screw or two loose, not much different to how he and his mother look at me most days to be totally honest…"

Outside there was a toot from the black car that had been patiently waiting outside the front of the house.

Nona pulled back the net curtain to look out through the window.

"Nothing to worry about, my dear," Kingston smiled," it's just my driver telling me that our free parking has run out."

The old man slowly stood, sighed and looked at Mel.

"Look - I can't make up for all the wrongs that my son and his wife have done to you and your daughter…" he began to say.

"I don't expect you to. I appreciate that you've taken the time to come and meet her though," Mel replied, extending a hand towards Roger Kingston.

Kingston accepted it, gratefully clasping his free hand around it.

"If you'd allow me to, I'd like to get to know my granddaughter more though, if it's all right with you?" he asked hopefully.

Mel looked down at her daughter, who was now leaning casually against Kingston's leg, licking her finger and using it to get the last of the sugar out from her sweet packet.

After a moment or two, Mel sighed and nodded. "We'd both like that."

A huge grin broke out across Kingston's face as he wrapped Mel in a great big bear hug.

"Excellent, excellent. Thank you, thank you..." he replied, Kingston's voice trembling slightly as he spoke.

"I want a hug too!" Nona demanded, holding her arms up toward him.

Kingston knees clicked as he slowly knelt to hug her before reaching beside the sofa for the package he'd brought with him.

"Here - this is Elsie," he smiled, giving it to Nona who excitedly pulled off the lid of the box she's quickly unwrapped before taking out a small, brown cuddly toy from it.

"It's an ellyfunk!" Nona giggled as she cuddled the toy tightly to her.

"Yes, it is," Kingston nodded, "would you like to come and meet the real one who lives in my zoo someday, Nona…?"

Chapter 4 – Happier Times

Scientists say that you clean up the memory database in your brain every seven years, but Nona believed she would never forget the first time that her newly found grandfather ever took her to Kingston's Kingdom.

The big black car which had brought him into her life a just couple of weeks before arrived bright and early one Sunday morning, hours before the zoo was due to open to the public. Nona and her mother said goodbye to Nona's great-grandmother before climbing onto the plush grey seats in the back of the expensive, executive vehicle.

Kingston's Kingdom, built on the site of an old military armoury near Woolwich by the banks of the River Thames was just a few short miles away. However, even though it was the quietest part of the weekend, London's traffic slowed the morning traffic considerably making the journey for a five-year-old girl, excited to be seeing wild animals for the very first time, seem like it was taking forever. Eventually, to her and Mel's relief, the car pulled up outside the entrance to the Kingdom. Nona gasped as she gazed up at the multi-coloured sign that greeted their arrival. Pictured on one side of it was a small group of penguins, who seemed to be staring down a couple of Red Pandas illustrated on the other side of the sign, the animals cleverly appearing to face one another each time the sign rotated.

"Come on sweetheart, this way," Mel had said, taking her daughter's hand, leading her past the main ticket office to a door set some way back from it, "your grandfather says we'll get our own private tour today if we knock here."

Mel curled her delicate hand and made a fist, which she rapped hard against the heavy security door. She winked at her daughter as they stood there and waited, Nona now bouncing up and down with excitement. It wasn't too long before the early morning silence was broken by the cheerful whistling they begun to hear grow louder behind the door.

"Owaya?" the greeting was as long and mysterious as its owner, "Oim Alan Doyle, head zookeeper of dis fine establishment, but me friends call me Doyley!"

"Are we your friends?" Nona asked, looking up at him.

"With those bush-baby eyes of yours, how could Oi possibly say no!" Doyley chuckled, "In yer come, yer grandfather's running just a wee bit late, so he's asked me to be yer guide until he arrives. Follow me!"

Doyley's long trench coat violently swung behind him as he turned, twirling around him like a superhero's cape as the three of them walked through the entrance corridor, passing a set of closed doors which led to the ticket office and gift shop their right before they reached a second security door. Beside it was a keypad, exactly like one that had been next to the first door they'd walked through earlier.

"Both deese doors have der same six-digit security code," Doyley explained, "Mr Kingston says dat Oim to give it to yer so dat yer can come to the Kingdom any time dat yer want…"

Nonas watched intently as Doyley whispered the numbers to her and her mother as he slowly pressed each key. "Noine – tree – seven – tree – four – tree…"

Instantly, a loud buzzing sound filled the air as the door's lock clicked loudly before Doyley pushed it open, holding it wide enough for Mel and her daughter to pass through.

Nona's eyes bulged as she struggled to take in every sight which filled her view as she stared at the colourful 3D cartoon animals who were positioned at several different points on the wide pedestrian pathway which wound ahead of them, each comic creature each having its very own speech bubble attached to it.

In all, there were six animated animals, all aimed to provide visitors with information and directions as to where they could be found in the grounds of the kingdom, along with *'their friends…'*
The signs read:

> ***"Hi! I'm Penny the Penguin. Come see all our animal antics in the Wet and Wild Zone!'***

> ***"Ronnie the Rodent at your service! Why not come see me, along with all the other super furry animals who keep me company!"***

> *Touché the Turtle says "Be shell-fish and visit me and the rest of my gang! I promise that I am always at home, as are many of my neighbours!"*

> *"Elsie the Elephant here...No need for you to stand on parade with this pachyderm! Head to the centre of the kingdom to find me!"*

> *"My name is Diana the Monkey and I am one of the rarest monkeys in the whole world! Make sure that you swing by and see me and the rest of my family of primates. No need to hurry though as we're always hanging*

> *"It's me - Syd the Snake...S-s-s-slither my way and s-s-s-see all my s-s-s-scaly s-s-s-superstars!*

Grinning happily, Nona's head had snapped back and forth as she looked in every direction a cartoon creature pointed.

"So, where'd yer like to go first den, lil' lady?" Doyley asked, wearing a huge, toothy grin of his own.

"The penguins!" Nona shouted, much to her mother's delight and amusement.

"As you wish!" Doyley smiled, "Oil just radio der office and tell dem to let yer granddaddy know where to meet us…"

Nona was beside herself as she excitedly stood watching the penguins begin to gather before her on the small, fake Antarctic Island in their enclosure. In all, there were probably around thirty of them in total, milling around as one of the other members of the zoo staff was going about their morning routine whilst cleaning the penguins' home out.

"Now yer sees, Nona," Doyley began, crouching down to talk to

36

her, "dere are tree types of penguins in dere – Humboldt, Magellan and Yellow Eyed. Can yer see the difference between any of dem?"

Nona peered closely, trying to see if she could spot what the tall Irishman was saying to her. Then she excitedly as she nodded and pointed towards of the penguins.

"That one has yellow around its eyes and on the back of its head," Nona said, before adding, "and that one has two black lines between its head and chest."

"Excellent - can you see the third one too?" a voice gently said behind her.

Nona and Mel turned to find that Roger Kingston had now finally joined them.

"Hello there, sorry I'm late." he smiled, "I hope Doyley has taken good care of you both."

"That he has, thank you," Mel replied, winking at the tall Irishman.

"Glad to be of service," Doyley said, doffing an imaginary hat at Mel and her daughter, "now if you'll excuse me, Oi have to go and carry out me final inspections before der gates open to der public today. Laterz, ladies..."

Nona waved as Doyley strode off, his long legs causing him to swagger as he quickly went on his way.

"He's smaller, has a black back and a white front," she said suddenly.

"Who does?" Mel asked, peering as the figure of friendly Irishman grew more distant.

"The other penguin. There." Nona replied, pointing at a penguin who was now waddling its way across to a bucket of small fish at the side of the island, waiting patiently to be fed by a young girl who'd just finished cleaning the penguins' enclosure.

"Well done - you're very observant young lady!" Kingston laughed.

"Nothing gets past my Nona," Mel smiled, adding, "she's as sharp as a tack this one!"

"So it would seem!" Kingston smiled, holding his right hand out for his granddaughter to take, "Now - shall we go and see what else we can find on our travels?"

Nona hopefully looked at her mother, who nodded to say it was OK before taking it. However, to make sure that Mel didn't feel left out, she grabbed her mother's hand with her other hand one so that the three of them could walk side by side, holding hands together.

The next couple of hours quickly passed as Kingston took great delight in telling Nona all about the rare, wild animals he cared for in his small but beautiful zoo. Nona was transfixed and gasped in awe and wonder as she gazed upon the many species that he kept there. Aside from the penguins, there were Red Pandas, various types of monkeys, different non-poisonous snakes and reptiles as well as a whole host small cats and rodents, lemurs and sloths, amongst other animals.

But, of course, Nona's favourite had been Elsie. She'd whooped and hollered with delight as her grandfather had called the old elephant over to where they were all stood, Elsie lumbering gently towards them. Nona giggled uncontrollably as the tip of Elsie's trunk tickled her as the elephant hoovered up the peanuts Roger Kingston had rested in Nona's hand as she stuck it through the bottom of the railings towards the grateful elephant….

Later that day, as they all sat under a large umbrella in the zoo café after Kingston's Kingdom had officially opened to the public, Kingston looked proudly at the little girl as she tucked into a giant ice-cream her mother had bought her, along with two large lattes for Kingston and herself.

"Thank you," Kingston said as Mel sat down at the table bedside him.

"It's the very least I can do, Nona's had a fantastic time today," Mel said, taking a sip of her drink.

"No, not for the coffee - for this…" Kingston smiled, gesturing towards Nona who was now devouring the large piece of flaked chocolate that stuck out of the top of her ice-cream.

"I have to admit I was in two minds," Mel replied, adding, "but today has finally convinced me that it would be good for Nona to get to know you better, even if I don't necessarily agree with wild animals being caged or kept in captivity!"

Kingston coughed and nearly spat out the mouthful of coffee he'd just taken.

"Really? Why's that?" he asked.

"I just think that they belong in the wild roaming free," Mel replied before continuing, "not kept confined and in cages just for the public to gawp at or gain amusement from."

"I understand and respect your point of view of course, Mel," Kingston smiled, "but please rest assured that the animals who live here are treated extremely well, given the best care and are kept in the best conditions possible."

"But they should be at home, in the natural environment," Mel argued, keeping a calm tone so as to not worry Nona unnecessarily.

"I agree," Kingston replied.

"You do?" Mel said, slightly taken aback, "Why run a zoo then?"

"When I first opened Kingston's Kingdom almost fifty years ago, I admit that, at first, it was to make me money," Kingston explained, "The prospect of showing off exotic animals in south east London at a time when most people had never even seen one in the flesh was just too good an opportunity to miss! But over the years, I've come to realise that the kingdom could actually help the animals that we have here instead."

"How?" questioned Mel, a sceptical look etched across her face.

"Have you seen any lions, tigers, gorillas or bears here? Or crocodiles even?" Kingston asked, "They're all huge money-making attractions if you purely wanted to make a handsome profit. No, Kingston's Kingdom sole purpose since the early days has been to provide a safe haven to as many animals or endangered species as we possibly can find and save."

Kingston took another swig of his latte, which was growing colder by the second as he continued.

"Each animal I have here is either endangered or listed as extremely vulnerable out in the wild," he said, "all I'm trying to do is keep them from being hunted for sport of profit as well as becoming extinct."

"Making lots of money whilst you're at it!" Mel replied, half-jokingly.

Kingston looked at the feisty but sceptical look on Mel's face.

I can see why my Ben liked you, he thought, realising it was probably best to keep that opinion to himself.

"Quite the opposite, Mel," he eventually replied, "Kingston's Kingdom is self-sufficient meaning that it survives purely on what it earns from the paying public. Initially, I used some of my family's money to set up the zoo…"

Mel listened intently as Roger Kingston explained how his father had made most of the family fortune from the Kingston KG8, a sports car which was especially popular in the swinging sixties with all the film and rock stars of the time and that he was more than happy to give Kingston enough money to build the park.

"A few years back, we sold off the Kingston car line to one of those large German manufacturers for a pretty tidy sum!" Kingston continued, "But I've not yet needed to use any of the profit we made to have to keep the kingdom going. Occasionally, I'll throw a few quid in here or there if any of the animals need anything or if we find any other species that are in urgent need of help or rescue."

Mel smiled, seeming to accept that what the old man was telling her was the truth.

"So, what's next?" she asked.

Kingston looked at Mel, a puzzled look now filling his face.

"Well, there's the gift shop I suppose..." he began to reply seeming to be flustered slightly.

Mel laughed. "No, I meant what's next for you and Nona?"

Kingston looked at the little girl who now seemed to have more ice-cream around her mouth and nose than in the cone itself. He sighed deeply, a slight frown creasing his face.

"I'd like to see even more of her, of course. But it's..."

"Here we go..." Mel replied, bristling slightly as she started to stand, "but you have a grandson already...Save it - I've been here before..."

"Please, Mel, sit-down...Please allow me to finish," Kingston said calmly, "Yes, I do and that causes complications as he knows nothing of you or Nona. I can't risk upsetting him as there's no telling what that mother of his will do to try and turn him against me, just like she did with his father.

Kingston smiled as though trying to reassure Mel turning to look at Nona.

"However, I'd like to find a way to get to know my granddaughter a whole lot better - with your blessing and permission of course," he added hopefully."

So it was that Mel agreed that Roger Kingston would be free to come visit Nona any time he wanted to at their home and that, in time, he would be able to take Nona on days out alone, just the two of them, should he ever wish to.

At that point, Mel had thought that the old man was going to burst into tears as he threw his arms around her.

"Thank you, Mel," he whispered, wiping a stray tear from his eye as he bent to pick Nona up, hugging her tightly, ignoring the melted ice-cream which brushed against his ruddy cheeks and coated his bushy moustache…

Over the next few years, as Nona grew, so did her relationship with Roger Kingston, or Grandpa as she eventually started to call him.

At first, he'd call by the house every few weeks, always bringing her a different stuffed toy animal from the zoo's gift shop.

Then, as the trust between Mel and Kingston grew, he'd take Nona out for the day, just the two of them as Mel had promised him. Invariably, when he asked her what she'd like to do, she'd always insist on going to the zoo. Often Kingston would take Nona secretly behind the scenes there so that she could help feed the penguins or hold a lemur or some other cute and cuddly creature. One time, Nona even tried to help clean Elsie but ended up with more soapy water on her and her grandfather rather than on the gentle and friendly elephant itself.

As the visits became more and more frequent, Kingston would always plan them around times when there were very few others in the grounds of Kingston's Kingdom so as to avoid any awkward questions as to who the little girl he'd grown so fond of and was completely besotted with truly was. Kingston had even prepared a false backstory for Nona just in case he happened to bump into his grandson or daughter-in-law, ready to say that Nona was Doyley's niece should he ever be asked, which, fortunately, he never was.

Nona also knew to never call him Grandpa when they were at the zoo, always Mr Kingston, believing that it was because he wanted all the zoo workers to still respect him as their boss as they walked around the zoo grounds. When Nona was old enough to make her own way to the kingdom on her own, she'd use the code Doyley had given her and her mother to let herself in so that she could just freely wander around, saying hello to all the animals who'd become her friends over the years.

Whenever Doyley knew Nona was around, he'd secretly let her into some of the safer enclosures so she could sit or play with whichever animal was in there whether it was hanging out with

Louie, the gentle old orangutan, or sitting on the tyre swing, which Elsie took great delight in spinning the giggling schoolgirl around on.

Often, when Roger Kingston himself knew that she was at the zoo, he would always find a way of breaking away from whatever he was doing to seek out his granddaughter, often ending up in the zoo café, where Nona would stuff herself with all the *wrong things,* causing her to come up with random excuses why she couldn't eat tea when eventually returning home that night!

Over the past seven years or so, Nona had got used to seeing her grandfather regularly in this way. As she'd grown older, she'd often thought about asking him about her father as her growing curiosity about Ben Kingston tried to get the better of her but - out of loyalty and respect for her mother - Nona had never quite summoned up the courage to do so.

A couple of times though, Nona had tried to broach the subject with Mel but had quickly and predictably been met with the standard response from her mother of *"he never showed any interest in you, you were best off not knowing him."*

Still, it felt like there was this gigantic hole in her life, a missing piece of the Nona puzzle. At least by getting to know and becoming close to her grandfather had helped to ease some of that longing she felt slightly.

However, over the past twelve month, Nona and her grandfather had begun to see less and less of one another. Admittedly, she'd been busy with her new school and hadn't visited the zoo quite as often as she'd once done but even when she had, her grandfather was hardly ever there. And when he did manage to see him, it was only briefly, with Roger Kingston looking older and more stressed-out with each fleeting visit, especially the last time they saw one another at the start of the Christmas holidays.

Her grandfather had still been pleased to see Nona of course but had seemed and distant pre-occupied when the two of them sat in the café, politely chatting about everything, and nothing in particular.

Whilst giving him a massive hug and wishing him a Merry Christmas before leaving, Nona had noticed that her grandfather had hugged her more tightly and for longer than he'd ever done before.

Sniffing slightly, Roger Kingston had then reached into his back pocket, taking out a small white box from it which he placed into the palm of her hand.

"Open it," he'd insisted as Nona looked down at it.

"But it's not Christmas yet, Grandpa," Nona had argued.

"Ho, ho, ho, do as I say - I might be a little busy come Christmas Day!" her grandfather had then joked, referring back to their first-ever meeting all those years before.

Nona opened the lid and gasped at the small silver necklace it contained. Hanging from a fine and delicate chain was a small key, like one you'd use to open an old mortice lock.

"It was your father's. I found it when I was going through some of his things," her grandfather had said as he'd helped Nona to put on the necklace, "We used to call it the key to the kingdom. I thought you might like it."

Nona gently touched the key which now hung around her neck before throwing her arms around the old man.

"Thank you, Grandpa," she said, gently kissing his cheek, "I promise that I'll never take it off..."

Now, as she lay in her bed just a few months later, Nona rolled the tiny key in between her thumb and finger. She'd been so busy with her friends, football and new school that she'd not been back to the zoo nor seen her grandfather since that late December day. It wasn't too long until the bitter tears of grief and regret came flooding back again, staying with her until the small hours when, drained and exhausted, Nona finally fell asleep, hoping to see her beloved grandfather once more in her dreams...

Chapter 5 – Where There's a Will…

A tense but expectant silence hung over the waiting room of Leadbetter, Leadbetter and Mole, the Kingston family's solicitors three weeks after Roger Kingston had met his sad and tragic end. Gathered there, waiting to be seen by the firm's founder and senior partner were Kingston's grandson, Lewis, his mother, Catherine and John Stafford, the Kingston family accountant.

"How much longer is that bumbling old idiot going to keep us waiting for, Lewis?" Catherine sniffed, "Haven't we waited long enough as it is to hear Roger's will already?"

"Patience, Mother," Lewis replied, patting her gently on the arm, "the police had to be thorough when carrying out their investigations to be certain that there was nothing at all unnatural about Grandfather's death - it was bound to delay matters."

"Yes, dear, I understand all that," Catherine huffed, "what I actually meant was that our appointment was at 2 pm - now it's two minutes past that. You know how I hate to be kept waiting…"

Lewis looked across the room to where John Stafford nervously sat, raising his eyebrows toward him. The accountant was about to reply when the oak-panelled door to Alistair Leadbetter's office slowly opened. An elderly man stood there, holding the door handle as he peered out into the waiting room.

"Sorry to keep you all," Alistair Leadbetter mumbled, his voice croaky and worn by his advanced years, "Please, do come in…"

Slowly Leadbetter turned and began to shuffle back to his desk, the backless carpet slippers he wore on his feet being completely at odds with the expensive brown but lived-in checked suit he wore.

Lewis, his mother and Stafford quickly followed Leadbetter as he made his way back to a large, antique desk which sat directly in front of a row of bookshelves that stretched from floor to ceiling, a large double-doored cabinet dominating the centre of it.

The Kingstons sat in the two leather armchairs that faced the desk, leaving Stafford to stand behind Lewis and Catherine as Alistair Leadbetter gingerly sat down, a large farting sound immediately filling the room as he did so.

Lewis, Catherine and Stafford shot each other a disgusted look as the old solicitor wiggled his bottom, trying to get comfortable in his seat, his leather chair continuing to make a succession of raspberry noises as he did so.

"I'm most terribly sorry," Leadbetter apologised, "my piles are giving me such awful jip at the moment. I just can't seem to get comfortable on this damned inflatable rubber ring my wife bought me to help ease the pain..."

As if to further emphasise the point, another fart-like sound ripped through the room, causing Stafford to bite down on his hand in order to stop himself from laughing nervously.

"That's quite all right, Mr Leadbetter, we understand," Catherine lied, trying hard to hide her anger and disgust, "as you may appreciate, the past few weeks have been quite trying, especially for my poor son who thought the world of his late grandfather..."

To make sure that Leadbetter completely believed the lie he'd mother had spun and to help him understand his supposed pain and suffering, Lewis looked down into his lap and sighed deeply, his chest heaving heavily as he did so.

"Of course, Mrs Kingston, I totally understand," Leadbetter replied, adding, "but as there were no witnesses to what actually happened to your father-in-law that night, the police had to be completely satisfied with the circumstances around Mr Kingston's death, especially as the security camera which covers the area where Mr Kingston fell from that night was not working so they weren't able to use any recordings from it to help aid their investigations."

"Did you know that, John?" Lewis looking up towards Stafford, "Grandfather's money-problems were so bad he couldn't even afford to carry out any running repairs on the zoo..."

"It's a crying shame it ever came to this," Stafford replied, shaking his head mournfully, "I repeatedly warned him how grave his financial situation was, but he chose to ignore them…"

"Hmmm, quite…" Leadbetter responded, looking over the top of his rimless glasses at the two young men before him, "Nevertheless the police are now of the firm belief that Mr Kingston must have tragically taken ill that fateful evening. As you are all no doubt aware, he'd been complaining of chest pains for a number of weeks before and was awaiting the results of hospital tests carried out. Therefore, based on this and having carried out a full and detailed forensic investigation, the police have concluded that the chest pains must have reoccurred and, feeling faint and dizzy from them, Mr Kingston went to lean against the railings near where Mr Doyle, the zookeeper, had last seen him that evening. Sadly, they believe that he must have then collapsed, accidentally toppling into the elephant enclosure in the process."

Catherine reached into her handbag and dramatically pulled out a handkerchief, which she theatrically held to her nose.

"How dreadfully tragic," she sniffed, "It's true - Roger had been complaining about feeling off-colour in the days and weeks leading up to that terrible night. If only we'd known how fatal it would turn out to be for him…. At least we can be comforted by the fact that his last moments were in the place he loved the most."

Alistair Leadbetter turned his head slowly so that he now directly looked at her.

"Yes, indeed," he half-heartedly replied, reaching into a desk drawer.

"Well, I suppose that does now mean that we can all finally try to get on with our lives whilst honouring Roger's dear memory," Catherine said, her mood seeming to brighten considerably as she made to stand, thrusting stuck out a hand in the solicitor's general direction.

"Thank you for all the loyal service, advice and guidance you have given the Kingston family over the years."

"You're most welcome," Leadbetter replied, remaining seated, "however, wouldn't you like to hear the contents of Mr Kingston's will and testaments before you leave?"

Catherine laughed and looked at Lewis, who smiled warmly back at her.

"Oh, my dear Mr Leadbetter, we are all fully aware what Roger's final wishes were to be in the event of his death," Catherine said somewhat patronisingly, "he always said that should anything ever happen to him, then everything would be left to my dear son, Lewis – Roger's only grandson…

Catherine turned to smile proudly at Lewis, gripping his hand tightly in hers as he sweetly grinned back at her before she continued.

"I can assure you, Mr Leadbetter, that there were never any secrets between Roger, Lewis and myself."

"Is that so…?" Leadbetter replied, leaning back in his seat, causing the chair to *phut -phut* as more air was expelled from his rubber ring, "I take it that you are fully aware of the changes Mr Kingston made to his will a few months ago then?"

Lewis, his mother and Stafford looked at the old solicitor and then one another before fixing their eyes on Alistair Leadbetter again. "Changes? What changes?" Lewis demanded, trying hard to contain the panic which was now beginning to build inside of him. Leadbetter slowly spun his chair around to face the doors of the cabinet which stood behind him. He then stood and drew them both open to reveal a huge flat-screen television hidden within it. "As I said, your grandfather came to see me and gave me this," Leadbetter said without turning, holding up a small USB stick in his hand. He turned the television on before struggling to insert the memory stick into the side of the set.

"What's that?" Catherine screeched, her posh, clipped tones now suddenly sounding a strange mixture of false, harsh and common. Leadbetter sat back in his chair, the obscene noises it produced now completely ignored by all present as the image of Roger Kingston's office filled the television screen.

"It's called a Living Will and it contains Mr Kingston's final requests," Leadbetter explained, "oh, look, there's Roger now..." The huge and imposing figure of Roger Kingston appeared from the side of the screen as he made his way to stand in front of the camera he'd secretly used to make his final recording.

"Hope this works - I've never been good with modern technology..." Kingston chuckled as he sat on the edge of his desk at Kingston's Kingdom before deliberately looking directly into the camera.

"Hello there," he smiled broadly, "if you're all sat together watching this then I must have passed, so welcome to I'm *A Celeb-Deaddy - Get Me Out of Here!*"

Kingston paused and stared, a fixed grin on his face as he stretched out both arms beside him. Lewis, Catherine and Stafford stared back at him, mouths wide open, as Kingston continued to stand there as though frozen in time.

Suddenly, Kingston jumped towards the screen, causing them all to jump in their seats, Stafford, in particulars, beginning to whimper a little as he did so.

"Too soon for a jump-shock? Sorry, but I'm having the time of my death here!" Kingston laughed loudly.

Again, another pause before he continued to speak to the camera and the unseen audience behind it.

"I'd really love to see the looks on your faces right now, I bet you all look like you've just seen a ghost and, in some ways, you have! Is that what they look, like Alistair?" Kingston asked, directly looking in the direction of the old solicitor who was sat to the right of the screen nodding.

"How the hell can he see him, Lewis?" Catherine whispered shakily.

"He can't, Mother, it's all just a sick act - you know what a showman Grandfather was," Lewis replied sulkily.

As though somehow having heard their whispers, Kingston stood and looked directly to where Lewis and Catherine both sat.

"Hello Lewis…Catherine… I suppose you're both dying to know why on Earth I felt the urgent need to change my will?" Kingston said, leaning towards the camera, his face now perfectly framed by the screen.

Lewis and his mother sat silently as Kingston appeared to look then up and down, before slowly moving away from the screen again.

"As you're doubtless aware, my finances have taken quite a bit of a battering over the past twelve months. Haven't they John?" Kingston said, looking up and out as though gazing into the distance, almost exactly to where Stafford was standing. The accountant gulped and swallowed nervously as he slipped a couple of fingers between his tightly buttoned collar and his throat, wiggling it loose as though in desperate need for more air. Kingston again paused as though waiting for a response which never came before returning his gaze to the centre of the screen as he continued,

"During this time, John has kindly tried to help to restructure my finances, sometimes with my permission, often not…"

Stafford now grew even more uncomfortable by the thought that Roger Kingston had been aware of some of the financial and dealings he'd done behind his back.

"Don't worry, John, I totally understand," Kingston said, adding, "desperate times require desperate measures I suppose, so I finally decided to follow your good advice and privately sold my house just a few short weeks ago…"

Lewis and Catherine Kingston shot each other a worried glance before looking accusingly at the accountant who now appeared to be disappearing deeper into his oversized suit jacket.

"Is that true, John?" Lewis said angrily, "Grandfather sold Kingston Manor?"

"I – I don't know - he never said a word of it to me!" Stafford stuttered now hoping that a sinkhole would open up beneath him and swallow him whole.

"Oh, it's quite true," Leadbetter butted in, "Mr Kingston came to me saying that it was a private and personal matter that he didn't want to bother any of you with it."

Before anyone in the room could respond, Kingston interrupted from the screen behind the solicitor.

"Please don't worry though," he smiled, "I've made certain that all the money from the house sale is safe and wisely invested…"

If looks could kill then John Stafford would have now been standing alongside Roger Kingston at the Heaven's Pearly Gates, such were the venomous looks with which Lewis and Catherine shot in his direction as on the screen behind them an even wider huge grin broke out across Kingston's ruddy face.

"Let's face it – all of you told me that the zoo was struggling to pay for itself and that if there wasn't some dramatic improvement in its finances then we would have to consider closing it," Kingston explained, "Well, by unfortunately dying I've completely solved that problem as all the money from the house sale has gone to the zoo."

Catherine flung the back of her hand against her forehead and slumped in her chair, moaning loudly as she did so whilst Lewis just sat there, silently seething as he listened to his grandfather continue to speak to them from beyond the grave.

"There should now be more than enough cash for the zoo to keep running for the foreseeable future," Kingston said proudly.

By now, Catherine had almost slid off her seat while Lewis' face had gone the darkest shade of red you possibly could imagine, making it look like an angry pus filled zit which was now ripe enough to burst.

"However, I that you'd still like to make absolute certain that you get your fair share of your inheritance now, wouldn't you, Lewis?" Kingston asked, his face suddenly taking on a far more serious appearance, "after all, you are your mother's son, aren't you?"

"How dare he!" moaned Catherine who just lay there whilst John

Stafford waved a crusty handkerchief over her face, trying to stop her from passing out as Kingston suddenly laughed loudly, the booming tone of his laughter sounding hollow and tinny through the cheap television speakers.

"Everyone knows that the Kingdom is the jewel in the Kingston family crown, the value of the land it sits on alone makes it prime real estate, its owner instantly becoming a multi-millionaire were it ever to be sold," Kingston said seriously, " Admit it, Lewis, the thought of selling the zoo must have crossed the minds of your mother and you more than once or twice now, hasn't it?"

Despite himself, Lewis found himself nodding back at the image of his grandfather as Roger Kingston continued to speak to him from beyond the grave.

"Therefore, once every animal has lived out their natural life in the Kingdom, then you and your sister can sell it to the highest bidder, provided you both agree on the terms of the sale to then split the proceeds between you…"

Suddenly, Lewis lurched forwards in his seat, his knuckles white from where they'd been gripping the leather armrests, his fingernails having been dug deep into them.

"Sister?" Lewis spluttered, "Did he just say, *sister*? What the hell's the old duffer on about, Mother?"

He turned to look accusingly at his mother who had miraculously risen from the depths of her chair and was now sat staring - open-mouthed - at the screen.

"Oops! Sorry Catherine – my bad… I think that I may have accidentally let the cat out of the bag, so to speak…" Kingston said, mockingly putting a hand in front of his mouth, "I actually meant to say your *half*-sister, Nona, but I think I might have said more than enough already so I'll let your mother or Mr Leadbetter fill you in on all the details about Nona Lancaster, Lewis… now, where was I…?"

Kingston sat on his desk again and held his chin as though in deep thought. "Ah yes, as I was saying, there are conditions attached to you and Nona inheriting the zoo, which must continue to operate as one after my death," he explained, "first, the animals there all get to live out their normal and natural lives, so no funny business, just in case anyone gets any ideas about offing them…"

Roger Kingston stood and moved closer to the camera which was filming him before continuing.

"Any animal which does die must be properly and thoroughly be examined by a zoological expert to make sure there was no foul play involved in their death as any living creature found to have unnaturally died in Kingston's Kingdom by either Lewis or Nona's hand," he explained, "will mean that person loses their share of the inheritance, it automatically reverting to the other. Secondly, no animals are to be sold to any other zoo or private collection - there's no profit to be made from them. Thirdly, if either you or your sister want to sell their share of the zoo, you can only sell it to each other, not to any third or outside parties..." Lewis furiously sat staring at his late grandfather as Kingston sat back at his desk and sighed.

"Finally, try to be your own man, Lewis. Deep, deep down inside of you, there's some good...somewhere," he smiled hopefully, "don't become cruel, bitter and twisted like your mother - be more like your sister, sorry, half-sister, Nona..."

The last sentence Roger Kingston had uttered finally proved to be too much for Lewis to take as he took his shoe off and hurled it at the television screen, it ricocheting off the glass and back past Leadbetter's nose, almost taking his glasses clean off his head in the process. His mother, Catherine, placed a hand on her son's arm to try to calm and reassure him, but Lewis immediately snatched it away from her, as though he'd been stung by her touch.

On screen, Roger Kingston, his facial features now slightly distorted from where the heel of Lewis' shoe had damaged some of the LEDs in the television set spoke for one, final time.

"Right then, I'd best be off," he smiled, pointing a finger skywards, "there's a new kingdom I've got to go see...Play nice now, Lewis, and remember to follow the rules... Mr Leadbetter and I will be watching you carefully - very carefully...Until we next meet again...Bye, bye..."

With his final words still hanging in the air, the television screen froze on one final image of Roger Kingston, his huge shovel of a hand raised in one final and silent farewell to his stunned audience.

"Doddery old git!" Lewis snarled, petulantly sitting back into his chair. "Watching me carefully...Yeah, right!"

Suddenly, the paperwork that had been piled high at the side of Alistair Leadbetter's desk lifted and violently flew through the air, covering Lewis Kingston and his mother like gigantic pieces of wedding confetti.

"I'm most dreadfully sorry," Leadbetter apologised, turning to the window beside him, "let me just close this...oh, it already appears to be shut..."

Ignoring the solicitor's apologies, Lewis angrily stood, the sheets of paper now cascading off him, scattering across the wooden floor of the office.

"Good day, Mr Leadbetter," he snarled, turning to march towards the office door, "come, Mother, you've got some explaining to do regarding this new *sister* of mine – a sister I'm *so* dying to meet…"

Chapter 6 – Not So Happy Families

'Good luck!' the Gestapo officer said to the nervous looking young civilian returning his travel papers to him.
'Thank you," Flight Lieutenant Andy MacDonald replied as he went to board the bus…

"No, Andy – that's the oldest trick in the book! Now they'll know you're one of the prisoners of war who've escaped from the prison camp…" Nona's great-grandmother screamed at the classic war movie playing on the TV.

Nona had lost count of the number of times that they'd watched the classic war movie *The Great Escape* together. But almost as soon as she'd walked in from school that night, Nona had heard its unforgettable theme tune loudly playing and immediately knew that her great-grandmother would be sat on the sofa with a gigantic bag of jelly babies waiting for her only great-grandchild to come join her. And, as usual, she would, Nona finding it impossible to ever say no to the adorable, but formidable, old woman she simply knew as Mim.

Mim was more a grandmother to Nona than her real one who lived over two hundred miles away in Yorkshire, having moved there with her new husband a couple of years before Nona was born, seldom returning. However, her absence mattered little to Nona as Mim had more than amply filled the void her grandmother had left.

A slight woman in her late seventies with a shock of frizzy hair dyed a vivid purply-black to cover all her grey, Mim still retained her thick and beautifully lyrical Welsh accent despite having lived in Ventham for well over half a century.

Annie Jones, as she was christened, had met Nona's great-grandfather Ivan Lancaster when he was on a pony-trekking holiday in the Black Mountains in her early twenties, immediately falling head over heels in love with the dashing young RAF officer and so had followed him back on the very next train to Euston Station after he'd returned home to Ventham, much to her parents' disgust and disapproval.

They were soon married, a happy marriage lasting over forty years, living in the same house all that time, the house that Nona and her mother now called home too …

"I tell you this, see, it always frustrates me how he could make such a silly mistake, child, after all that hard work in digging the tunnels to escape in the first place," Mim sighed, still struggling to understand as to why the character would make such a careless and fatal error once again, "he wouldn't have made that blunder had he been a Welshman, mind…"

"Dinner will be ready in about half an hour you two," Nona's mother Mel called from the kitchen, trying hard not to laugh at her grandmother's strange observations once again.

Nona was just about to pause the DVD to ask Mim exactly how many times she'd actually watched *The Great Escape* before when their ancient doorbell rang, it now sounding more like a cat being strangled as the baldly distorted tones of *Greensleeve*s slowly ebbed away.

"I'll get it!" Nona shouted, jumping from the sofa, sprinting to the door in the hope that it would be one of her friends who'd come to call for her.

However, her excitement soon gave way to one of caution as she opened the door to find two men both dressed in suits stood there on the doorstep, one young and weasly looking, the other man looking as old as time itself being bent slightly at the waist as though carrying the whole weight of the world on his shoulders.

"Hello, you must be Nona," the young man said, his voice high and nasally.

Nona knew not to reply to strangers so immediately called for her mother instead, Mel soon joining her daughter on the doorstep, wiping her hands on the tea towel she'd brought with her.

"Miss Lancaster?" the older gentleman asked, producing a crumpled card from the pocket of his waistcoat before thrusting it towards Me, "My name is Alistair Leadbetter, I represent the estate of the late Roger Kingston. This is his grandson, Lewis Kingston. May we come in?"

Mel looked carefully at the business card and nodded cautiously, stepping back to allow the two men inside, Lewis aggressively pushing past the elderly solicitor before striding into the front room. There he was met by the fearsome sight of Mim standing before him, walking stick raised high above her head making her look like a wild Celtic warrior ready to attack rather that the meek and mild old woman she looked on first impression.

"We've nothing of value here, see, so you best be on your way, boyo if you know what's good for you!" she hissed loudly.

"It's all right, Mim," Nona called as she followed Lewis into the front room, Leadbetter slowly shuffling close behind, "he's not here to rob us, Mim, you can let him in."

Mim looked at Lewis, who had his hands raised to show her that he meant no harm. Slowly, Mim lowered the stick and sank back into the sofa.

"I don't trust him though, you hear?" she muttered, "His eyes are a bit too close together for my liking, see?"

Alistair Leadbetter stood and waited awkwardly until Mel returned from the kitchen with two chairs which she placed opposite the sofa for the men to sit on.

"Please," Mel said gesturing to the chairs, as she sat in the armchair near to where Nona and Mim sat together on the sofa.

"Thank you," Leadbetter replied as he gingerly took his seat, placing the briefcase he carried with him on his lap before unclipping its locks and opening it.

Lewis Kingston chose to remain standing, resting his back against a wall as he smiled at Nona and her family, his smile fixed firmly on his mouth without ever seeming to reach his eyes.

"Ladies," Leadbetter began, pulling a pair of rimless glasses out of an inside pocket of his suit jacket, "it is my solemn duty today to inform you about the contents of the last will and testament of Mr Roger Kingston…"

"…and, finally, should either sibling wish to sell their share of the zoo in the meantime, they can only sell it to the other, not to any outside interests or third parties…" Leadbetter concluded, removing his glasses as he looked across the room before continuing, "Do you have any questions?"

Nona, her mother and Mim sat in stunned silence, trying to take in everything the elderly solicitor had just explained to them. Nona looked up at Lewis Kingston, who was still stood looking at her, still wearing the false welcoming grin which he hid his true nature behind.

"So, you're my brother then, Lewis?" Nona finally asked.

"Half-brother," Lewis snapped before quickly catching himself and regaining his friendly demeanor, "but what difference does that even make anyway? I'm just sorry that I didn't know about you much earlier, Nona…"

"*Duw, duw, duw,*" Mim muttered in Welsh under her breath, rolling her false teeth around her mouth as she did so.

"Let me get this perfectly straight," Mel said, leaning towards Alistair Leadbetter, "You say that my daughter now owns half of the zoo."

Leadbetter nodded. "That is correct."

"And this ain't a joke?"

"No."

"And it ain't gonna cost us anything?" Mel asked.

"No – not a penny," Leadbetter smiled reassuringly.

"But she can only sell it to her brother should she wish to?"

"Half-brother!" Lewis repeated somewhat wearily.

"Whatever," replied Mel, "Wow…"

"Wow, indeed," smiled Leadbetter, continuing, "now I understand that young Nona is just twelve years old -"

"I'm thirteen in October," Nona interrupted, suddenly finding her voice again.

"My apologies – thirteen…" Leadbetter replied, "However, due to her still being a minor, it does mean that a parent or guardian will need to help her make any financial or business decision regarding the running of the zoo until Nona reaches the legal age of sixteen. Therefore, as her only surviving parent, which would mean you, Miss Lancaster, if you're willing to of course…"

Nona looked pleadingly at her mother, angry that by some quirk of fate, her young and tender age meant that she wouldn't have complete say in the running of the zoo, and fearful that Mel would say no.

Fortunately, that was never going to be the case…

"My daughter is old, wise and smart enough to make the necessary decisions regarding the running of Kingston's Kingdom," Mel replied, adding, "which I will then be more than happy to communicate to you."

Nona smiled as Mel winked back at her.

Suddenly, Lewis Kingston sprung forward, clapping his hands together.

"Well, if that's the case, I'd like to make you both a very generous offer here and now!" he said, grabbing the empty chair before him, spinning it around to sit astride it as a jockey would when riding a horse before continuing.

"I know all of this must have come as a much of a shock to you as it has me. Let's face it, it's not every day you find out you've inherited a zoo. I mean, it's almost as bad as discovering that your dad had another secret kid!" Lewis chuckled, his laughter sounding both false and hollow. "Anyway, all joking aside, I'd like us to get to know each other properly without the added burden of having to run the zoo together. I'd us to be able to do normal brother and sister things together instead."
"I'd like that very much too," Nona smiled excitedly.
"Great, so, let's make this awful situation far less complicated for you, Nona. Therefore, I'd like to buy your half of the zoo off you!" Lewis announced, clicking his finger at Alistair Leadbetter, who fumbled around in his briefcase before finally producing an official looking document.
Lewis snatched the papers from Leadbetter and thrush them into Mel's hands.
"As you can see, it's a very reasonable offer and will save you all of the headaches attached to owning a failing zoo," Lewis continued as Mel began to carefully flick through the wad of paperwork she now held, "Once you sign the zoo over to me, I will then arrange for my accountant to transfer the money directly into your bank account. Then we'll be free to concentrate on getting to know each other properly, Nona, without any other silly, time-consuming distractions."
"£450,000!" Mel exclaimed loudly.
"Yep!" answered Lewis, seemingly pleased with himself, "four-hundred-and-fifty-thousand smackers!"
"*Duw, duw, duw!*" Mim repeated, standing and peering over her grand-daughter's shoulder at the figure written in bold on the paperwork.
"Is that a good offer, Mum?" Nona asked.
Mel nodded and looked at her daughter. "It's a very generous offer, sweetheart, in fact you could say a life-changing one."
"That it is," Lewis interrupted, "you could buy a new house for you and your family - all you have to do is sign on the dotted line, right next to the X…"
Nona looked at her mother, then at Mim, before turning back to look at Lewis Kingston once again.
"I'm quite not sure what to do…" she said nervously.
"What's there to even think about?" Lewis replied, now seeming

to slightly lose his patience, "Just take the money – go get yourself a bigger and better home to live in…Lord knows you need to, judging by the state of this place…"
Unfortunately for Lewis, his words instantly riled Nona's great-grandmother who shot him a fierce and ferocious look.
"Now, look here, boyo," Mim growled, "I've lived in this house ever since I came up here from the valleys, you hear?"
"And God it shows!" came Lewis' curt response as she turned to look at Nona, "Look, don't you owe it to the old girl to make her last years as comfortable as possible, Nona love?"
"Listen here you - I've got a good few years left in me yet, you jumped up streak of pi-" but before Mim could complete her sentence, her walking stick now wildly swinging around her head, Nona quickly intervened.
"Thank you for your kind and generous offer, Lewis," she began to say quietly, "but the zoo is all I have left of both father and my grandfather..."
Nona paused before turning to look at her mother.
"Sorry, Mum, but Grandpa really loved that place," Nona said sadly, "it's down to me to love it for him now that he's gone…"
Behind them, Lewis jumped from his seat, desperately trying to conceal the anger he felt rising within him.
"I totally understand how your feeling, Nona," he replied before adding, "but as Mr Leadbetter said earlier, it really is for the adults to decide, isn't that right, Mel?"
Mel Lancaster looked at her daughter, whose eyes looked pleadingly back at her. She started to nod slowly, causing Nona heart to sink, sighing heavily as she expected the worst.
"Yes, you're right Mr Kingston," Nona's mother finally replied, "Mr Leadbetter, whatever decision I you have to accept as per the terms and conditions of Roger Kingston's will, right?"
"As I previously stated, you have the final say on Nona's behalf until she reaches the age of sixteen, Miss Lancaster," the old solicitor nodded.
Mel paused for a moment at first as he looked at the contract that she still held in her hand before looking around their home, where pieces of wallpaper curled away from the walls here and damp patches grew larger there. Finally, Mel looked over at Nona again and smiled sadly before eventually replying.
"Thank you, Mr Kingston for your very generous offer, as well as

thinking of us at such a difficult time," she replied, "but I think Nona's grandfather would have wanted her to look after the animals he loved so much in his tragic absence."

At first, it appeared that Lewis Kingston had fallen into some sort of trance as he stood there, motionless, with not so much as a hair moving for a good minute or two. Slowly, he then began to nod and stood, pushing the back of the chair he sat on away from him.

"I completely understand," he finally said, "my grandfather gave his life for zoo animals so it's vitally important that we all do everything we can possibly do to honour his legacy and memory."

Lewis stepped forwards to first shake Mel's hand, then Nona's, only stopping when he saw Mim spit in her hand before she thrust it toward him. He then turned to walk back towards the front door, Leadbetter shuffling behind him.

Suddenly he stopped and turned as though seeming to have remembered something.

"Please, may I ask whether either of you would have any problem with me continuing to run the zoo on a day-to-day basis?" Lewis smiled, "After all, I have grown up with it! Of course, Nona will be free to come and go as she pleases, which I understand she has often done before in the past..."

"I think Grandpa would be really pleased to know you were looking after things for him, Lewis," Nona replied, adding, "after all, what would I know about running a zoo at my age? But I'm more than willing to learn if you'll help teach me..."

Suddenly, without warning, Nona leapt off the sofa and ran over to Lewis, wrapping her arms around him in a great, big bear hug, before continuing. "Brother!"

The unexpected gesture completely caught the young man off guard as Lewis just stood there, arms raised, looking like a clean-freak terrified of touching even the slightest a speck of dust. Eventually, he gently patted Nona on the head, as though he were pacifying an over excitable beagle.

"Yes, yes," he answered, nervously trying to break the death grip Nona still had on him, "all in good time. First things first – I'll have to quickly get a business plan in place as to what happens next with the Kingdom to try to keep it profitable. Are you happy for me to do whatever is absolutely necessary so that we lose no more money in order to keep Kingston's Kingdom open?"

Both Mel and Nona smiled and nodded back at him.

"Of course, I completely trust your judgement, Lewis," Nona replied, "after all, we're family now, aren't we…?"

It was only after the door to Nona's house had shut behind him, Alistair Leadbetter had driven off in his small, electric car and Lewis was sat in the backseat of the vehicle driven by John Stafford, the accountant, that Lewis finally spoke again.

"All she has left of *'her father and grandfather…'*" Lewis spat, slamming the bottom of his fist against the car window in anger, "he wasn't ever her father - he was mine!"

Tears of rage filled his eyes as he stared out of the car window and up at the angry sky.

"I hope you're looking down from up there, Grandfather," Lewis snarled, "Don't you even begin to think that you and she will be able to stop me - I've got a deadline to meet…"

Stafford nervously looked at Lewis in his rear-view mirror, swallowing hard before speaking.

"I take it that she said no to selling the zoo then?"

Lewis fixed Stafford with an icy glare as if to confirm the stupidity of the question, causing Stafford to pause and think carefully before asking his next one.

"So, what next?" the accountant eventually said.

"We go to plan B," Lewis calming replied as he reached for his cigarettes, "if that damned girl won't sell the zoo because of the animals, then we'll have to make sure that there are none left for her to have to worry about…"

Chapter 7 – A Family at War

The camera crews and reporters jostled for position with one another at the entrance to Kingston's Kingdom early the following morning, having scarcely had enough time to prepare for the hastily arranged press conference Lewis Kingston had unexpectedly called that day.

Soon, the hum of anticipation in the crowd turned to an expectant silence as Lewis walked to the rostrum which was positioned perfectly in front of the zoo's welcome sign to stand alongside Alistair Leadbetter. To the side of the rostrum, out of the cameras view, stood several key members of the zoo's staff, with Catherine Kingston and John Stafford in close attendance beside them.

It was Alistair Leadbetter who then spoke first once a hush had fallen over all the assembled members of the press.

"Thank you all for coming here this morning on such short notice," the old solicitor said, "First, I'd like to introduce you to Lewis Kingston, one of the new co-owners of Kingston's Kingdom…"

Lewis' smile flickered briefly at the mention of the word *co-owner*, but he quickly regained his composure as Leadbetter continued.

"He will now read to you a short, pre-prepared statement before taking a few, brief questions." Leadbetter smiled and slowly shuffled away from the rostrum to be replaced by the young man dressed in yet another ill-fitting suit.

"Thank you, Alistair," Lewis Kingston began, coughing to clear his throat before reading from the hand-written papers he held, "I would like to read you a short statement regarding the sad and devastating loss of my grandfather as well as the future of his beloved zoo…"

Pausing briefly, Lewis bit down on his trembling lip, mainly to give the impression to those watching that he was struggling to control his feelings and emotions, but, in truth, it was to cause himself enough pain to cause his eyes to fill with crocodile tears…

"I'm sorry, but as you can imagine, this has been an incredibly difficult time for me and my family, having to come to terms with the loss of a such a huge and important part of our lives," Lewis sniffed before continuing, "but we must move forward and continue to honour him and his final wishes."

Lewis paused and looked at his mother who titled her head in mock motherly concern, part of the act they'd agreed upon earlier that day to help to sympathetically paint Lewis to all the reporters present.

"As you are no doubt aware, the kingdom has struggled financially over the past few years with only the hard work, generosity and goodwill of my grandfather keeping it afloat financially," Lewis sighed, "however, there comes a time when one says enough is enough and he knew this, making his wishes clear in his will which left Kingston's Kingdom in the care of myself and my half-sister Nona Lancaster…"

At the mere mention of Nona's name, a flurry of whispers and mummers passed around the audience, but Lewis calmly continued to read out his statement.

"Therefore, with her blessings and verbal agreement we have both together taken the painful, but absolutely necessary decision to close Kingston's Kingdom at the earliest opportunity…"

Cameras suddenly began to flash incessantly as dozens of hands raised at his shocking and unexpected announcement.

The zoo's employees - Doyley amongst them - shook their heads in complete disbelief, with a few of them openly sobbing. Lewis raised both hands and waved them up and down to try and regain the silence he first had when he'd begun to read out his statement.

"Please, please, allow me to finish," Lewis loudly pleaded, "however, as per my grandfather's final wishes, the Kingdom will remain open until the very last animal has lived out its natural life nor will any animals be sold or rehomed, of that I promise," Lewis smiled, his vampire-like skin now making his teeth stand out, causing them to appear more yellow than they already were.

An almost audible and collective sigh of relief came from the zoo's employees with the petite figure of the trainee vet, Hayley Maguire, spontaneously hugging Doyley, her head pressed against his stomach, scarcely above the Celtic Cross belt buckle which topped his skinny black jeans. He patted her gently on the back like she was a favoured favourite pet before the young vet realised what she'd just done, suddenly releasing Doyley before quickly moving away, her face as red as one of the many baboons' bottoms she'd been examining the previous day.

Before Lewis could continue there was a loud round of applause, which had again been pre-arranged beforehand, and was led by his mother and their accountant.

"Stop, you're all too kind!" Lewis asked humbly, "All we are doing is honouring my grandfather's last wishes. That concludes my statement, I will now take a few brief questions. Please raise your hand and when selected, confirm your name and the news organisation you work for…"

A sea of hands instantly shot up with loud cries of '*Mr Kingston*' ringing out amongst all those gathered together that day.

Looking at all the expectant faces jostling to be chosen, Lewis somewhat predictably pointed to the prettiest face first.

"Yes, you gorgeous – in the red jacket."

The female reporter frowned at the lack of respect Lewis Kingston had shown her.

"Mr Kingston, Jill Whelan, UK News Network. What are your predicted timescales for closure?"

"As I've already stated," Lewis smarmily grinned, "that will be determined by our animals' health and welfare."

"So, it won't be driven by the proposed agreements that you already have in place to redevelop the land?" Jill Whelan pressed. Her question threw Lewis a little.

What does she know? he thought to himself as he adjusted his tie and leant closer to the microphone.

"Agreement to develop the land? I'm sorry, I'm not quite sure I understand where you are coming from?" Lewis replied.

"I'm asking if there is any to truth to the rumours that you've already agreed to sell Kingston's Kingdom to Aleksander Kashlotov, the Russian oil oligarch, to develop the land into a luxury housing development?" the reporter asked, scrolling across the screen of her handheld mobile device.

How does she know that? Whose tongue has been wagging? thought Lewis, feeling a little uneasy that the secret discussions he'd been conducting with the notorious Russian gangland leader had somehow been leaked to the British press.

"May I ask who your source may be?" he smiled.

"I'm not at liberty to say…" the reporter replied, smugly smiling back.

"Well, I'm not at liberty to even entertain such nonsense," Lewis grinned whilst feeling slightly annoyed, "beyond looking after the welfare of the animals in the Kingdom, I haven't given a second thought as to what will happen next. Their welfare is my ultimate concern and so, to that end, I have hired one of the world's leading zoological veterinarians to conduct a full physical examination on every animal to ensure they are in peak physical health and condition."

Lewis angrily gathered up his papers and tapped them firmly on the rostrum before continuing.

"Unfortunately, due to the aggressive, negative and ill-informed manner of Miss Whelan's questions, I've no alternative but to now declare this press conference over. Thank you."

Despite the appeals for him to stay and continue, Lewis quickly stepped down from the rostrum and briskly walked past his mother towards his grandfather's old office, Catherine Kingston closely following behind.

John Stafford stayed and watched as Alistair Leadbetter was almost overwhelmed by the remaining reporters who were all jostling with each other, thrusting their microphones and voice recorders at him, hoping for a quotation or soundbite they could use for their paper, website, blog, radio or television station. The accountant then turned to the zoo's employees who remained stood beside him.

"Mr Kingston has asked me to reassure you that all of your jobs are of course safe until the zoo closes," Stafford whispered, "in the meantime, please go about your daily business as usual - we've still a zoo to run."

"Yer heard der man," Doyley declared, "Let's get cracking guys!" Slowly, the small group began to disperse, muttering to one another before heading off in their different directions before Stafford next spoke to those remaining.

"Mr Doyle, Mr Kingston has asked for your immediate presence, along with that of both Mr Richards and Miss Maguire."

"Why does he want to see the three of us?" Tom Richards, the zoo's vastly experienced head vet asked apprehensively.

"All will soon be revealed, Mr Richards," Stafford replied, adding, "but I suggest we hurry - Mr Kingston is not a man who likes to be kept waiting…"

Stafford and the three summoned zoo employees found Lewis Kingston sat in his grandfather's chair, feet raised and resting on the desk. In his hand he held a photograph of Roger Kingston taken shortly after the Kingdom had first opened. Upon seeing his visitors arrive, he placed the picture, face down, on the desk and stood whilst trying to smooth out the crumples in his cheap suit as he did so.

Stafford gestured to Doyley, Maguire and Richards to shuffle to stand directly in front of the zoo's new owner whilst the accountant went to join his employer on the other side of the desk.

"Thank you all for meeting with me at such short notice," Lewis began to say, wearing the sincerest smile he could muster.

"Your henchman didn't exactly give us much of a choice!" Richards moaned, pointing at John Stafford.

The accountant smiled - he'd been called several things, many of them extremely rude, before in his lifetime, but he'd never once been called a *'henchman'*...

I quite like that - makes me sound a little dangerous...Stafford thought to himself as Lewis ignored the remark and continued regardless.

"I'll get right to the point Kingston's Kingdom is doomed," Lewis declared, "attendances have been falling steadily over the years. People have so much to choice in what they spend their leisure time doing nowadays we simply can't compete anymore and, to be honest, zoos are rapidly going out of fashion."

"But the news conference today will surely help to generate much more interest, Mr Kingston," Hayley Maguire replied, raising her hand like a schoolchild asking permission to speak to her teacher.

"You're quite right Miss Maguire," Lewis nodded. We'll have an initial bump in attendance figures, which is good news of course, but we won't be able to maintain that for long. Sooner or later, we'll be back to square one, that's why closure is the best thing all round."

Tom Richards stood quietly for a moment, his arms crossed as he defiantly looked at Lewis Kingston.

"Be that as it may, but you've just made a commitment to allow the animals to live out their natural lifespans," the head vet finally said, "some of them, such as our giant tortoise have quite a few years left in them, so, as I see it, you won't be closing anytime soon, Mr Kingston."

"That I know only too well..." Lewis replied, lifting a small yellow notebook from his desk, thumbing through its pages before adding, "Not only are they long-lived, but they are also extremely rare and valuable to the right, interested parties…"

Richards, Maguire and Doyley looked at each other uneasily.

"I don't see what difference that makes," Richards argued.

Sighing, Lewis laid the notebook down on the desk walking around it to sit on the edge of it in front of the three zoo employees.

"There's one way we can save the animals, close the zoo and all still make a pretty penny out of it for our troubles," he smiled.

"How would yer do dat den, Mr Kingston?" Doyley asked, now slightly confused by the direction the conversation was suddenly heading.

"What if the animals slowly started to die? Or there was a sudden disaster that hit the zoo and wiped them all out like the dinosaurs…" Lewis asked, a mischievous glint now sparkling in his eye "We'd have no other alternative but to close the kingdom down then, would we?"

"Firstly, they're all incredibly rare and endangered species, so we pay extra special care and attention to them regarding their welfare," Richards frowned before adding, "and, secondly, the animals in the Kingdom are all in excellent health thanks to the team of vets that we currently have looking after them."

"True, but what if we were to give nature a little bit of a helping hand…?" Lewis asked.

"I'm not sure that I follow, Mr Kingston," Tom Richards, "you're not seriously suggest-"

But before Richards could complete the sentence, there was a single, sharp, knock on the office door and a tall, well-built man purposely strode in, nodding at Lewis and Stafford as he moved across the room to join them. The stranger wore a tight-fitting short-sleeved shirt, which made his muscles appear even larger than they already were, and had an unnaturally smooth, tanned face framed by a golden mane of unruly hair and a thick and bushy beard.

"Perfect timing!" Lewis laughed, grabbing the stranger's hand before shaking it firmly, "Allow me to introduce all of you to one of the world's leading zoological veterinarians - Doctor Henrik Au."

Doctor Au nodded, his features showing no signs of emotion, as though his face had been carved out of stone.

"Doctor Au has perfected a unique technique where he can put an animal so deep into sleep that its vital signs are virtually non-existent and undetectable…" Lewis continued.

"Catalepsy," Au added.

"Yes - what he just said," Lewis replied.

"But why would you want to do that?" Richards angrily asked, looking to Doyley and Maguire for some sign of moral support which sadly failed to materialise.

"Transportation!" Au barked, his accent thick and heavy, a mixture of dialects aggressively battling with one another, "If wild and dangerous beasts are the problem, then I'm the solution."

"But there's nothing here in the kingdom that's that dangerous to move!" Richards argued.

"True, not dangerous but highly valuable to the right bidder instead…" Lewis whispered.

For a moment or two a silence fell over the room as Lewis and Richards locked eyes on one another, as though playing a serious and deadly game of *Chicken*. Eventually, it was Tom Richards who blinked first…

"You're not seriously suggesting…" he again began to say.

"I think he's finally got it!" Lewis laughed, eagerly clapping his hands together.

"Oim sorry, but Oi tink Oi must have fallen asleep or sometink as Oive absolutely no clue as to what yoos two fellas be on about!" Doyley asked, shaking his head slowly.

The room immediately split into two – the sound of laughter echoing around Lewis, Stafford and Au whilst confusion and disbelief filled the air surrounding the figures of Tom Richards, Doyley and Hayley Maguire.

"I believe," Richards began to explain to Doyley and Hayley, "Mr Kingston would like us to help convince everyone outside these four walls that the animals are dying in Kingston's Kingdom."

"Got it in one!" Lewis laughed, pointing at the head veterinarian.

"How?" Maguire asked, still struggling to fully understand what was going on.

Doctor Au stood and opened his arms wide.

"It's quite simple," he began to explain, "we simply give the animal an injection which safely lowers its body temperature and heart rate below the point where it can be read. We can then declare it '*dead*' and carefully prepare it for transportation, away from any prying or suspicious eyes."

Maguire screwed up her eyes, her brain now completely confused. "But why would you want to do that?"

"Profit, Miss Maguire," Stafford calmly said, "cold, hard cash. As per the cruel terms of his grandfather's last wishes, Mr Kingston cannot be seen to sell off any of the animals, nor is he allowed to put them down. But were it to appear to the outside world that they've all died naturally…"

"I don't default on the will and can then sell the animals off to the highest bidder!" Lewis laughed before continuing, "Of course, you will all be richly rewarded for your help, receiving a generous percentage of the money I make on each animal, plus a large cash bonus upon the sale of the kingdom when the zoo is animal-free. All I need you to do is keep quiet, prepare the animals for sale and for Mr Richards to counter-sign the fake death certificates Doctor Au creates for each animal we ship out. So, do we have a deal?"

"No," Richards firmly replied.

"I'm sorry?" Lewis replied.

"You heard me - I'll not be a party to this. What you suggest is highly illegal as well as being morally wrong!" the vet said, visibly struggling to control his anger.

Lewis nodded, "Yes, it is, but then so is living with someone who is staying in this country illegally…"

"What? I – I don't know what you're on about…" the head vet spluttered.

But Tom Richards' guilty face betrayed him as he slumped into one of the armchairs which were positioned opposite the desk. Lewis Kingston walked over to him and gently rested an arm on his shoulder as Doyley and Maguire looked on, fearing to speak.

"It's all right, Tom, I won't say a word about you and Kristina," he whispered into the vet's ear before adding, "as long as you don't say anything about my plans for the animals either…"

After a moment or two, Richards reluctantly nodded his head in both defeat and resignation.

"Excellent!" Lewis grinned, "I tell you what – why don't you take some time off, Tom, an extended and fully paid leave of absence."

Richards bowed his head and slowly nodded again as Lewis stood to look directly at both Doyley and Maguire.

"Do either of you have any problems with my proposal?" he asked.

Doyley and Maguire shook their heads which pleased their new employer greatly.

"Fabulous!" Lewis smiled, "And to show you my appreciation, Miss Maguire, I'm promoting you to acting head veterinarian in Mr Richards' extended absence, assisting Doctor Au for the foreseeable future."

Maguire looked across at her despondent boss, but Tom Richards just raised a hand to tell her that it was all right, the fire in him having been dosed and put out, the fight having been knocked out of him as well.

"Thank you, Mr Kingston," Maguire replied, not really sure if she was really grateful for being mixed up in something so deceitful, dishonest and, potentially, illegal.

"And you, Mr Doyle?" Lewis Kingston asked, again pressing the head zookeeper standing quietly behind Maguire for an answer.

Tugging at his earlobe, Doyley shrugged his shoulders nonchalantly.

"Yer der boss - what yer says goes. Why bite der hand dat feeds yer?" the Irishman replied, his answer immediately causing the biggest smile of the day to fill Lewis Kingston's face.

"Terrific! All you have to do is go about your business as usual," Lewis replied, clapping his hands loudly together again before continuing, "Remember - if you're asked any questions or are invited for interview by the press, then politely decline and refer them to the three of us."

He then shook both Doyley and Maguire by the hand, ignoring the forlorn vet who still quietly sat in his chair, his head low as he continued to stare at the floor.

"Good to have you all on board," Lewis then said, "you keep your mouths shut, we'll all then make a shedload of money…"

The water in the sink had hardly drained away after dinner later that day as Nona dried the last dish with a tea-towel whilst her mother used her finger to try to get rid of a few stubborn food remnants down the plughole when the front doorbell cried in anguished submission once again.

"Be a love and go answer that," Mel asked.

Nona put the dish down on the counter, slung the tea-towel over her shoulder and jogged to the door. There she was met by Doyley's tall frame blocking her view of the street.

But before Nona could manage to greet him, the normally cheerful Irishman spoke to her more seriously than he'd ever done before. "Dere's sometink yer ought to know about what dat brother of yers is planning to do wit' der zoo, Nona…"

Sleep did not come easily to Nona that night, her thoughts dominated by Doyley's words, telling her and her mother everything that had taken place that morning at the zoo.
Earlier, Nona had stormed off to bed angry and frustrated, first by the lies told to her by her *brother*, then by her mother's response that night after Doyley had left them.
Her mother had announced that there wasn't much they could do to stop Lewis as all they had was Doyley's word as to what was allegedly said. She'd then also declared that even if it were true there'd be no way that could stop him as they didn't have the sort of money needed to go up against Lewis Kingston and his family. But the biggest source of frustration Nona felt was the fact that she was just a kid and had to rely on others to act on her behalf, supposedly in her best interests. Nona was certain Lewis would have thought twice had she been an adult and confronted him with what she now knew.
However, playing these fantastical scenarios over and over in her head just before falling asleep had only caused her to become even angrier as she tossed and turned, waiting for sleep to find and claim her. Eventually, when it crept into her room and stole her away for the night, Nona found that her sleep was fitful, with lots of wild broken dreams which she couldn't quite remember every time she awoke.
The only dream which lasted any length of time after she woke was one of her and her grandfather sitting across a table from one another, eating ice-cream with long spoons out of a large glass they both shared. Nona was wearing her favourite all-red football kit as usual, while her grandfather was, unusually for him, dressed from head to toe in white.

"It's not fair, Grandpa," Nona had said, "everything was going so well and then you up and die on me."
Her grandfather took a large mouthful of ice-cream and winced slightly.
"Ooh, brain freeze!" he laughed before adding, "I'm sorry my

dear, trust me - it wasn't by choice. Here..."
He lifted a cherry off the top of the ice-cream and started to make lots of plane noises, before planting it into Nona's open mouth. She grinned for a moment, but the smile soon disappeared from her lips.
"I miss you so much!" she cried, pushing the ice-cream away from her.
"I miss you too, but please don't be sad," her grandfather had replied, pushing it back towards her.
"I can't help it. Every time I think about you, I just want to cry," Nona sniffed.
Nona's grandfather moved around the table and wrapped an arm around her shoulders.
"Do you think I'd want you to be sad every time you thought of me or remembered all the times we shared together?"
Nona shook her head, "No, but it's so hard."
"So, every time you think about me, think of something I said, or something we did that makes you happy instead," Roger Kingston smiled, "that way I will forever live in both your heart and mind."
Nona smiled and hugged him tightly, "I'll try, I promise."
"That's my girl," her grandfather replied."
"It's just that I always knew that no matter whatever problem I had, you'd always listen and try to help me find a solution to it," Nona said, taking another huge mouthful of ice-cream.
"And I always will, Nona. I'll never leave you, no matter what..." her grandfather smiled as he wiped the remains of his ice-cream from his lips, "just trust yourself, dear - you'll know exactly what to do when the time comes..."

When Nona rolled over in her bed with a contented smile on her lips from being with her grandfather again, the sheet she'd restlessly discarded at the end of the bed earlier rose up from the floor and gently fell across her sleeping form again....

A few hours later, the early morning sunlight broke through the gaps in the bedroom blinds to gently wake her. Nona immediately sat up, quietly confident that she now knew of a way to keep her grandfather's wishes, as well as his memory, from disappearing forever...

Chapter 8 – So it Begins

"You're seriously telling me that you're gonna steal the animals?" Luca almost spat out his sandwich during lunchtime the following day as Nona shared her grand plan with Keeley and him.

"Technically, it's not stealing as the zoo was equally left to me and my brother," Nona replied.

Luca and Keeley looked at one another. They'd shared their friend's original excitement when she told them about the zoo, having visited it with Nona on several occasions in the past. And like Nona, they were outraged when they first heard about Lewis' devious plans. But neither one of them could ever have imagined the extreme of action Nona now planned to take.

"How are you gonna manage to get them out, Nona?" Keeley whispered, looking around the school dinner hall to make sure that they weren't being overheard.

"Got the idea from an old war film my nan keeps watching over and over again. All these prisoners escape from a German prison of war camp by building tunnels, climbing fences and cool other stuff," Nona said proudly.

"You're gonna dig a tunnel into the zoo!" exclaimed Keeley, "That will take you ages!"

"No, I'm using the film as an example," Nona replied, shaking her head, "I've a much simpler and easier plan. We'll walk in and grab a couple of the animals, hide them and then walk right back out of the zoo again!"

"But that's still stealing!" Luca gasped, "I thought that by coming to this school, we'd finally have gotten away from being around people like that. You'll be no better than them if you do this, Nona."

Having just taken a huge bite out of her tuna and mayo roll, Nona waited until her mouth was completely empty before replying. "The zoo was left to me by my grandfather which means that half of the animals are mine too. We'll just be taking what belongs to me won't we?"

"That's twice you've said *'we'll'* in as many sentences..." Keeley frowned, "so, who's gonna help you?"

"You two of course," Nona smiled.

"Us!" Keeley said loudly, instantly causing Luca to spit out some of the fruit juice he'd just sipped from his carton.

"Of course -who else could it be?" Nona asked.

Luca and Keeley looked at each other in disbelief as their friend continued to share her plans with them.

"You two could take it in turns each time we go there," Nona explained, "one could be the lookout whilst me and the other one each nab an animal."

"So, you're only planning on taking two animals at a time?" Luca asked, curiously.

"Yeah."

"Two by two?"

"Yeah - so?" Nona frowned.

Luca started to laugh uncontrollably as tears began to roll down his cheeks.

"What's so funny?" Nona asked, beginning to feel slightly annoyed.

"Sorry, I just suddenly pictured you with a long grey beard whilst holding a wooden staff," Luca giggled, "it won't be long until you'll have to change your name to *Noah* Lancaster too!"

With that, Luca erupted into a second bout of laughter as he slowly slid down between the bench and table.

"Ha, ha, very funny!" moaned Nona as a tall, forbidding looking woman slowly approached the table.

"Would you care to share the joke, Master Bonnetti?" the woman enquired in a clipped and well-educated voice.

Almost immediately, Luca rose from beneath the table and sat on the bench, his back as straight as a ruler as it were standing to attention.

"No Miss, sorry Miss," he replied sheepishly.

"What about you girls?" Would you like to explain what has tickled his funny bone so much?" the woman said, turning to Nona and Keeley.

"It was nothing Miss Bridges," Nona replied, "we were just having a bit of banter, that's all."

"Hmm," said Miss Bridges, pinching the end of her nose slightly as she always did when she was thinking.

Nona looked up at her and swallowed hard hoping her feeble excuse would be enough to appease Trinity Free School's first headteacher…

A tall woman in her late fifties, the tall and elegant figure of Sheila

Bridges was topped off by an uncontrollable shock of frizzy grey hair which surrounded her normally sunny, warm and friendly face. But if you were to ever fall foul of Miss Bridges, you did so at your own peril for she was known to possess a quick and ferocious temper. This fury had first been witnessed by a worldwide TV audience many years before during the Los Angeles Olympics.

The clear favourite for the marathon, Britain's best gold medal hope Sheila Bridges had entered the stadium twenty metres ahead of her nearest rivals with certain victory just a lap away. However, a combination of exhaustion, plus the incompetence of one of the stadium officials meant Miss Bridges had started to run the wrong way around the track, only realising her error after the chasing group had entered the arena and were battling for the medal places. Despite a brave and valiant effort to close the gap after turning around and sprinting after them, Miss Bridges eventually finished fourth, just missing out on the medal she'd spent a lifetime dreaming of and training for, as well as a place on the winners' podium.

But rather than throw herself to the track in anguish and dismay, Sheila Bridges continued to run around the track until she finally found the official who had originally misdirected her...

The photograph of her chasing him, before kicking him firmly up the backside made the front pages of newspapers all around the world, garnering her with instant celebrity, with fame and fortune following thereafter.

As Ventham's most famous former resident, Sheila Bridges was the natural and perfect choice to front and run the free school being an ex-athlete herself.

"I do like a good joke," Miss Bridges finally smiled before continuing, "just make sure that it's not when someone is eating, my dear – we don't want anyone choking now, do we?"

"No Miss Bridges," smiled Nona, relief now sweeping over her.

Miss Bridges nodded, pinched a crisp from Keeley's packet and walked off cheerfully whistling loudly as she strode away from them.

When she was convinced that Miss Bridges was out of earshot, Nona leant across the table and whispered to her friends. "So, are you in?"

Luca turned to look at Keeley, who smiled back and nodded.

"Of course," he smiled before looking back at Nona, "so when do we start...?"

It took the three of them just over half an hour to cycle to Kingston's Kingdom from school the following night, each of them carrying a small, backpack filled with scrunched up newspapers to make them seem like they were already full.
When they arrived at the zoo, Nona, Keeley and Luca rested their bikes against some metal railings beside the entrance Doyley had first shown little Nona and her mother through all those years before.
Since then, Nona had come to let herself and her friends into the zoo on countless other occasions without ever having to meet the friendly Irishman on their arrival. But no visit to the kingdom had ever been as secretive or important as the one they'd planned that day...
"Ready?" Nona asked as she stood in front of the door, her two friends nodding nervously as she began to enter the six-digit code she'd memorised and used repeatedly in the past onto the keypad.
"Nine – three – seven – three – four – three!" Nona said, her voice unconsciously adopting taking on a slight Irish burr as though she was channelling Doyley himself.
The lock slowly clicked as she pushed the door open just enough for Luca and Keeley to ease past her, before Nona followed them both in. The three friends quickly walked through the corridor past both the ticket office and gift shop doors as they'd done so many times before without ever drawing attention to themselves.
At the end of the corridor Nona quickly re-entered the code into the keypad on the second door, holding her breath just in case someone had somehow miraculously read her mind and knew their plans, changing the access code to something entirely different. It wasn't long though before Nona exhaled in relief as she heard the familiar click of the lock allowing her to push it open for the three of them to pass through unchallenged and unnoticed.
As usual, Kingston's Kingdom was quiet at that time on a school night, there hardly being any visitors, except for the odd couple here and there, as well as an occasional parent or grandparent pushing a buggy or trying to control the mad stumblings of a toddler who was trying to escape their clutches.

Nona hadn't actually realised just how quiet the zoo was before then and now began to understand just why she'd seen less and less of her grandfather during the last few months of his life whilst he'd battled to keep his beloved zoo open.

"You all right, Nona?" Luca asked, snapping Nona out of the quiet trance she'd suddenly appeared to have fallen into.

"Yeah, sorry. Was just thinking about Grandpa that's all," Nona replied, looking at her watch, "right, follow me…"

Now resembling a ninja, Nona crouched down low and began to jog up a pathway to their left, towards where the large, cartoon figure of Diana the Monkey stood, the cartoon cut-out beckoning the zoo's visitors to call by and see the animals in her area. Luca and Keeley looked at one another as they shook their heads and jogged casually after her, still laughing at the stealth-like stance Nona had adopted just ahead of them.

It wasn't long before the three of them stood outside a small enclosure, fenced off from the public but still large enough for its inhabitants to have plenty of freedom to run, hide and climb in the bushes and trees which grew inside the pen. Luca looked closely at the sign stuck in the ground just behind the mesh fencing in front of him…

Being elusive and reclusive, the Red Panda is extremely difficult to find in its normal surroundings, which are the bamboo forests of the Eastern Himalayas with fewer than 10,000 of these beautiful creatures remaining in the wild today. Their existence is threatened by a combination of the loss of habitat, pressures from grazing, illegal hunting and poaching.

However, Scarlet and Rhett were the first two Red Panda cubs born in captivity here in the UK and have enjoyed many happy years with us in Kingston's Kingdom…

"Why these two?" he asked as Nona made her way to a door at the back of wooden viewing area marked *'Employees Only.'*

"I thought as this is our first rescue mission we'd best off start small…" Nona replied, laying her backpack down on the floor before continuing, "The two of them ought to fit perfectly into our backpacks, plus, as all they do is sleep and eat, they'll hardly make a sound so we should be able to smuggle them out easily."

Nona began to punch the keys on the door's keypad.

"Gotta love Doyley and the simple but memorable access codes he's programmed into every door!" she laughed, gently punching on the keys.

$$R - 3 - d - P - 4 - n - d - 4 - 5$$

Another soft *click* and the door popped ajar slightly.

"Come on, Keeley, you and me up tonight," Nona winked, "Luca - you're the lookout."

"What do I do if I see anyone?" asked Luca, suddenly terrified by the responsibility which had now been thrust upon him.

Nona turned and smiled. "Make some sort of panda sound," she said before quickly disappearing, Keeley closely following behind.

Luca stood there, momentarily reassured before suddenly realising he'd no clue as to what sound a normal panda would make, let alone a red one, before rushing to look inside the enclosure. There he found Nona and Keeley ducked down in the undergrowth as they quickly emptied the crumpled-up newspapers from their bags. Keeley glanced up and was alarmed to spot a CCTV camera fixed to one of the tree trunks that crisscrossed the panda's enclosure. She patted Nona anxiously on the shoulder, pointing to it once she'd got her friend's attention.

"Don't worry - it's a dummy camera. Nona smiled, "plus, we've an insider if we ever need any help whilst in here."

Nona winked reassuringly at Keeley, secretly hoping that Doyley would stay true to his word when saying he'd help her in any way he could when he'd visited her and her mother at home.

Around them, the enclosure was eerily quiet with nothing but the sound of the gentle breeze brushing past the leaves and reeds in there. Keeley strained her eyes, desperately trying to see the two little creatures they'd come to *rescue*.

"I can't see Scarlett or Rhett anywhere?" she sighed.

"Me neither," Nona replied, before rummaging around in the bottom of her backpack.

"Well, how are you going to catch them if we can't find them?" Keeley asked.

"Like this..." Nona triumphantly declared, producing a large tin and plastic pot covered with clear film. "I brought a tin of bamboo shoots and mushrooms from the supermarket. Now, watch this..."

Nona slowly peeled back the lid of the bamboo shoots and, pulling a spoon from her back pocket, began to gently tap on the side of the tin.

At first, there was still no sign of the red pandas, but after a moment or two, some leaves in one of the trees to the far right of them began to rustle. Keeley smiled as a small animal with reddish brown and black fur cautiously began to crawl down the trunk towards the two of them.

"That's Scarlet," Nona whispered, "her face is little darker than Rhett's, he won't be too far behind her though..."

Sure enough, a second panda soon began to make its way down another trunk not too far away from its furry friend. The two creatures stood on all fours a little way from Nona and Keeley, trying to decide whether there was any danger ahead of them as Nona tapped the side of the tin again, causing the pandas to rise up on their hind legs.

"Are they going to attack?" Keeley asked nervously as the pandas fell back down onto all fours again.

"Nah, they know it's me," Nona smiled as the two little creatures began to run towards her, stopping just in front of the two girls as Nona first poured the bamboo shoots onto the ground before taking the cellophane off the mushrooms. She began to scatter them as first Scarlet, then Rhett crept forward sand began to pick up the food with their little clawed hands.

"Can I stroke them?" Keeley asked, looking on in amazement at the two incredibly cute animals before her.

Nona nodded so the two girls sat there momentarily, gently stroking the pandas' backs as Scarlett and Rhett happily nibbled the treats that they'd just been given.

"They're quite friendly," Keeley whispered, as Rhett finished the mushroom he held between his paws and flopped into her lap.

"They've known me for long time," answered Nona, gently picking up Scarlet, "besides, Grandpa told me the way to win their love and affection was to them bring plenty of food and to rub them on their tummies!"

The two girls happily sat rubbing the pandas' soft underbellies for a few minutes until a loud voice called out from behind them.

"Hello there - remember me?" Luca shouted from behind the fence.

"Shush - we'll be done soon, they're nearly asleep," Nona tutted before turning to Keeley, "Once they're sleeping, we'll gently put them into the backpacks."

"Won't the zookeepers miss them though?" Keeley asked.

Nona shook her head as she reached into her bag with her free hand to produce two small, red, cuddly soft toys.

"We'll position these somewhere in the enclosure," Nona whispered, "everyone who visits moans that they never see them anyway, so these should keep them all happy for a while…"

She looked down at Scarlet, who was now fast asleep with a full and fat contented look on her face.

"She's out for the count," Nona whispered, gently lifting the panda up before placing her in her backpack whilst wrapping Scarlet up in an old fleece she'd packed earlier.

"Wanna hand with Rhett?" she then said, turning to Keeley.

"Please," her friend replied, trying to lift the weight her red panda had become.

Rhett was trying hard to fight off sleep, but as soon as Nona began rubbing his stomach he too succumbed, soon snoring gently as the two girls lifted him between then up to lay him in Keeley's backpack.

After he was safely tucked in, Nona and Keeley carefully climbed through the undergrowth to find the best positions to place each of the two soft toys Nona had brought with her. They decided to use Luca as a casual observer to tell them which locations were best to place the toys so as to fool anyone passing by.

At last, after Luca had told them that even he'd struggle to say whether the toys were real or not from where he was standing, the three of them readied themselves to leave.

But as the girls picked up their backpacks, Nona, Keeley and Luca were quickly forced to hide and take cover as a young couple began to approach the enclosure. Fortunately, the two lovebirds were far more interested in kissing one another than looking at the red pandas as they slowly passed by, Nona and Keeley holding their breath as they lay flat to the floor, whilst Luca hid behind the vending machine which stood to the right of the enclosure.

The three of them nervously waited until the young couple had finally smooched their way out of sight and had heard Luca's best attempt at a panda cry before deciding it was now safe enough for Nona and Keeley to scurry out of the panda enclosure, their backpacks secured safely in place.

As Nona slowly closed the door behind her, Keeley turned to look at Luca.

"What on Earth was that sound meant to be?" she asked.

"It was my best panda impersonation," Luca said proudly.

"Sounded more like a constipated puppy!" Nona chuckled as the three friends began to make their way back to the zoo exit.

By now, the kingdom was even quieter than it had been earlier, but that still didn't stop the three of them feeling incredibly guilty every time they passed the occasional visitor or employee. In fact, Keeley lost count of the times she said *'Evening, lovely weather'* as she nonchalantly walked along, trying to appear as though she didn't have a care in the world whilst Nona just smiled and nodded at people as they passed. Meanwhile, Luca felt that the casual *hands-stuck-in-pockets-and-whistling* approach would be best for him, especially as his palms were constantly soaked with sweat.

Eventually, after what seemed to be an absolute eternity, the three of them arrived at the employee's corridor again. Stood there, leaning against the wall, his thumb scrolling the screen of his mobile phone was Doyley, looking as cool as ever. He looked up as the three children approached him.

"Owaya, Nona?" he drawled, an almost knowing look etched across his face.

"Awright, Doyley," Nona replied, not quite knowing if he knew just what their bags contained.

Still, she needn't have worried as Doyley's eyes soon returned to the screen, the Irishman no doubt looking at the replies he'd received against his profile on the numerous dating sites he was subscribed to.

Without further worry or difficulty, Nona, Luca and Keeley quickly negotiated their way through the door-corridor-door combination exit and were soon outside the zoo again where the girls took a brief peak into their backpacks, both relieved to find the pandas still curled up and fast asleep inside them.

"We did it!" Keeley squealed excitedly, before remembering that they'd yet to fully clear the shadow of the zoo buildings which loomed around them. Nona nodded cautiously as they all unlocked their bikes and began to walk back up the pavement, pushing their bikes as they made their way from the zoo.

After a few anxious minutes, when they were certain that they were far enough away from the kingdom to be safe from capture,

the three of them stopped and fist bumped one another excitedly.
"That was wicked!" Luca laughed, adding, "It was way easier than I expected too."

"Told ya," Nona replied cheerfully, "nobody suspected a thing! If we stay smart, sensible and careful, we should just be able to walk in, rescue a couple of the animals and walk out with them anytime we want!"

"What's next then?" Keeley asked, strangely surprised at how thrilled she'd been by the whole adventure.

"Well, if you're both free after school tomorrow, I thought we'd come back and grab a couple of the pygmy three-toed sloths," Nona replied, "they sleep even more than the pandas! We'll have to watch out for their claws, mind, they're lethal!"

"I'm up for it!" Keeley replied, looking at Luca hopefully.

"Me too," he nodded before adding, "so, where we taking the pandas to then?"

Nona suddenly stopped with her mouth wide open.

"I – I hadn't thought about that!" she spluttered.

"Seriously?" Luca gasped, "You've gone to all this trouble to break them out and you've not already planned what you're going to do with them next?"

"I got so carried away in planning *how* to get them out that I didn't think of *where* we'd go with them if we did…" Nona sighed, pleadingly looking at her friends, "unless one of you would…"

"No chance!" Luca interrupted, crossing his arms and shaking his head, "I get busted trying to sneak a friend in my house, let alone a freakin'' panda! How about you, Keels?"

Keeley could feel her friends' eyes burning on her.

"I'd love to help, Nona, but my dog goes absolutely mental anytime he hears or smells anything different in our house," Keeley said sadly.

"Well, that's just peachy!" moaned Nona, "It looks like I've drawn the short straw tonight then, doesn't it?"

"That'll teach you not to think of every possible angle, you budding criminal mastermind, you!" laughed Luca, almost slapping his friend on the back before suddenly thinking better of it.

"Help me get them back to my place then," Nona said, sitting astride her bike, "I'll have to hide them both in my room for the night."

"What if your mum finds them though?" Keeley asked as she and Luca climbed onto their bicycle seats.

"Don't you worry about that - Mum knows better than to enter my room without either my knowledge or permission!" winked Nona as the three of them pushed off and began to pedal slowly and gently, so as to not wake the two furry passengers Nona and Keeley secretly carried in their backpacks

Chapter 9 – Best Laid Plans…

If Nona had thought she'd slept badly the night before rescuing Scarlet and Rhett from the zoo, then it was nothing in comparison to the night's sleep she'd eventually have after the two red pandas unexpectedly became her fugitive roommates…

Getting into the house with them was relatively easy - Luca waiting outside Nona's home with their bikes whilst Nona and Keeley ran inside, shouting *'Hello, only us'* before they hurriedly rushed upstairs with their backpacks, Nona and Keeley's excited arrival not that unusual in itself for the Lancaster household who'd experienced it many times before.

No, the problem the girls faced was in actually getting the pandas *out* of the backpacks, their legendary elusiveness playing out in full and frustrating effect as Scarlett and Rhett stubbornly refused to leave the safe confines of the girls' bags.

After fifteen joyless and fruitless minutes of teasing and coercing, Keeley told Nona that she had to go home and so, wearing an entirely different backpack, she'd sped off down the stairs and out the door, shouting *'Goodbye'* hoping that Mel and Mim wouldn't notice the quick switch in her bags. Fortunately, the two women didn't, their eyes glued to the television and yet another dreary reality TV show.

Whilst her mother and great-grandmother sat transfixed by a cast of D-listers trying to outsmart each other – a challenge in itself - Nona continued to try and prise her two reluctant guests out of their hideaways with little success, eventually having to conceded defeat and go downstairs from dinner when Mim had summoned her to the table in her best Welsh sergeant-major's voice.

Once her food had been served, Nona's mother and great-grandmother chatted around her as she wolfed down her food, either giving monosyllabic or one-word responses to questions asked about her day so desperate was she to get back upstairs to the red pandas.

Having asked to be excused from the washing up as she'd a ton of homework to do, Nona quickly put her bike in the backyard before rushing back up to her room, flipping her door sign over to read *'Enter at your peril!'* as she closed it behind her.

She hurried over to the backpacks which still lay on her bed and let out a quiet little shriek of despair when she found them both empty. A sense of panic soon began to set in, but Nona quickly calmed down by reassuring herself that the window was closed, as had been the door when she returned to her bedroom.

They've got to be in here somewhere, Nona thought as she looked around the bombsite which was once her room, clothes being strewn everywhere whilst drawers and wardrobe doors had been left open wide whilst her dirty washing pile grew steadily higher in the corner of room.

The chaos which was Nona's room was done to the agreement she'd struck with her mother that her bedroom was Nona's domain and strictly off-limits to any adult entering it without her permission or knowledge. Therefore, whatever Nona chose to do with her room was her entirely business, provided her dirty dishes which needed washing were returned to the kitchen and any laundry placed in the basket in the bathroom, which Nona was neglecting to do with more regularity recently…

Normally, lived Nona happily in this pre-teen jungle of a bedroom where she was queen of all she surveyed without having to answer to anyone. However, she now realised that her room was the perfect haven for two shy and reclusive animals to comfortably hide in. Try as she might, Nona could not find them but was quietly comforted by the odd little *huff-quack* sound – like a bark - that they made, along with the occasional noise of the pandas' claws scratching on her wooden floor. Eventually, having finally caught sight of a ringed tail waving about on top of her wardrobe, Nona breathed a huge sigh of relief and was ready for sleep, whilst being totally exhausted from the events of the day.

However, she soon realised slumber was easier said and done once the lights went out, Nona being immediately confronted by two pairs of eyes beadily staring at her, glowing brightly when caught by the light of the streetlamp which shone through a gap in Nona's blinds. If that wasn't bad enough, Nona had also completely forgotten that Scarlet and Rhett were nocturnal creatures as they spent the next few hours chasing one another around her bedroom playing hide and seek with one another, safe in the darkness, only stopping to hide again whenever Nona turned on her bedside light, which she did repeatedly.

"Shush!" Nona continuously whispered, pressing an index finger to her lips, fully expecting the racoon-like creatures to completely understand English and then stop their night-time activities. But no matter how many times she told them off, as soon as the room plunged into darkness again, red panda play began again, the pandas immediately having the zoomies once more.

By the time the sun rose early the next morning, the rings around Nona's eyes were as dark as the rings the pandas wore on their tails. She awoke to find Scarlet lying flat on her back at the end of the bed, with Rhett lying on the pillow beside her, both completely exhausted by their nocturnal escapades. Nona smiled to herself despite her lack of rest, only for the smile to disappear almost as quickly again when she saw the long wavy trail of yellow liquid which traced its way along the floor by one of the walls of her room.

"Ew, gross!" Nona gasped, pulling the top of her window down a fraction to try and help clear the room of the musky smell the red pandas' scent had created. She dashed to the bathroom, tore off a long strip of toilet paper and returned to try to wipe the sticky substance off her wooden floor, taking several attempts at doing so before she was satisfied it was completely clear of panda pee.

However, the time she took in doing so, as well as showering, having her own breakfast before tipping out the contents of yet another container of bamboo shoots as well as putting down a saucer of fresh, drinking water for Scarlett and Rhett's first meal of the day, meant that Nona was already running late for school that morning.

Usually, Nona liked to walk or cycle in the mornings, meeting her closest friends on the way to Trinity, but as she was in real danger of missing registration, had to cadge a lift off Marilyn, one of her mother's friends, who drove Mel to and from school every day where they both also worked. Nona hated travelling with them normally as she liked to keep her home and school life separate. But today, she was more than grateful for the offer, closing her eyes in the back seat of the car as Marilyn drove at her usual snail pace during the school-run/morning rush hour traffic.

"Drop me here please," was Nona's only conversation of note, asking to be set down on the corner just before her school so as to keep the fact her mother worked at Trinity as a teaching assistant a secret from those who didn't know for just a little while longer. The school day itself passed in a bit of a blur for Nona as she fought off the tiredness which was threatening to take total control of her weary and aching body, the lessons she attended that morning failing to register with her at all, Nona's performance in drama '*limp, lifeless and lacking energy,*' according to the views of the strange and eccentric Mrs Allen.

Maths was no better, Nona's work-rate low, her calculations careless and inaccurate, resulting in a *'We need to revisit this, Nona'* comment being left on the bottom of her worksheet by Mr Maynard-Keynes her Maths teacher.

Not only that, Nona also almost fell asleep in assembly and barely spoke more than two words at lunchtime, save agreeing to meet with Luca and Keeley as agreed after school.

Even during hockey practice that afternoon, another sport she was talented at and loved hugely, Nona failed to play with her usual zeal, energy and competitiveness, volunteering to go in goal for the match they played at the end of training, much to the amazement and disappointment of Miss Kerly, Trinity's hockey teacher and other Olympic medal winner. However, without her intimidating and imposing presence on the pitch, Nona's side were on the end of a hammering with Charmayne Cunningham, the school hockey team captain, having a field day, scoring seven times past the listless and lethargic Nona.

"I don't think keeper's your best position, Nona," Charmayne smiled as she walked off the pitch, a consoling arm wrapped around her friend's shoulders at the end of the game.

But Nona didn't mind as she was just grateful that she'd somehow managed to make through all of her lessons that day, saving what little energy she had left for her greatest challenge after school that night – smuggling some more animals out of Kingston's Kingdom.

After showering and changing, Nona raced out of the changing rooms round to the front of the school where Luca and Keeley stood with their bikes patiently waiting for her.

"Where's your bike, Nona?" Keeley asked.

Nona almost swore at herself, remembering the lift she'd had that morning, meaning that her bike was where she'd left it - back at home.

"Sorry, I forgot it - had a long night," Nona yawned.

"Don't worry," smiled Luca, "We can go twosies on my bike if you sit behind me, I'll have to leave my bag here though."

"Thanks," Nona nodded as Luca dashed back into the school to put his bag in his locker.

"You look dreadful," Keeley said as they waited for their friend to return.

"Love you too!" came the curt and tired reply.

"Did our little friends keep you up last night by any chance?" Keeley whispered as a number of children and school staff passed by them as they made their way home for the evening.

"You might say that…" Nona yawned again – Keeley mirroring the gesture - as Luca sprinted back toward them.

"All done. Ready?" he smiled…

Nona was quite actually relieved that she wasn't cycling home that night, resting her head against Luca's back as he took the strain of the journey, expertly weaving in and out of the traffic, closely followed by Keeley.

So smoothly did his riding make the journey for her that Nona almost nodded off a couple of times, despite the sounds of the vehicles they passed and the roads that they travelled along. Eventually, the three of them arrived at the intended destination, chaining up their bicycles and smoothly negotiating their entry for a second night running into the almost deserted zoo.

Once inside, there seemed to be even fewer visitors than previously, which suited their plans, but this worried Nona as it gave extra merit and purpose to Lewis' plans if the zoo continued to lose money heavily.

Nona and her friends briskly walked towards the area which housed the habitat that had been especially created for the rare pygmy three-toed sloths who called the Kingdom their home.

The three friends casually walked past one of the zoo's employees who was carrying two buckets of feed - a man whose face was crumpled up into a wrinkled squint, a small pair of glasses perched on the end of his nose.

Nona couldn't recall ever having seen him before, but said, *'Hello'* anyway. The man just grunted, sounding more like one of the wild animals in his care and protection than their carer as he continued on his way, glancing suspiciously over his shoulder back at the children.

As Luca had left his bag at school, it was again down to Nona and Keeley to smuggle out the animals once they'd reached a large oval, mesh cage which housed the sloths.

Whilst Nona worked on the lock, as both Luca and Keeley watched the pathway in either direction.

"Got it!" Nona exclaimed as the lock popped open, allowing the two girls into the cage, Luca standing on guard by the entrance to the enclosure.

Crouching down, Nona and Keeley quickly made their way to the far side of the cage where three of the sloths hung side by side from the long, bare branch which arched into the centre of the cage.

"OMG, they're so adorable!" squealed Keeley as she stood and considered the face of one of the sloths, its cute, tan-coloured face bearing a dark band across its forehead, a long shaggy fringe making it look like it was wearing a hood.

"Aren't they?" Nona agreed as she knelt to open her bag, Keeley immediately copying her friend.

However, Nona exclaimed loudly as soon as she looked into her backpack.

"Noooo!" she cried, slapping her forehead hard enough to leave a red mark on her skin.

"What is it?" Keeley asked nervously.

Nona pulled out the hockey kit, shin pads, shoes and towel she'd only just used in school that afternoon.

"I've only gone and brought the wrong freakin' bag!" she moaned.

"What do we do now?" Keeley replied.

"We can't waste this opportunity," Nona said, looking her, "we'll have to swap bags and only take the one sloth tonight. It'll be better than nothing, I suppose."

"Oh, OK," Keeley replied, passing her bag to her friend.

Nona quickly unzipped it and, reaching high up above her, gently began to prise a sloth's hand off the branch it tightly clung to, the permanent smile it wore on its face made it quite difficult to tell whether it minded being disturbed or not as she gently pulled it to her shoulder. Nona briefly cuddled the pygmy sloth to reassure it, before gently placing it into the backpack, the sloth's eyes not opening once as it continued its contented slumber.

"Right then - let's get going," Nona said, gently slipping both of her arms through the bag's straps so it comfortably nestled on her back, sitting perfectly between her shoulder blades.

"All clear," Luca called as Keeley placed a small stuffed toy her mother had made for her years before onto the branch.

"Nice touch!" Nona smiled as she secured the door to the cage before quickly walking away with her friends, relieved that everything had gone so smoothly once again.

As they approached the exit, they again passed the man they'd met earlier that evening, the buckets he carried now empty and stacked inside one another. Again, the three children smiled at him as they made their way towards the door, pausing momentarily until he had eventually disappeared around a corner and safely out of view.

Nona typed in the codes needed to pass through the doors again and soon they were back outside, standing beside the fence where they'd left their bikes earlier.

"Sorry guys - I dropped the ball tonight," Nona admitted as first Keeley moved her bike and climbed into the saddle, followed by Luca, who was now positioned behind her so that Nona could ride his bicycle with her precious cargo.

Nona was just about to climb aboard it when a gruff voice behind her shouted *'Stop right there!'* as a chubby and grubby hand grabbed her firmly by the shoulder.

"Get out of here!" Nona shouted at Luca and Keeley.

Her friends needed no further instruction or encouragement, frantically pushing down on their pedals to propel them away from the danger that Nona now found herself in.

"So, what have you been up to then, young lady?" boomed a voice as Nona turned to see her face reflected in a pair of thick, lensed glasses which were perched on the end of a large and bulbous nose – a nose peppered with so many blackheads that it resembled a strawbrry.

"N-nothing," stuttered Nona as the man's free hand first unzipped the backpack, and then reached inside it.

Gently, he pulled out the sloth who looked sleepily back at him.

"Nothing, eh?" the man replied as the sloth slowly wrapped its limbs around his raised forearm. "Mr Kingston may view matters differently…you're coming with me, young lady…I think you've got some explaining to do…"

Chapter 10 – Another Fine Mess

The phone call she received that day couldn't have come at a worse time for Mel Lancaster, especially as she was balanced precariously on a ladder, helping Marilyn put up a giant display for Mr Light, Nona's form teacher at the time. Normally, Mel hated doing displays, but as it was for him, she found herself unable to say no.

If truth be told, Mel had developed more than a soft spot for the charismatic young teacher and it was because of him that she'd, in part, gone back into education after vowing never to ever set foot in a school again to work.

There she'd stood on the Trinity playground, along with all the other apprehensive and expectant mothers the previous September, patiently waiting for the arrival of their children's new teacher. Most of the other teachers in the new school were already known to the parents, having taught their subject specialisms in other schools in and around Ventham, but Mr Light was a mysterious and completely unknown quantity, being new to both Trinity Academy and the local area.

Mel was stood with Nona and Mim, who was impatiently sat on her disability scooter beside them, all anticipating the arrival of a short, middle-aged man, who probably would be wearing an old and worn tweed jacket with leather patches on his elbows, just like any other traditional and stereotypical secondary school teacher.

So, when the tall, dashing young man purposely strode out of the classroom door towards all the parents that morning instead, a large number of gasps and sighs could audibly be heard from the women, as well as some of the men, who were all gathered there awaiting his arrival.

"Ooh Mel, he's just like a film star, isn't he?" Mim whispered to her granddaughter as Mr Light walked toward the line of children who stood nervously waiting for him.

"Hush now, Mim!" Mel blushed as she turned her face away as the teacher stopped a few feet away from her to address his admiring audience.

"Good morning, parents," Mr Light had said confidently, "my name is Mr Light and I am very much looking forward to teaching

all your children this year. Come on kids - follow me!"
And with that he turned and walked off, followed by a long line of excited and chattering children - Nona included - looking to all and sundry like a modern-day Pied Piper in his slim-fitting olive-green suit.
Mel and Mim waited until the children had safely disappeared from view before they began to make their way back across the playground away from the school.
Above the whirring sound of Mim's scooter motor, Mel could just about hear some of the other parents exchanging comments about their child's new teacher.

'He's soooo gorgeous…"
"Didn't know teachers could be that good looking…"
"Definitely be coming to parents' evening this year…"
"I wonder if he's married…"
"You don't think he's gay, do you?'
"I hope so – he's dreamy…!

But Mel kept her own counsel as well as her thoughts to herself, not even telling Mim how much she fancied Nona's teacher too.
So it was that when an advertisement appeared later that term for additional teaching assistants needed at Trinity, Mel didn't hesitate in applying, knowing that with her teaching degree and previous school experience, she'd have more than a good chance of getting a job in the school, even though she hadn't taught for years. Fortunately, her best friend Clive was already working at Trinity and put in a good word for her with the headteacher, so Mel soon found herself working with Miss Mackenzie in Year 7.
As time went by and she got to know Mr Light better, Mel found herself liking him even more, his laid back, friendly nature making him loved by all at the school.
Therefore, when in the staffroom that lunchtime as he asked those there having their lunch for any help they could give him in putting up a new year group display later that evening, Mel hadn't hesitated in saying *'Yes'* as she had no plans of her own at the end of that school day - at least, she hadn't until her mobile phone rang violently in her pocket…
"Hello, Miss Lancaster?" a voice Mel thought sounded vaguely familiar asked.

"Yes?" Mel replied cautiously.

"It's Lewis Kingston here," came the formal reply.

"Oh - good afternoon, Mr Kingston," Mel replied, now slightly taken aback as she carefully began to make her way down the stepladder she'd uncomfortably been balancing on.

"Please, call me Lewis," the smarmy voice, "I'm so sorry to disturb you at work, Mel - you don't mind me calling you Mel, do you?"

"No, I suppose not," Mel quietly replied.

"That's OK then, Mel, like I said, I'm sorry to have had to call you, but it's about our dear, little Nona…"

A wave of fear spread through Mel's body like a forest fire.

"Nona? Is she all right?" she asked anxiously.

"Yes, yes, of course, forgive me - I didn't mean to worry you…" Lewis replied with more than just a hint of sarcasm in his voice, "Actually, she's sitting here with me now at the kingdom, all safe and sound. But I'm afraid to say that she has got herself into a right bit of a pickle today..."

"How?" Mel asked, now beginning to fear the worst.

There was a long pause before Lewis eventually replied, his voice now adopting a far more serious tone.

"I think it's probably best that we meet here at the zoo to discuss this in more detail in person. We'll both see you soon…" Lewis said curtly.

Then, before Mel could reply, the line suddenly went dead.

"Everything all right, Mel?" Marilyn asked, a piece of display border sticking out of her bottle dyed blonde hair.

"I'm not altogether sure, Marilyn," Mel replied, "would you be able to give me a lift, please? Nona's got herself into some sort of trouble…"

Mel didn't know what was worse, the random thoughts which were running through her head as they made their way through the rush hour traffic in Marilyn's battered little car, or Marilyn's careless and erratic driving itself. Mel tightly held on to her armrest as Marilyn sped in and out of traffic, her aggressive and frenetic driving in total contrast to the cautious approach she normally took to life, Marilyn now seemingly being possessed by the spirit of a long dead Formula 1 racing driver…

Therefore, it was with much relief when they eventually came to

a screeching stop in the customer car park at Kingston's Kingdom.
"Do want me to come in or wait for you here?" Marilyn asked as her car engine hummed and idled around them.
Mel shook her head. "No thanks – you'd best get off home to James and the kids."
"How will you get two back?" asked Marilyn, a concerned look now filling her kind but haggard face.
"We'll probably walk home, I suppose," Mel replied, shrugging her shoulders."
Marilyn immediately reached into the back of the car to retrieve her handbag as Mel undid her seat belt and opened the door to get out.
"Here, get an Uber," Marilyn said, thrusting a twenty pound note firmly into Mel's hand.
"Marilyn, I can't..." Mel began, but Marilyn just closed her eyes shook her head back at her.
"You can, and you will," Marilyn smiled back, "text me later to let me know how you both got on."
"I will," said Mel, "thanks, Marilyn."
Marilyn smiled again as Mel closed the door then drove off, her car bunny-hopping slightly across the tarmac before she eventually found the right gear and sped away, her tyres screeching wildly, leaving Mel to stand alone, save for a few zoo sponsored vehicles, in Kingston Kingdom's vast but empty car park. She quickly made her way to the entrance to the kingdom and was met by John Stafford who was impatiently stood waiting for her.
"This way, Miss Lancaster," he said unsmilingly, "your daughters in the office with Mr Kingston..."
There, Mel found Nona sat in one of the large chairs which were positioned opposite Lewis Kingston, looking pretty sorry for herself. Mel was also surprised to see that there were others present there too.
As well as Lewis Kingston, who was sat at his desk, and John Stafford, there were three other men, positioned at various points around the office. Instantly, Mel recognised the familiar figure of Doyley, who tugged a bit of his fringe towards her as she passed him, but didn't recognise the two other men who stood either side of the window that she now reluctantly faced.
The first man was tall and powerfully built, wearing a tight fitting

short-sleeved shirt, his long golden hair and thick, bushy beard cascading wildly over its collar. Across from him stood the second man who was quite the polar opposite being soft around the middle, his shapeless green shirt threatening to allow his stomach to escape at any minute. He also seemed to be sneering at Mel through the glasses which were perched on the end of his huge, bulbous nose.

"Mum!" Nona exclaimed at seeing Mel, raising herself slightly from her seat.

Mel quickly made her way over to Nona and wrapped her arms around her daughter.

"I'm so sorry," Nona said quietly.

"It's OK," Mel replied, "as long as you're safe and well then, that's all that really matters…"

"Oh, is it that so?" Lewis interrupted, "Why did I not expect anything less from you, *Miss* Lancaster?"

Mel released Nona from her embrace but still held her hand gently as she sat on the arm of the chair facing Lewis.

"You have me at a huge disadvantage here, *Mr* Kingston," Mel replied sharply, "exactly what is my daughter supposed to have done?"

"Theft…" Lewis spat, standing up, trying to make his slight frame look far more imposing than it actually was, "your precious daughter here was caught by Clarke, one of our new employees with an item of my personal property outside the zoo grounds."

"It's not your property nor mine - it's a living, breathing creature!" Nona shouted back at Lewis, anger now overtaking the fear she'd first felt when being captured earlier.

Lewis smiled. "See, she readily admits doing it with no remorse whatsoever..."

Mel looked at her daughter disappointedly. "Nona, what on Earth have you one and done?"

"I caught her trying to escape the kingdom with one of the three-toed pygmy sloths hidden in this," the man who must have been Clarke said, holding a backpack high above his head.

"That's not her school bag," Mel argued, not recognising the backpack Clarke held proudly like a prized trophy.

"Be that as it may, madam," Clarke grunted before continuing she was wearing this bag and was attempting to leave the zoo with two other individuals when I made my citizen's arrest."

"Is this true?" Mel asked looking at Nona with a look that only a truly disappointed mother can give.

Nona nodded, dropping her eyes to the floor.

"And to top it all, she refuses to say who the other two damned thieves were!" Lewis shrieked, dramatically throwing his arms high up into the air for good measure, "I've a good mind to call the police to come and sort this whole, sorry mess out!"

"But they're my animals too," Nona argued, "I was only trying to save them from *you*!"

Lewis leant across his desk, his face just a few inches from the surface of it.

"Me?" Lewis Kingston asked innocently, "Why would the animals need saving from me?"

Nona was about to reply when she caught sight of Doyley tilting his head as he raised a hand to scratch his pierced eyebrow, his head shaking slightly as he did so, as though warning her not to say anything more than she had to.

"Because…" Nona hesitated slightly, deciding on what lie to tell to protect the Irishman before continuing, "because you don't love them as much as Grandpa did."

Lewis leant back in his chair, chuckling as he did so.

"Oh, is that so?" he smiled, "Then why have I employed Doctor Au here to make sure that all of the animals are properly taken care of now that it's my zoo?"

Turning slightly, Lewis then held a hand out in the direction of the thin, tanned figure who had stood unmoved throughout the entire heated exchange before continuing.

"I think it would be best for all concerned if we do involve the police in this matter," Lewis sighed before adding, "it's now painfully obvious to me that little Nona isn't at all sorry in the slightest for the harm and distress she's caused me, let alone that poor, defenceless animal she stole…"

Nona went to answer but stopped when she felt her mother's hand firmly squeeze her knee.

"Mr Kingston…" Mel began to reply.

"Lewis - please," Lewis interrupted.

"Mr Kingston," Mel continued, ignoring the request, "I'm very sorry for any inconvenience caused by my daughter's childish and reckless actions, but seeings as she's your sister…"

"Half-sister," Lewis abruptly corrected.

"Half-sister," Mel repeated, adding, "surely it would be best for all concerned if we amicably resolve this matter between ourselves - after all, I'm sure that we can come to some sort of mutual agreement where we don't have to involve the authorities?"

Lewis sat silently for a moment, seeming to ponder Mel's words carefully before he slowly nodded his head.

"I agree, Mel, it wouldn't be in anyone's best interests to publicise this - just think what a criminal record would do for Nona's future life prospects," he sneered, exposing his hideous teeth again.

"Thank you, Mr Kingston," Mel said, relieved that the whole sorry episode that appeared to be drawing to a happy and peaceful conclusion, "come on Nona, let's get you home."

"However," Lewis added as Nona and Mel stood to leave, "there is one condition for me not going to the police...Nona is to never to set foot in this zoo again unless she is accompanied by a responsible adult and then only through the main entrance. No more secret lone visits for her and her, ahem, *friends*…"

"But…" Nona protested.

"No *ifs, buts* or *maybes,* sister dear, you've proven you're not to be trusted when coming or going when left to your own devices," Lewis snorted.

"Agreed," Mel replied before Nona had even had a chance to protest further.

Nona shot her mother a furious and defiant look but quickly dropped her tear-filled eyes to the floor as Mel looked back at her daughter with her, *don't you dare argue with me, young lady'* face.

"Good, I'm glad we've sorted this messy little business out so quickly and smoothly," Lewis smiled, holding a hand out for Mel to reluctantly shake. "I expected it to be a lot more difficult given your background and history..."

Mel stopped and quickly released his sticky and clammy hand as she stared back at him.

"Given my background and history?" she repeated.

Lewis smiled smugly as he stood and pushed his chair back under his desk.

"Oh, you know…a home-breaking, money-grabbing, benefit claiming single mum with a thief for a daughter who sponges off her demented nan. Living on a rough estate like you do, I was a bit worried things could have gotten nasty at having to deal with the grubby likes of *you*…" Lewis sat turning his face away from her as he pointed to the door, "you both know your way out…"

Mel just stood there, shocked and speechless for a moment. She was about to sharply answer back but immediately thought better of it as she looked down at her daughter's face.

"Let's go home Mum, please…" Nona pleaded.

Nodding, Mel bit her lip and took Nona's hand as she angrily walked towards the door.

"God knows what my father ever saw in that woman…" Lewis said in the direction of the tanned man who still stood silent and motionless by the office window.

Unable to stop herself from doing so, Mel stopped and turned back to look in Lewis Kingston's direction.

"Don't begin to think that you've heard the last of us, Mr Kingston," she snarled.

"Oh - I'm so scared…" Lewis mocked, holding his hands up in fake surrender before continuing, "Now, run along back to your dingy little council house, Miss Lancaster – that psycho nanny of yours is waiting…"

Mel made to head back to the desk when she felt Doyley's hand gently clasp her arm.

"Come along now, Miss Lancaster," he said softly, "let me show yer and Nona out. No good will come of dis, mark me words."

Mel shook her arm from his grasp and, shepherding Nona through the door ahead of her, began to march down the stairs, her feet taking her anger out on the wooden steps as Doyley closely followed behind them.

Lewis waited until the sound of their footsteps had faded away before speaking again.

"Thank you for your help, Mr Clarke," he smiled, "we appreciate your diligence - they'll be a nice little bonus in your pay packet this month. Good evening."

Clarke nodded, taking this as his cue to leave as he began to walk across the office.

"Of course, we expect not to speak of this to anyone…"

"As you wish, Mr Kingston," Clarke replied.

"Excellent," Lewis smiled before adding, "Stafford, please show Mr Clarke to his car."

Stafford gestured to the door and followed the shabby little man

down the stairs, leaving Lewis and Au alone in the office.
"You handled zat very well, Mister Kingston," Au finally said with barely a flicker of emotion in his tight and taut face.
"Actually, it's worked to my advantage," Lewis smiled, "I needed a way to stop that little irritant from having any involvement in what goes on at this zoo. Now they'll be too scared to do anything in case I get the law on to them. It's a win-win situation."
Lewis opened the bottom drawer of his desk and produced a bottle with a dark-coloured liquid from it. "Drink?"
"I thought you'd never ask," Au grinned as Lewis poured the liquid into two small glasses before handing one to the Doctor.
"Let's make a toast to our future successes, Doctor Au!" Lewis said, raising his glass before pouring its contents straight down his throat, the Doctor instantly mirroring the gesture.
Lewis poured them both a second glass before continuing. "Now tell me how our plans are progressing?"
"I've injected the Iberian Lynx with my unique solution, Mr Kingston," Au began, continuing, "the beast will then fall into a trance-like state within twenty-four hours, its vital signs so faint and minimal that it'll appear to all the world to be as good as dead."
"Excellent!" Lewis said, slapping a hand down hard on the desk, "Make sure the Maguire girl confirms the animal's *'death'* with you. She's so inexperienced and desperate that she'll say *anything* to keep her job here. Once the *official* paperwork has been completed and filed, we'll pack the lynx up and ship it off to its new owner - a popular little Spanish actress who's paid a pretty penny to have a big cat all of her own…"
Lewis Kingston raised his glass to his lips again but a sudden gust of wind appeared from out of nowhere, sweeping it from his hand before shattering the glass against the office wall.
Au looked on in shock and surprise at Lewis who just sat there, grinning.
"You never did meet my grandfather now, did you Doctor Au…?"

"It'll be here any moment, Miss Lancaster," Doyley said, referring to the taxi he'd called just a few minutes before.
Mel just stood in silence, holding Nona's hand, refusing to acknowledge that the Irishman was even there with them. Doyley was used to uncomfortable silences though, after all, he was now

an expert at sitting across the table after dozens of blind online dates, having exhausted the conversation whilst trying to get to know yet another ill-matched and unsuitable lady. However, this was totally different, the guilt he felt at being unable to intervene upstairs in the office earlier completely overwhelming him. Finally, Doyley could bear the silence - nor the way that Nona looked at him - no longer.

"Look, Oim so sorry 'bout der way dat he spoke to yer two," he said sheepishly.

"I didn't hear you say anything to stop him though," Mel finally replied, still looking into the distance, refusing to make any eye contact with him.

"Oi wanted to, but Oi couldn't," Doyley replied before adding, "not if we are going to save deese animals. Someone still has to have Lewis Kingston's trust."

"I understand why you didn't say anything Doyley, but that was so humiliating back there," Mel sighed as she finally turned to look at him, "the way he spoke to me and my daughter was disgusting…"

Just then, a big black London taxi pulled up to the kerb as Doyley stepped forwards to open the door for them both. As Nona and Mel climbed into their seats and buckled up their safely belts, Doyley placed a hand on either side of the door frame and leant in the vehicle.

"Look, anytink yer two needs, just ask. He'll not get away with any of dis, you mark me words," the Irishman said softly.

He then reached into his waistcoat pocket and pulled out a scrap of paper before passing it to Nona.

"If yer or yer ma needs me or wants me to do anytink, just give me a call," Doyley smiled, "Oil help in any way dat Oi can - dat's a promise dat is."

"Thank you, Doyley," Nona smiled sadly as he closed the taxi door and patted it on the roof as it drove away from him.

Nona turned and looked out of the rear window and waved at the tall Irishman, who slowly waved back at her.

"Don't be angry with him, Mum," she said as she sat back in her seat, "he means well and has always been so good to me before."

Mel sighed and turned to look at her daughter.

"I'm not angry at him - I'm angry at the trouble you've now gone and got yourself into. How could you have been so stupid?" Mel growled, "Whatever possessed you to go do something as foolish as that?"

Nona looked down into her hands, suddenly looking like a lost little girl.

"I had to do something, Mum," she said quietly, "he can't get away with what he's planning, and you wouldn't help -"

"Couldn't help," Mel corrected, "there's a big difference."

"Is there?" Nona argued, "Luca, Keeley and I were able to do something!"

"Yes, and you got caught…"

"Yes - the second time-" Nona replied before suddenly realising her careless error.

Mel immediately turned to look at her daughter again. "Second time? Exactly what do you mean by 'the second time…'?"

By the time their taxi had pulled up outside their house and the driver had asked for his fare, Mel was laughing uncontrollable despite her best efforts, genuinely amazed and quietly impressed at the ingenuity her daughter and her friends had used the night before and on their previous visit to the kingdom.

As she stood searching for her house keys in her handbag by the front door, she slowly shook her head in disbelief.

"So, we've Red Pandas in the house then…" Mel chuckled.

Nona nodded, trying hard not to smile. "Yes, we do – they're called Scarlet and Rhett."

Mel shook her head again as she put her key in the lock.

"And you, Keeley and Luca did this all on your own you say?"

"Uh-huh – with a little help from Doyley of course…" Nona nodded proudly.

"And you were genuinely planning to smuggle out two animals at a time?"

"Yep"

"That would have taken you absolutely ages," Mel said as they stepped across the threshold of their house, Nona quietly closing the door behind her so as not to wake Mim, who was fast asleep in her armchair in the front room.

Nona sat at the table in the kitchen as her mother put the kettle on. "What were you planning to do with all the animals once you'd rescued them?" Mel asked, "You wouldn't have been able to keep them all in your room now, would you?"

Nona shrugged her shoulders and rested her head on the table as her mother sat down opposite her.

"You gonna need a lot more help and a much better plan for you to be able to get all those poor animals out of Lewis Kingston's clutches," Mel finally said as the kettle began to boil.

Nona looked up at her mother and smiled as Mel winked and grinned back at her.

"Do you mean you'll help us…" Nona began to ask hopefully as Mel nodded back at her.

"Of course I will, Nona," Mel replied, "it'll be worth it just to see the look on Lewis Kingston's face once we've stripped his zoo bare…"

Chapter 11 – The Escape Committee

Nona excitedly made her way to school with Luca and Keeley the following morning, filling her friends in on the events of the night before as well as telling them about her mum's unexpected yet much welcome offer to help Nona put Lewis Kingston firmly in his place and to teach him a lesson he'd never forget.

Whilst she was doing so, her mother Mel was travelling separately to Trinity with Marilyn, telling her pretty much the same thing…

"What a horrid little toad!" the normally mild-mannered teaching assistant said as she carefully drove her car through the large wrought iron gates which led into the school staff car park.

"I can think of far worse things to call him than that," Mel replied, continuing, "honestly, Marilyn, he made Nona and I feel like we were this small…"

Mel held her thumb and forefinger close to one another, showing a small gap of about an inch between them to help to further illustrate the point.

"I'm surprised you didn't give him a right good slap!" Marilyn responded, showing Mel a feistier side of her she never knew existed.

"Trust me, I was sorely tempted, but I'd have only been playing straight into his hands if I had," said Mel as the two of them made their way into the school, adding, "as ludicrous as Nona's idea to rescue all the animals seems, I couldn't help myself from saying that I'd help her to do so. But now, in the cold light of day, I'm not exactly sure how I can."

The two women stopped and put their bags in their named lockers just outside of the staff room before taking their school lanyards from them.

"What you need is to form an escape committee, just like the British prisoners of war did when they were trying to break out of the German prison camps in World War II."

"Have you been speaking to Mim recently?" Mel asked, a wry smile teasing her lips.

"No, why?"

"Oh, no reason…" Mel grinned before continuing, "Anyway, what you suggest would be a whole lot easier said than done. So far, our '*escape committee*' is made up of three twelve-year-old school kids and an overworked and underpaid single mum."

"Don't forget Mrs Henderson, the gorgeous and vivacious teaching assistant!" Marilyn smiled, theatrically tossing back her long, shaggy blonde hair.

"Thanks, Marilyn, but I wouldn't dream of asking you to get involved in any of this," Mel protested as she slipped the name tag and lanyard over her head.

"Nonsense!" Marilyn laughed as she copied her friend's actions, "James has been moaning at me to find a new hobby ever since the girls left home - looks like I've finally found the perfect something to keep me busy for the next few weeks or months."

Mel and Marilyn left the staffroom together and began to make their way down the corridor toward their respective classrooms before Mel stopped at the door to her classroom.

"Are you absolutely certain, Marilyn?" she asked, checking to make sure that they weren't overhead, "It could be quite dangerous were we to get caught."

Marilyn placed a reassuring hand on Mel's arm.

"Danger, my dear, is my middle name - along with Gertrude, of course..." Marilyn grinned, "Leave it with me, I'll make a few, discreet enquiries. Then, let's meet at the end of the day in the Media Suite and I'll tell you how I've got on. Be sure to bring Nona and her friends too..."

When Nona unexpectedly received the message during morning registration to go to the Media Suite at the end of the afternoon, she initially panicked, thinking that she was being summoned to an after-school detention. But - try as she might - Nona she couldn't think what on Earth it could be for.

Her confusion was compounded when both Luca and Keeley confirmed at breaktime that they'd both received the same summons to be at the Media Suite for 3.45 pm that day.

"You don't think your brother has got in touch with the school, do you?" Luca asked as they made their way across the courtyard in between the two school blocks that were being used the most in the school's infancy, especially as the former private school buildings Trinity Academy had inherited were old and forbidding, built in Victorian times and had housing hundreds and thousands of children in nearly two hundred years of its existence.

However, as the fledging free school slowly continued to grow, many of its buildings stood empty and unused, awaiting renovation and redecoration whilst the school's pupil numbers continued to slowly grow.

Nona shook her head. "I don't think so. Anyway, even if he did, he doesn't know who the two of you are and I swear I never told him either of your names..."

The mystery of the message continued to prey on Nona's mind until lunchtime when she caught sight of her mother from across the dinner hall.

Mel raised a thumb and mouthed *'Are you OK?'* to which Nona nodded.

Then Mel mouthed *'See you in the Media Suite later,'* which Nona's lip-reading skills badly made out as to be *'Salami Sweet Letter'* until her mother slowly lip-synced her message again upon seeing her daughter's confused face stare blankly back at her…

When Nona, Luca and Keeley finally walked into the hugely impressive looking Media Suite shortly after the final bell of the school day, they were immediately confronted by four adults who they knew well, all sitting patiently for them at various points around the room. Whilst at school, they were known to the students as Miss Lancaster, Mrs Henderson, Mrs Brightside and Mr Tilley, but when away from Trinity, Nona called them Mum, Marilyn, Sue and Clive respectively...

Nona thought her mother looked a little nervous as the three children entered the room, Luca the last in, closing the door quietly behind him. However, Marilyn's beaming white-toothed smile immediately helped to reassure them all slightly.

"Excellent, excellent!" Marilyn said, clapping her hands, "And with the three of you, we make a most secret seven. Magnificent!"

"Ooh yes!" Sue Brightside, a short, rotund but cheery looking woman sat next to her piped up. "Just like the western where a group of cowboys, outlaws and gunslingers are hired to save a small Mexican village from an evil bandito and his ruthless gang of desperados!"

"Let's hope we fare a whole lot better than they did, eh?" Clive Tilley replied, scratching his wiry beard, "Most of them ended up dead in the end!"

Nona's mother gave her best friend a playful punch on the shoulder as though to remind him that the three worried children now sat before him would not understand his dry sense of humour.

She was right, the colour instantly draining out of Keeley and Luca's faces as they only knew Clive as Mr Tilley from his joint roles as the school's computing technician and site manager.

"Apologies, Miss Forbes and Master Bonnetti, I forget you don't know me as well as little Nona here," Clive said, winking at his goddaughter, who flushed as little with embarrassment.

"Yes – do behave yourself, Mr Tilley," Marilyn rebuked before continuing, "We don't want to scare the children now, do we? They've been through quite enough as it is this week."

Clive nodded and held his hands up in apology as Marilyn continued.

"Now, I've asked you and Sue here to listen to what Nona has to say as both she and her mother need our help..." Marilyn said, standing to walk over the children, holding a small white paper bag out in front of her, "Jellybean anyone...?"

As Nona, Keeley and Luca rummaged around in the bag, doing their best to avoid the colours they didn't like, Marilyn continued speaking.

"Having spoken to your mother, Nona, I understand you've inherited something very precious to you from your late grandfather recently."

Nona, her mouth bulging with the handful of jellybeans she'd just grabbed and thrust into her mouth nodded.

"That's right - his zoo," she mumbles, "he left it in his will to me and my brother, Lewis...."

Clive and Sue looked at Mel, their mouths open as Mel slowly nodded back at them, confirming what her daughter had just said.

"Trust me," Mel sighed, "it's complicated but he's no son of mine, let me assure you..."

"And I understand that he hasn't been entirely honest with what he intends to do with it?" Marilyn asked, pacing across the floor of the Media Suite, like an actor questioning a witness in a television courtroom drama.

Nona could feel the tears well in her eyes as she shook her head. "He wants to get rid of all of Grandpa's animals despite his final wishes," she moaned, looking to her friends, "so we've been trying to save them..."

"It's OK dear," Marilyn smiled gently, "just tell us what you've been doing and the reasons for doing so."

Nona looked at her mother, unsure as to how much of the recent

events she should share with the others.
"Tell them everything you can remember, Nona," Mel nodded, "I'll chip in with what I can recall too. Don't worry, sweetheart, we're among friends here - you can trust them all with your secrets…"

Clive Tilley exhaled deeply after Nona and Mel had finally finished sharing every last detail with them, aided by the odd comment or remark made by Luca and Keeley in support of their best friend.
"You should have told me earlier, Mel!" Clive barked, "What an evil little sh-"
"Clive! There are children present!" Sue interrupted.
"Shyster!" Clive replied, quickly correcting himself.
"My thoughts exactly! Marilyn added, "Now can you see why I asked you both here tonight?"
Sue and Clive looked at each other and nodded.
"He can't be allowed to get away with any of this," Clive tutted.
"And you say there's no way you can afford to get a solicitor involved to help you with all of this?" Sue asked.
"No, for two reasons mainly," Mel replied, "the most obvious one is the fact we can't afford one…"
"There are ways and means you could…" Marilyn began to reply.
"True," Mel nodded, already knowing what her friend was implying, "but I won't take charity from anyone thanks. No, the main reason is the simple fact we have no real proof of what he plans to do with the animals. It was Nona's friend, Doyley at the zoo who heard it all originally. Lewis would just deny saying it and Doyley would lose his job as it would be his word against Lewis Kingston's. We'd then have no one at the kingdom who we could trust to be on our side in all this."
"But why would he not keep Kingston's Kingdom open instead?" Sue asked again, "Surely he'd make more money from having a profitable and successful zoo rather than closing it down forever?"
Mel and Nona shrugged their shoulders, as Clive took a mobile phone from his pocket and began to lightly type on its screen.
"How much did he offer you to sell your share of the zoo to him, Nona?" he asked.
Nona furrowed her brow, trying to recall the exact amount.

"I think he said four hundred and fifty thousand pounds, Uncle Clive," Nona immediately flushed at her brief slip of the tongue as Keeley and Luca giggled beside her.

She'd known Clive Tilley for as long as she could remember and had had real difficulty in calling him Mr Tilley after she joined Trinity, given her genuine fondness for him.

When she was younger, Nona had hoped that her mother and Clive would eventually get married, even telling Mel of her hopes and dreams when she was about seven. Her mother had smiled and said it was *'a lovely idea'* but they were *'just good friends'* and *'besides, Clive is gay.'*

Nona still didn't understand why they couldn't get married though just because the dictionary she'd read at school the following day said that *gay* meant that Clive was *incredibly happy*.

Mel had had fun at the table that night explaining to Nona what she really meant by the word she'd used to describe her best friend, Mim sat roaring with laughter beside her.

When Nona was old enough to fully understand what it was to be gay, it didn't change in the slightest the way she felt about the cuddly, teddy bear of a man who gave her the best hugs and piggy-back rides ever...

"£450,000 you say, Nona," Clive repeated as he scrolled down the screen on his phone.

"Yes, I know it's a lot of money, but I couldn't just sell it as it is all I have left of Grandpa." Nona looked at her mother who smiled and nodded back at her.

Clive puckered his lips, as though sucking on a boiled sweet, his eyebrows furrowing as he looked closely at the screen.

"It's a damned good job that you didn't, kiddo," he eventually replied, "it's a pretty pathetic offer really, especially as the land the zoo sits on could be worth almost fifty times the amount he's offered you were you to sell it to him..."

If eyes could really pop out of heads, then Mel's would have shot out of the window and made it all away across the other side of the Thames, such was the look of disbelief on her face.

Seriously?" Mel finally managed to blurt out after her initial shock had worn off.

Clive passed her his mobile phone and pointed to its screen.

"I can't be exact, but based upon a couple of articles I've found on the internet," he said before adding, "plus using an online land

value calculator, I'm fairly confident I'm in the right ballpark on figures."
Mel began to scroll through the screen on Clive's mobile, hardly noticing that Sue, Marilyn and the three children had gathered around her, eager to see whether Clive was being truthful or was merely pulling their legs again, which he had a long and successful history of doing. But as soon as she looked at the phone now in her hands, Mel knew that Clive was being deadly serious. The first webpage which filled the screen was an online encyclopedia, filled with details about the history of Kingston's Kingdom. Mel, as well as the small audience who were peering over her shoulder, quickly scanned through the text, Mel's eyes only slowing when she came to the sub-heading entitled *Zoo Origin*. Now she read aloud directly from the page…

'After his time in South Africa, Kingston returned to London fully intent on bringing the wild to the inner city for the children there to be able to share in his love of the exotic. He successfully purchased 13 acres of the Woolwich Warren from the Ministry of Defence in 1966, the land having formerly been used for various highly classified or top-secret military training events and exercises. However, after eventually being granted planning permission, Roger Kingston built his animal kingdom on the former army site, opening it to the public the following year…'

"Now, click on the second tab that's open on my phone - the one titled *The Woolwich Warren*," Clive said, picking his teeth for a piece of leftover lunch he'd saved from earlier that day.
Without needing further instruction, Mel did as she was told, bringing up an old news item from their local newspaper, The Ventham Gazette. The article detailed the opening of a brand-new golf course directly next to Kingston's Kingdom on the remaining land, sold off by the Ministry of Defence many years later after the closure of its final military base on The Woolwich Warren in 1997. Mel quickly skimmed through the article until she came across one line of particular interest to her.

'Having initially bought the land at Woolwich Warren for a fee of £2.5 million, the new owners have since spent a further £1 million to produce the state-of-the-art 18-hole golf course without it losing any of its natural features or original character. Over time, the developers hope that their ground-breaking and unique

sporting and leisure will both service the playing needs of hundreds of keen amateur golfers on this side of the river as well as offering even more opportunities to those new to the sport.'

"Clive," Mel sighed, shaking her head, "you really need to work on your maths. Yes, it's a huge amount we turned down, but £2.5 million is only between 5 and 6 times larger than what we were offered for it."

"Check the date of the article before clicking on the last tab that's open on my phone," Clive answered, smugly crossing his arms.

Mel squinted at the screen, trying to find the date in the tiny text.

"There, Miss Lancaster," Luca shrieked, pointing over Mel's shoulder at the mobile phone screen, "17th June 1987."

"That's almost forty years ago," Marilyn added.

"Precisely," Clive replied, continuing, "next screen please, Mel..."

Tapping on another tab, Mel pulled up a page directly from a local estate agent's website. The page itself read *'Land for sale for redevelopment'* and showed a photo of a large, unoccupied strip of land Mel and Nona vaguely recognised located somewhere between Woolwich and Ventham.

"It's just a piece of barren ground," Nona said, disappointed at the result of their findings.

"Yep, just an ordinary piece of land now but one where its usage can be changed from commercial to residential..." Clive nodded.

"Huh?" Nona said, Keeley and Luca nodding in unison beside her.

"What Mr Tilley means," Sue Brightside chipped in, "is that you can knock down all of the work buildings or shops on a piece of land and get planning permission to then build houses on them."

Nona nodded her understanding, feeling slightly less confused than before but still not entirely sure where all this was going.

"Now- look at the starting price per acre..." Clive repeated.

"£1 mill – a million quid per acre!" Mel shrieked, leaping from her seat, almost knocking over those around her.

"My work here is almost done – Mrs Mackenzie would be so proud of your maths, Nona!" Clive laughed, "The zoo sits on approximately thirteen acres of prime real estate in London which backs onto the River Thames itself. Were it ever to close and be sold off for redevelopment, the landowner would stand to make a tidy little fortune from it. No wonder he's so keen on keeping you away from the zoo, Nona…"

Nona didn't respond – no, she couldn't respond…

£13 million…how many zeroes were there in £13 million? The knot she already felt in the pit of her stomach grew larger as she realised how sneaky and devious her newly found brother had been when making his original offer to her.

"Not only is he trying to destroy my grandfather's legacy and ruin his zoo - he also thinks that we're complete idiots in trying to buy us off cheaply!" Nona finally said, her face a barely contained ball of pent-up fury, "He needs to be taught a lesson or two in manners…"

"Quite right dear," Marilyn replied, clapping her hands in delight, "And we're all going to help you do it."

"We appreciate that you want to help us, Marilyn," Mel replied looking at her friend sadly, "but, realistically, there's not an awful lot we can do with just the seven of us."

It was now Sue Brightside's turn to interrupt.

"True - except it isn't just the seven of us now, is it?" she smiled.

"I'm not quite sure I follow?" Mel said, now slightly puzzled by her friend's remarks.

"We're the heads of the escape committee - the planners and the organisers," Sue continued, "therefore, we bring on board others who we carefully select and trust to help us. That way it won't be long before we have a secret network of people who can help teach that evil little man a lesson he'll never forget..."

Now Nona understood why Marilyn had asked for Sue Brightside's help, for she was one of life's do-gooders, always being the first to put her name down on sponsorship forms handed to her or to buy raffle tickets or to raise her hand whenever anyone asked for help.

Not only was she a dinner lady and lunchtime supervisor at Trinity, Sue was also the head of the PTFA and the school's Chair of Governors, having been one of the original proposers for the free school, Sue Brightside having driven the application to the Department of Education from start to finish, canvassing the support of residents and businesses in and around Ventham, constantly haranguing and harassing the DoE until they were eventually granted permission to open Trinity Academy.

It was a long-standing joke locally that the school was only opened to stop the civil servants and government ministers from getting endless hourly phone calls, texts or emails from Mrs Brightside! Not only did Sue somehow combine all those roles with being a mother of three Trinity students in Years 8, 9 and 10 herself, she was also the treasurer for Ventham Football Club, which was where Nona knew her best from.

It always amazed Mel and Nona how Sue found enough time to sleep, let alone juggle her multiple roles and responsibilities in helping her local community. However she did it, Sue Brightside always did so with a sunny smile and a friendly word for anyone she ever met...

"Thanks, Sue," Mel responded, "but, as I was saying, realistically we are somewhat limited in what we can actually do."

"But, Mum," Nona argued, looking at Keeley and Luca, "if the three of us could manage to get the red pandas out of there on our own, just think what we could do if there was more of us..."

Mel looked at Nona and smiled knowingly.

"True, but you were caught the second time, weren't you?"

"We were careless," Luca chipped in, "we should have paid way more attention to who was watching us."

"Yes, Miss Lancaster, we forget to have a proper lookout," Keeley agreed, "like we did the night before."

"Keeley's right, Mum," Nona added, "it was all my own fault I got caught, but if there's more of us involved in future, we can set up diversions, have warning systems and change who does what and when..."

"That the Lancaster spirit!" Marilyn laughed, punching the air in delight, "Come on, Mel - you were all for this earlier!"

"Yes, and I still am, but once I started to think of the practicalities, then I realised that it's not that simple," Mel sighed.

"Like what?" Clive asked.

"Like where do we keep the animals once we've rescued them?" Mel replied, "It's all right having a couple of stinky red pandas hiding out in Nona's room but I'm not sure my house, or Mim for that matter, would cope with orangutans, chimpanzees or the like swinging from the bannisters!"

"Then we'll keep them here," Clive said calmly, causing all of the children and women with him to look on in surprise.

"I'm sorry," Sue replied, "but did I just hear you right? Keep the animals here at the school - with the children?"

"Yep - you heard right, Sue," smiled Clive, "most of the buildings aren't currently being used and have been fenced off, ready to be gutted and renovated over the next eighteen months or so. It's not ideal, but it'll be a damned sight easier to hide and care for them here until we find them all a permanent home. There are loads of deserted classrooms, two large portacabins, the old gymnasium and an indoor pool as well as several other unoccupied rooms we could use…."

The room was eerily quiet when the site manager eventually stopped speaking, Clive looking at the stunned faces who were all staring back at him, awaiting their response. Unsurprisingly, it was Mel who broke the deafening silence.

"Once again, I can't tell if you're taking the mickey or not, Clive?" she finally said.

"I'm deadly serious, Mel," her friend replied, "unless you all want your houses full of animal sh-"

"Clive!" Mel, Marilyn and Sue shouted simultaneously.

"Shedding their hair, fur or skin as well as dropping their dung everywhere!" Clive winked, quickly correcting himself.

Nona noticed the faintest flicker of a smile surf across her mother's face before instantly disappearing as soon as she spoke again.

"But what about Miss Bridges?" Mel asked anxiously.

"I know she can be a bit fierce sometimes, but she's no wild animal!" Clive quipped, "We wouldn't need to keep her here as she has got her own home after all!"

"Seriously, Clive," Mel shouted as her friend sat smiling back at her, "you know what I mean…"

"Mel, don't worry," Clive grinned, "you leave Auntie Sheila to me…"

Now Nona finally understood how the lovable, but lazy, work-shy technician and site manager had somehow managed to get a job at the school with no previous experience - he was Miss Bridges' nephew!

"She's more than enough on her plate as it is with the pupils on roll as well as the buildings that are already open and ready for use in Phase 1 of the Trinity School Development Plan," Clive, added, "which means that C, D and E Blocks are at least twelve months away from being ready or needed. Plenty of time to help you and Mel sort that little bug-, I mean, bully, out!"

Nona, Luca and Keeley looked hopefully at Mel, also noticing that Marilyn and Sue were both doing the same.

Finally, the smile which had been playing hide and seek somewhere in Mel's stern face broke cover again causing her famous and infectious smile to dazzle as brightly as it ever had.

"Well, it seems like we have an escape committee everyone. Thank you - all we have to do now is decide which of the animals we rescue next…" she beamed.

"Already one step ahead of you, Mum," Nona said cheerfully before turning her gaze to Sue, "But we're going to need some of your football team to help us with this, Mrs Brightside…"

Chapter 12 – A Grand Day Out

Rain, normally the most feared and dreaded of weather conditions when planning a school trip, grand day out or sporting event - except for the fact that it was absolutely essential for the next rescue attempt from Kingston's Kingdom.

Initially, when Nona had shared her idea with the newly formed escape committee, the adults couldn't help but smile at such a ridiculous but audacious plan.

It was so ridiculous that you could say that it was, in fact, quite brilliant coming as it did from the mind of a twelve-year-old girl. But so daring and ingenious was it meant everyone agreed that nobody at the zoo would expect anything so outrageous to be attempted, giving it every possible chance of success. To pull it off would mean that they would have to rely on some key factors to come into play all at once.

First, they would need a zoo insider and it was perfectly obvious to all present who that person needed to be…So, as soon as the escape committee had ended their very first meeting, with all those present given different tasks in readiness for when they were needed, Nona had immediately called Doyley.

However, before she had even outlined exactly what they planned to do and what help she wanted from the Irishman, he'd already said 'Yes, text me when, what and where.' No further questions were asked nor was any more persuasion needed…

The next part involved Sue Brightside and some of the girls who played for Ventham Football Club.

As soon as their first escape committee had ended, Sue had dashed home and then spent the next couple of nights phoning parents, saying that *'as a reward for their efforts this season, we would like to take a selected number of players nominated as player of the season to the zoo as a special thank you.'*

The parents were even happier when told that there would be no cost to them Sue concluding each conversation with a *'but please be on standby as to what night it may be as we are waiting for the zoo to confirm availability for group bookings.'*

Another little white lie, the reason for the short notice offered being the third piece of the jigsaw they needed to help make their break-out attempt a complete success…

The weather...

It was critical to the plan for it to rain when they all went to the zoo next. Not simply a few spots or a light drizzle either... no, it had to be full-on biblical rain, the sort of rain which makes you think you're parting heavy bead curtains as you walk through it... Without this, the escape committee who have little to no hope of success.

They needed to be patient though as it took well over a week, but, eventually, the 5-day forecast from the BBC confidently predicted *'heavy, persistent showers,'* to fall in the capital the following Thursday. That meant that Sue could finally agree with the parents the date and time of Ventham FC's end of season rewards, confirming that the children would have their tea at the zoo before the parents came to collect them when finished.

Sue ended each telephone conversation by telling the parents not to worry about the weather conditions predicted that day as she would make sure that there were more than enough Ventham FC raincoats and hats available to keep all the children warm and dry. However, the final part of the planning puzzle which needed solving was proving to be problematic - how to transport everyone - rescued animals included - away from the zoo that night.

Given the numbers involved, the escape committee were struggling to find a vehicle large enough to carry the whole thing off. Marilyn then suggested they use the school minibus which could carry seventeen adults, driver included. Clive had said it was possible to borrow it but there was no way he'd be able to drive them all after school as he had to be on site every night until 6 pm at present due to Trinity having after-school clubs which used both the hall and playing fields.

"Besides," Clive added, "you'll need me here to let you and the animals in through the back of the school grounds."

"Who else has a licence to drive it then?" Marilyn asked, expecting a lengthy list of suspects to choose from.

"Other than me, there's just Miss Bridges and Mr Light," came the reply.

"Well, that narrows our choice down quite a bit, doesn't it?" Mel sighed, knowing that there was only one other potential mini-bus driver that they could approach and then use...

So, it fell to Marilyn and Mel to sweet talk Mr Light and find out if he was free that night to inadvertently help them with their plan.

The new teacher couldn't have been nicer when Marilyn and Mel explained about the *'girls'* football team outing' especially with many of them already attending Trinity, several girls being in Mr Light's form...

"Of course, I'll drive you all," the teacher replied when eventually asked, "Thursday's a good night for me anyway as there's no school fixtures so the bus will be free for you to have. You have already cleared this with Miss Bridges, no doubt?"

Mel and Marilyn shot each other a furtive look before Marilyn eventually replied.

"Didn't need to, Mr Tilley gave us permission as he is the prime key holder."

That was a good enough answer for Mr Light.

"Just tell me where and when then and I'll be there," he smiled, winking at Mel, causing her to blush slightly.

"Kingston Kingdom's main car park, Thursday, 6pm," Mel answered, adding, "thank you again, Mr Light."

"How many times have I told you before, Mel - call me Lawrence." he smiled back at her...

Mel could have throttled Marilyn in the car on their way home as she teased her.

"Ooh, just call me Lawrence, Mel...!"

Thursday dragged as Nona, Luca and Keeley distractedly went through the motions of their school lessons. Generally, they really loved being at Trinity, but today they couldn't wait for the day to end so that they could finally put Nona's latest plan into action.

They all ran to meet Mel and Marilyn in the staff car park straight as soon as the end of day bell rang, Nona already wearing her bright yellow waterproof windcheater and a baseball cap, both emblazoned with Ventham FC's official club crest on them.

"You ready for this?" Nona's mother asked whilst the three children squeezed into the back of the car, the rain drumming a heavy metal rhythm on the roof of it.

"You betcha!" her daughter grinned excitedly...

Sue Brightside was already waiting at the zoo with some of the girls from Nona's football team when the five of them climbed out of Marilyn's car. Nona smiled and nodded at Kirsten, Mya, Paige, Amy and Kylie and who were stood in line like a row of damp daffodils, dressed as they were from head to toe in yellow, along with the jovial figure of Sue who wore her oversized club coat whilst holding a huge umbrella above her head.

When Nona had told her team-mates of her escape plans at the under 13s training session the previous Monday, the girls couldn't have been more eager to help. Now, as the six of them stood in the incessant rain, a nervous, but excited tension filled the air.

"Thanks, girls," Nona said, walking past her team-mates, high fiving each of them as she did so.

"Thank us later," Kirsten replied, winking.

"The others should be here any minute," said Sue, handing Mel a large yellow jacket and cap like the one she too wore, "put this in your bag for later, Mel."

Just then, a small group of girls, each one holding an adult's hand, came around the corner and approached Nona and her friends.

"Excellent!" Sue Brightside boomed, "Welcome my fabulous and unbeatable under 8s! As a special treat for your fair play and sportsmanship this season, we're going to have a tour of the animals before having our tea in the zoo! Now, partner up with one of our under 13 players who are helping out as young leaders today..."

The younger children excitedly said goodbye to their parents and walked towards Nona and her friends, who were now stood waiting with outstretched hands for them all to take.

"Oops - almost forgot..." Sue added as she rummaged around in her Ventham FC backpack, "make sure you put these on over your raincoats. We can't be too careful with the weather as it is now, can we...?"

Carefully, Nona and her team-mates all helped their little charges put on the waterproofs, guiding heads away from armholes as well as making sure that they were on the right way around.

Sue chuckled, as she looked at the group of children, each now covered from head to toe in yellow windcheaters which were far too big for any of them.

"I've only gone and brought the wrong size with me!" Sue laughed, winking knowingly at Nona, "Silly me...!"

"We'll be off then," Mel said, hugging Nona tightly to her, "take care and be safe - we'll meet you all later, as agreed."

"You too, Mum," Nona replied, squeezing her mother just a little tighter than usual.

"Remember - any sign of trouble and we go straight to Plan B,"

Marilyn whispered as Mel finally let go of her daughter.

Nona nodded and waved as she watched her mother, Marilyn, Luca and Keeley walk towards the zoo entrance, looking just like any other visitors to Kingston's Kingdom.

"Let's give them five minutes," Sue said, looking at her watch, "then we'll make our own way in…"

Now normally, five minutes isn't long in the grand scheme of things… I mean, you could boil one and a half eggs, just about run a mile - if incredibly fit - or listen to a modern pop song, with time to spare if you wanted to...

But having to wait five minutes when you are planning to do something you're not supposed to can feel like an absolute eternity, especially when you're a kid...

"Can we go in yet?" Nona asked impatiently after her mother and the others had disappeared from their sight.

"Not yet, dear," Sue replied, "we need to make sure they are a good way ahead of us…"

A few moments later…

"Now can we go?"

"Not just yet."

Seconds after that…

"What about now?"

"Nona, patience dear! I'll tell you when!" Sue said firmly.

An uneasy silence hung over the group of girls as they watched Sue Brightside, who calmly stood, looking at her watch, waiting for her to give them order to finally move.

"Now we go!" Sue eventually declared, not a second before or after the five-minute deadline she'd set.

Slowly, the yellow-coated group walked off, two by two, led by Sue who proudly strode off ahead of the girls, her umbrella thrust high above her head, Nona pulling the peak of her cap down over her face so as to not be recognised by anyone she happened to pass.

Upon arriving at the entrance, Sue made her way to one of the ticket office windows, leaving the children stood a little way behind her, each pair of girls looking like a *before and after* commercial, one tall girl holding the hand of a miniature yellow version of themselves.

"Sue Brightside, Ventham FC group booking. Here's my E-ticket," Sue declared, thrusting a badly folded and poorly printed sheet of A4 paper through the window hatch in front of her where spotty faced youth wearing a Kingston Kingdom sun visor peered closely at it.

"It says one adult and twelve children," he replied, revealing a mouthful of teeth trapped behind a cage of metal braces.

"That's correct, young man," Sue answered patiently, "me and my twelve girls here."

She gestured to the children, who all waved back at her, the smaller girls having to tilt their heads up to peer out from under the windcheaters.

"How old are they as they all need to be under 14 to get the discounted rate and some of them look a bit big to me," the teenage ticket attendant mumbled.

"Half the group are under 13 players and the other half are under 8s," Sue smiled through gritted teeth, trying hard not to show her displeasure.

The lad in the ticket office stared at the children and was about to ask for proof of age but thought better of questioning the honesty of the stern looking woman stood in front of him.

It's not as though we're that busy anyway, he thought to himself as he pushed a button hidden under his counter.

"Push your way through the turnstile, one by one mind," he finally declared before adding, "I hope you enjoy your visit to Kingston's Kingdom."

"Thank you, young man, you've been most helpful. Come along now, children, let's hurry!" Sue called, shepherding Nona and the girls towards the turnstile, making sure each one passed safely through it, before squeezing through the tight gap herself.

Nona moved to the head of the line and waited until Sue had joined her again.

"What time's it now, Sue?" she asked.

Sue glanced down at her watch. "A little after a quarter past four."

"Perfect! Right - let's make our way to the Penguin House, everybody," Nona said, adding quietly to Sue, "Doyley will meet us there at half-past…"

Once inside the penguin house, the older girls laughed almost as much as their younger counterparts did as they watched the Humboldt Penguins scurry and scamper around after the fish that were being thrown at them by their keeper. Nona herself was still amazed at how graceful these lumbering creatures always looked after they'd dived into the water to chase the sprats which eluded them in their artificial Antarctic world.

"Ain't dey sometink grand?" a familiar voice whispered behind her. Nona turned to look up into Doyley's friendly face, his lazy eyes and mouth smiling back at her.

"Yes, they are," she replied.

"Just give der word and we'll get dis done," Doyley said, looking around them to see if there were any other visitors about. Fortunately, as was all too common at the kingdom nowadays, there were none.

"As soon as Mum and the others arrive, we'll get going," Nona replied.

It wasn't too long before Mel, Marilyn, Keeley and Luca entered the Penguin House themselves, the two children quickly positioning themselves at both entrance points as lookouts. Mel looked over at Sue and nodded her readiness to proceed with the second part of Nona's daring plan, taking out the yellow raincoat and hat her friend had given her earlier.

"Right then, my darling little under 8s," Sue said loudly, "it's time for the next exciting part of our trip to see the creepy crawlies! Unfortunately, Ventham's under 13s are incredibly squeamish and scared of the bugs we'll see so they are going to visit another part of the zoo instead. However, we're extremely fortunate that Mrs Henderson is here to come along with us, as well as Keeley, one of the top dancers from our school, and Luca, the star of the famous Soft-Botty nappy commercials on television when he wa a baby..."

"Thanks for that, Mrs Brightside!" Luca shouted sarcastically without once turning his eyes away from the direction they were now staring in.

"But before we head off children, I think it'll be safe for us to remove our hats and waterproofs now," Sue smiled, continuing, "as I think the hoods on our raincoats will be sufficient for the rest of our visit, especially when we go for cakes and ice-creams later this afternoon."

The loudest cheer of the day rose from the young girls at the mere mention of food as Nona and her team-mates took off the hats and windcheaters their smaller counterparts had been wearing. It wasn't long before the six younger girls all stood in their normal rainwear again, Sue and Marilyn holding the hands of two girls each, leaving Keeley and Luca to have a child of their own once they left their lookout positions.

"If we don't manage catch up with the rest of you later," Sue said, winking, "We hope you all have a fruitful and memorable visit of your own…"

Mel, Nona, Doyley and the rest of the girls waved as Sue and the others left, now looking like just another ordinary family group out on a family day out.

"Do you still have to wear nappies?" Nona heard a ginger-haired girl with freckles ask Luca as they made their way out of the Penguin House, causing her to chuckle and she watched the last of the younger group exit the Penguin House.

When she was certain that they were now completely alone, Nona asked Amy and Mya to go to either entrance, ready to take up lookout positions vacated by Keelly and Luca. She then looked at Doyley and nodded at the Irishman who took out a large set of keys from his coat pocket to let himself in through one of the doors which led into the feeding area for the penguins, stooping low as he did so.

"Owaya, Tom?" Doyley said, placing a long-fingered hand on the shoulder of the keeper who was already inside feeding the penguins, "Here Oi am, bang on time as promised, ready to take over from yer."

Tom turned and smiled at Doyley.

"Cheers, dude," the penguin keeper grinned," I've been trying to get tickets for this band for ages and Oxford's the closest venue to here that we can get to see them play live."

"Well, yer best be going den if yer don't want to miss dem!" Doyley laughed, "Oil finish off in here for yer, plus as some of dem have to have their routine checkups with Miss Maguire, Oil sort dat out for yer as well."

Tom frowned for a moment, causing Nona and the others to watch from afar to worry that he might suspect something was up. But no sooner had the lines appeared on his face than they'd disappeared again, now replaced by a happy and grateful grin.

"No worries, Doyley," Tom replied, "and thanks again! Me and the missus owe you one."

"Tink nothing of it, just go and enjoy yerselves, wee man," Doyley winked.

Mel, Nona and the rest of the girls busied themselves outside, pretending to be doing nothing other than watching the penguins feed as the penguin keeper exited the enclosure, tunelessly singing one of his favourite band's songs as he did so.

Nona immediately signalled to Amy and Mya as she, her mother, Paige, Kirsten and Kylie stood by the door with raincoats and hats in their hands. Doyley soon opened the door and gestured to them to come inside to join him and the penguins. The inner part of the enclosure was deceptively cold, causing the girls to shudder slightly as they entered it where around twenty Humboldt Penguins were still moving about, darting in and out of the water. The Irishman pointed to another group of penguins to the left of him who were stood watching the activities of the others in the water.

"Deese guys are der ones that we will take," Doyley said quietly, "dere der the tamest and will do anytink for deese…"

He slipped a hand into his long coat and pulled out a fish, one slightly larger than the sprats the penguins had been feeding on earlier.

"All yer got to do is walk beside dem and every once in a while, wave one of deese in front of dem - they'll follow yers anywhere den!" The Irishman winked.

"Er! It's dead!" Kylie gasped, wrinkling up her nose in disgust.

"Well, yers going to have a hard job keeping a live one in yer coat pocket now, don't yer tink?" Doyley said, more than a little exasperated for once.

He quickly handed everyone a fish which they all gingerly slipped into their raincoats, along with a couple of spare ones for Mya and Amy's penguins.

"Now follow me," Doyley said as the six of them, waterproofs in hand, made their way over to the docile group of penguins who looked quietly and curiously back at them.

It was surprisingly easier for Nona and the others to put the waterproofs over the penguins than it had been with the younger children earlier.

Initially, the camouflaged effect was promising, the windcheaters comfortably covering the penguins' bodies so that no part of them could easily be seen. When their hats were then placed atop their heads, so perfect was the illusion that you'd have struggled to physically tell that the six under 8 girls had been replaced with six penguins.

However, moving them proved to be an entirely different matter altogether, the penguins being so slow that it was proving extremely difficult to move them as quickly as the younger girls had moved especially as holding the penguins' flippers through the arms of the waterproofs was proving to be almost impossible, their oily, waterproof texture of them causing the flippers to regularly slip from the girls' grasp.

Eventually, Mel came up with the idea of them all walking single file, each one of the group in front of a penguin, holding the fish Doyley had given them all behind their backs, just out of the reach of the penguin's beak. This approach proved to be much more effective, the penguins now desperately shuffling after each girl, the fish they held in their hands proving elusive enough to be a tempting and teasing bait for each penguin to follow obediently.

Nona and the rest of her teammates followed walked behind Mel, fish in hand, a weird procession of yellow figures quickly shuffling along in the heavy rain as they gradually made their way to the exit, Doyley following at a safe distance behind them, casually acting as their lookout.

As they approached the exit, Nona began to feel a tightness in her stomach, the Irishman now breaking away from the group to watch their departure from a safe distance. Fortunately, upon their arrival there, they found the exit was completely unmanned with only a couple of other people hastily leaving at that time having been caught out by the sudden deluge of water that afternoon.

But as they all passed through the exit, one of the penguins reared its head so that its beak poked out of its hat for the briefest of moments, causing the spotty youth in the ticket office to do a double take, before shaking his head and return to the magazine he was reading.

A sudden surge of relief filled Mel as she led the yellow conga line slowly out in the rain, towards the car park where she was mightily relieved to see the white school minibus waiting for them, with the words *'Trinity Academy'* emblazoned along its side.

"Almost there, girls…" Mel called behind her, the sound of her voice almost being drowned out by the flip-flapping sound of the penguin's feet on the wet concrete.

Having seen the line of children begin to approach him, Mr Light had immediately jumped down from the driver's side of the school vehicle and made his way around to the passenger side of the minibus, sliding open the door behind the main cab.

"Hey," he cheerily called as Mel and the others quickly approached the minibus, "I hope you all had a good time and didn't get too wet in there!"

Mr Light laughed and watched as a long, yellow and wet line of figures began to form in front of him, Mel Lancaster carrying out one final head count before quickly moving to the head of it.

"Are we good to go then?" Mel asked, anxiously checking over her shoulder.

"Yep, just as soon as the children are on board and safely strapped in," Mr Light replied.

"Great," said Mel climbing in through the open door, expecting the lead penguin behind her to instantly follow.

It didn't - instead, it chose to stand and curiously look at the small metal step in front of it.

"Come on," Mel said urgently, gesturing for the penguin to follow her into the vehicle, again with no luck.

"Let me give you a hand, little one…" Mr Light said gently as he moved towards the transfixed penguin.

"No, Sir - don't…" Nona cried, but it was already too late as Mr Light's arms wrapped around the penguin's ample waist.

"My, you're a chunky, little thing, aren't you?" the teacher said as he tried to get hold of the slippery creature who was wearing an even more slippery raincoat.

Eventually, after no little effort, Mr Light managed to lift the penguin onto the minibus, but not without revealing the penguin's ample black behind first.

"What the devil…?" Mr Light stammered as the penguin turned and made a sound, one somewhere between a honk and a squawk as though it were impersonating a donkey, "I've just p-p-picked up a p-p-penguin!"

Suddenly, as though playing a strange version of *'Follow the Leader,'* the other penguins all quickly broke rank and waddled and hopped their way out of the line of girls, jumping up onto the minibus to join their friend who was now happily honking inside the vehicle.

Mr Light could only stand there, open-mouthed, as the girls all then followed, each sheepishly saying, *'Thank you, Sir'* to him as they too climbed aboard to then sit with a penguin directly beside them.

Once the girls and penguins were all safely in place, Mel jumped down from the minibus and slid the door shut. She placed her hand on Mr Light's arm, who was still stood there, water dripping from his hair, transfixed, as he watched three of the penguins' heads poke out of their hats and bob up and down through the minibus windows honking excitedly as they did so.

"I promise that I'll explain everything once we're on our way back to the school," Mel whispered, "but we really need to go now…"

Slowly, Mr Light turned and looked at her.

"Mel, have you honestly just stolen six penguins - dressed in waterproofs - from the zoo?" he asked in disbelief.

"Technically, yes…" Mel replied, with more than a hint of urgency in her voice, "but it's way more complicated than that. For now, please trust me and just get us the hell out of here…"

Chapter 13 – A Chink of Light

Lawrence Light liked to believe that he could cope with the most stressful of situations, having worked in several different high-pressured work environments prior to teaching. He'd never really settled on one career choice though until finally re-training to be a teacher just five years earlier.

However, nothing he had ever done before had prepared Lawrence for the stress and strain of driving a minibus full of children and penguins through London's manic rush hour traffic, Mel Lancaster nervously chattering away beside him, leaving no detail out in explaining the incredible and almost unbelievable chain of events which had led them to this point in time.

The honks and horns of cars, vans, buses and lorries merged with the laughter of the girls and the honk-squawks of the Humboldt penguins as they bobbed up and down behind Lawrence and Mel, the minibus windows now steaming up with condensation. Not only that, but the air inside the school vehicle also stank of raw fish thanks to the last meal the penguins had consumed moments before their *'escape'* from the zoo.

All in all, Lawrence was more than just a little relieved to eventually see the familiar but imposing sight of Trinity School looming in the distance.

"Almost there," he said tiredly.

"Fab, can you turn right, just before the main entrance and drive us around the back of the school. Clive said he'll meet us there."

"Mr Tilley is in on all this too?" Lawrence said, shaking his head in disbelief.

Mel nodded as the minibus turned down the one-way street which led to the unused buildings at the rear of the school site.

"The two of us have been best friends forever…" Mel replied before quickly adding, "There he is, pull up over there, please…"

The minibus came to a grinding halt just before the steps to the Sports Block where Clive Tilley was stood holding an umbrella, sheltering him for the rain which now lightly fell. He nodded as Mel waved at him through the front windscreen as the engine of the minibus suddenly fell into silence. The site manager then turned and quickly walked up the steps to open one of the main doors, wedging it open as both the driver and passenger doors on the minibus cab slammed behind him.

Once satisfied that the door wouldn't move of its own accord, Clive turned back to where Mel and Lawrence were now stood in front of the minibus.

"Did it all go as planned?" Clive asked as Mel made her way round to open the side of the vehicle.

Mel smiled and nodded as she slid the door open, the muted sounds of the penguins suddenly filling the early evening air.

Clive looked at Lawrence as Mel began to usher the girls out of the minibus, the penguins honking excitedly as they bounced around inside the vehicle.

"I take it Mel has filled you in on why we're doing this all this?" Clive said to the young teacher who just stood and watched as the first penguin gingerly hopped down the minibus step towards Nona, who still held her fish in front of her to help coax it off the vehicle.

"Yeah, but I'm still not exactly comfortable with all this," came the subdued reply.

"Yet you still drove the minibus here rather than turn around and go straight back to the zoo. I wonder why that is, Mr Light…?" Clive winked as he nodded his head in Mel's direction.

He grinned as Lawrence wordlessly blushed before walking towards the group of children and penguins who were growing larger in numbers in front of the two men.

The girls gently removed the penguins' waterproofs, causing them to shiver and stretch once their bodies were free of the tight and restrictive material they'd been forced to wear.

"Come on," Clive called, looking anxiously around him, "let's get them indoors before anyone sees what we're up to…"

The inside of the Sports Block smelt cold and damp from months and months of abandonment and disuse as Clive led the line of children and penguins down the corridor which led to a pair of heavy double doors at the very end of it, the sound of foot and flipper steps echoing off the polished wooden floors around them. Nona took the lead with Mel and Lawrence following at the rear, the line of penguins and people stopping as Clive pulled out his keys once more to unlock and open the doors to reveal a massive swimming pool hidden behind them.

"I got here at lunchtime to check the pool water was completely chlorine free as well as putting on the air conditioning," Clive said as the temperature around the group of people and animals suddenly plummeted.

Whereas the penguins had been reluctant to board the minibus earlier, they now needed no second invitation to dive into the welcoming pool, Nona and her friends whooping with delight as they watched the six penguins swim and cavort freely, leaping out of the water like mini torpedoes occasionally. Even Lawrence Light managed to raise a smile as he watched the animals curl and twist, cutting their way through the water ease and grace.

"They're so beautiful," Lawrence eventually said.

"Aren't they, Sir?" Nona agreed, beaming back at her teacher. "Thank you so much for your help, Mr Light."

Mel hugged her daughter as she turned to Lawrence, smiling. "Yes, Thank you Mr Light."

"I don't necessarily agree with how you're going about this, but I'm beginning to understand why," Lawrence sighed. I'm just worried about what will happen to all of us if Miss Bridges were ever to find out."

"You leave her to me," Clive replied, "What my aunt don't now won't hurt her..."

"Clive Tilley and Miss Bridges are related...?" Lawrence spluttered, looking at Mel in utter disbelief.

"She's his Auntie Sheila," Mel smiled before adding, "long story... Anyway, keeping the animals here will is only a temporary measure until we can find somewhere that is able to house them permanently. It'll also give us time to make sure that they're safe and happy there and not just sold off to the highest bidder."

"Like I said, I can't argue with your reasons," Lawrence began, "but I'm not sure how much more I can do to help you do other than drive the minibus."

"That's more than enough, Mr Light," Nona replied.

"I agree," added Mel, "we couldn't have done ever of this today without your help, Mr Light."

Lawrence sighed again but much more heavily this time.

"Why do you still insist on calling me Mr Light, Mel?"

"I dunno," Mel replied, "I suppose it's because your Nona's form teacher..."

"That should make no difference," Lawrence interrupted, "we do work together after all.

"True, but to be honest, it's quite a long name to have to wrap your tongue around," Mel confessed, adding, "perhaps if I could shorten it to something like Lol…or Larry…or Lawrie instead…yes - Lawrie, I like that…"

"No, Lawrence replied firmly, "definitely not Lawrie…"

"Why ever not?" Mel teased, nudging him, "I quite like it actually…Lawrie, it doesn't sound as stuffy or posh as Lawrence now, does it?"

"You can call me whatever you want, Mel - within reason, of course…" Lawrence shook his head, "but please don't call me Lawrie…"

Mel and Nona looked at each other for a moment of two, still desperately trying to understand why the young teacher had such loathing for the shortened version of his first name. Then Nona's eyes suddenly lit up like lightbulbs.

"Oh…my…god…" she exclaimed, looking directly at her teacher with a more than a little hint of mischief in her eyes.

"Don't you dare, Nona Lancaster…" Lawrence warned, much to Mel's confusion.

"What? What am I missing?" she asked, now noticing Lawrence's face had begun to grow redder.

"Lawrie Light…" Nona laughed, "Lawrence Light would then become Lawrie Light…*Lorry* Light….? *Lawrie* Light, geddit?"

Mel put her hand to her mouth and looked at Lawrence, whose face was now flushed with embarrassment.

"Oh - I'm so sorry, Lawrence," she gasped, "I had absolutely no idea!"

Lawrence shook his head and smiled.

"I know you didn't, Mel, but it's almost been worth it just to hear you finally call me Lawrence!" he laughed before bending to down to directly look into Nona's eyes, which were wet with laughter as she continued chuckling away to herself.

"And as for you, young lady…" Lawrence said, playfully jabbing his finger towards her, "if anyone finds out about my secret, they'll soon find out all about yours…"

Nona immediately stopped laughing as Lawrence stood up and winked, unseen, at Mel.

"Yes, Sir, sorry Sir," she said stiffly causing her mother to smile warmly at Lawrence before they all turned to gaze at the pool, standing silently as they watched the penguins continue to frolic before them.

A short while later, the double doors swung open behind them, causing all those present to anxiously turn towards them before relaxing again as Marilyn, Sue, Luca and Keeley walked in. Keeley gasped loudly as the penguins continued to swoop past the other girls, whose shoeless feet now dangled in the water at the edge of the pool, giggling as the penguins swept past them.

"Oh - how marvellous!" Marilyn clapped.

"Yes, I agree," Sue replied, adding, "I hope you don't mind, but we've brought some company..."

Just then, the doors opened once again and in strode the tall, imposing figure of Doyley, carrying a large bucket of fish and a net, alongside a small but pretty girl, dressed in what resembled a medical uniform.

"Owaya all?" the Irishman drawled, "Oive brought dem sometink to keep dem going for der next couple of days. Diss is Miss Maguire from the zoo...don't worry, she knows all about Mr Kingston and yoos all!"

Everyone turned and looked directly at Miss Maguire, who giggled nervously and waved back at them.

"Please - call me Hayley..." she said before continuing, "what I think Mr Doyle is trying to say is that he's told me everything about Lewis Kingston and his plans. I'd like to help too, after all, you're going to need someone to keep an eye on the health of the animals who are still in the kingdom - that's if you'll have me of course...?"

Nona looked at her mother, then back towards the young vet and nodded.

"To be honest, Hayley, the more help we get to secretly and successfully do this, the better," she smiled happily...

Chapter 14 – Two by Two

Nona absent-mindedly sat gazing out of the classroom window. *It's been a helluva a week,* she thought to herself as she watched a class of year 3s play Kwik Cricket outside on the school field. Her grin grew even wider when she recognised two of the young Ventham FC players who'd inadvertently helped with the second stage of her secret rescue plan.

Knowing that the penguins were absolutely thriving in their makeshift environment, helped by Doyley and Hayley Maguire's regular visits of course, had spurred Nona and the others on to ramp up their efforts in order to release as many animals as they secretively could.

She once again tried to concentrate as Miss Miller droned on about the hidden message in Shakespeare's play Macbeth, but Nona's mind kept wandering, reliving everyone's efforts over the previous seven days, ever since the penguins' release a week ago that day...

The Zooper Troopers – a name conjured up by Marilyn (an ABBA music fanatic) to describe their ever-expanding escape committee – now totalled eleven regular members. This number included Mr Light who, although initially reluctant, had shown an increasing keenness and willingness to help out, alongside a growing number of close and trusted friends, both young and old, who'd all played their own minor parts in helping to free the animals of Kingston's Kingdom.

As the rest of the class lowered their heads to continue reading the study guides they'd been given by Miss Miller, Nona replayed in her head some of the week's events - events which had included the Humboldt Penguins having new neighbours to hide within the disused school buildings, under Uncle Clive's ever watchful eyes...

Nona then chuckled to herself as she also recalled how the escape committee had accidentally and surprisingly, gained its eleventh and most unexpected of members...

They'd all gathered at her house on the previous Saturday to quietly discuss, agree and map out which animals were to be moved out next, and when.

After an extremely productive meeting, Nona and her mother had just waved off Doyley and Hayley Maguire, the last of the Zooper Troopers, when they heard a piercing scream escape from the bathroom.

"Mim!" Mel exclaimed as the two of them rushed upstairs, both Nona and her mother fearing the worst, expecting to find that their elderly relative had slipped and fallen whilst trying to get in or out of the bathtub.

However, as they thrust open the bathroom door, neither of them could have prepared themselves for the scene that they then saw slowly unfolding before them.

There, still sat in the bath, was Mim, a bath cap covering her newly dyed purple hair, whilst soap suds, a small flannel and what looked like soggy toilet paper were covering her modesty as well as sparing her blushes.

"Whatever's the matter, Mim?" Nona asked as her great-grandmother just sat there, her denture-free mouth wide open, pointing across at the slim bathroom cabinet which stretched from the bathroom floor to its ceiling, now partially hidden behind the open door.

"Th-there!" Mim finally managed to shriek, her Welsh accent becoming ever stronger as the fear coursed through her raspy voice, "W-what in God's name is that *thing* over there?"

Nona and Mel slowly closed the door so as to be able squeeze themselves into the tiny bathroom which was normally only just about big enough for the one person. The two of them slowly turned to look at the cabinet which usually housed scented candles, numerous bottles of bubble bath and body lotions, as well as the various bathroom accessories and spare loo rolls needed by their family of three.

Nothing seemed to be out of place or order on first inspection. Mel shrugged her shoulders at Nona and was about to question both her grandmother's eyesight and sanity when suddenly she caught sight of a bushy, ringed tail sweeping backwards and forwards between the toilet rolls which were stacked on the very top shelf.

"See - there it is!" Mim exclaimed again, waggling her finger in time with the swishing of the Red Panda's tail, "What on God's Green Earth is that and why's it here in my house, throwing quilted bog roll at me when I'm in nothing but my birthday suit?"

Mel rolled her eyes and looked at Nona, who quickly opened the door to look at her bedroom door directly opposite, which was ever-so-slightly ajar.

"Oops - my bad!" Nona blushed as she closed the bathroom door again and leant against it.

Upon hearing Nona's voice, the frightened little red panda leapt from the cabinet and hid in Nona's hoodie, knocking more toilet rolls down into the bath as it did so.

"It's the devil himself, I tells you!" Mim wailed again, raising her knees up in the bath, causing more sodden tissue and water to slosh onto the floor.

"No, Mim, he's, not…his name is Rhett and he and his sister needed our help," Nona replied, stroking the tail which was now curled above her mouth, making it look like she'd grown a giant, red, bushy moustache.

"Hand me a towel," Mim snapped, "I think you both have some explaining to do, don't you…?"

It took Nona the rest of the evening to clear up the bathroom, calm her great-grandmother down and explain what was really going on - but that was only after Nona had managed to get one red panda out of a hoodie whilst trying to find the other, who'd already decided to play a never-ending game of hide and seek using the whole house.

Therefore, it came as some relief when Mel finally found Scarlett fast asleep in the washing machine just as she was about to load the drum with all the wet towels the two of them had used to mop up the bathroom floor.

Finally, once the two red pandas had been safely tucked away again in Nona's bedroom, the three generations of Lancaster women sat quietly around the kitchen table, drinking their hot chocolate.

"Why didn't you just tell me?" Mim finally said as she cleaned her glasses which had been misted up by the steam from the hot milk, "Secrets is for strangers, not family, see?"

Nona shrugged her shoulders as Mim slowly turned to look at Mel, her piercing stare now asking her granddaughter the very same question.

"We didn't want to have to involve you in any of this," Mel began to explain, "especially as we could get in a helluva lot of trouble if we were to ever get found out."

"We're family, *cariad*," Mim sniffed before sipping her drink, "and a trouble shared is a trouble halved - have you learnt nothing?"

"Sorry," Mel smiled sadly knowing how disappointed her grandmother was with her lack of honesty and trust.

"Still, no harm done, except to my pride and the bathroom lino!" Mim smiled, the lines on her face creasing even more as she did so. "So, what can I do to help...?"

Nona chuckled quietly, pretending to read the Macbeth text before her, scarcely believing how successful their repeated raids on the zoo had been ever since her great-grandmother had been welcomed into the fold.

Every day since the weekend, with the zoo generally being much quieter during the working week, a different group of Troopers, ably supported by Doyley and Maguire, had managed to smuggle a different set of animals out of Kingston's Kingdom, without suspicion, challenge or capture. Whilst Miss Miller continued to drone on in the background, Nona silently recalled each moment of every rescue mission and raid on the zoo with pride.

She'd even given each one its own film title, creating a playlist for the season of Hollywood movies Nona daydreamed would be one day made and released in cinemas and on streaming services, telling all about their daring exploits.

Her imaginary '*Now Showing*' movie features list read like this...

MONDAY – *Invasion of the Lemur Snatchers*.
TUESDAY – *Bush Babies in the Hood*.
WEDNESDAY – *Slothbusters!*
THURSDAY – *Monkey Business*.

The next set of rescues had begun with Sue Brightside and her small but highly elite and efficient team of PTFA mums. Sue normally didn't work on Mondays, so had arranged to go to the local supermarket with some of her most trusted friends – all school mums who Nona's mother, Mel, also knew quite well.

All of them had arrived at the zoo carrying one of those bags for life supermarkets were regularly issuing, in line with the government's ban on free plastic shopping bags. Each of the bags carried several everyday food items you'd normally expect to find on a supermarket shelf - sliced bread, dried fruit, cup-a-soups, biscuits, crisps etc.

All of them had then left Kingston's Kingdom with the contents of their shopping bags intact, along with the addition of a blue-eyed black lemur in each bag. The lemurs had come courtesy of Doyley who'd placed one of the little creatures carefully in amongst the groceries as each PTFA mum had casually passed the enclosure he'd deliberately located himself in for that morning.

Sue and her team then enjoyed a hassle-free journey on the number 49 bus back to Trinity where they were met by Clive Tilley who'd quickly ferried them into one of the school's many unused and unoccupied buildings. There they soon discovered that most of the contents of their shopping bags had been consumed by the lemurs, who were sleepily lying there with huge, contented grins on their faces...

The following evening, Nona, Keeley and Luca were joined straight from school by the girls who'd previously helped them smuggle the penguins out of the kingdom. And, as before, Mr Light drove the minibus, with Mel and Marilyn sitting in the cab alongside him. This time though, the easy-going young teacher was now fully aware of the reasons for the journey to and from the zoo and was there as a willing participant and fully paid-up member of the escape committee.

Even though she'd been warned off from going to Kingston's Kingdom ever again by her vile brother, Lewis, Nona had insisted that she was going to go in again to help the others liberate yet more of the animals and nothing that the others could say to her dissuade her. So, led again by Marilyn, Nona took her place alongside the other children – all of them wearing their Trinity School hoodies - as they patiently queued up for their entry ticket. She deliberately turned her face away from the ticket office window when the time came for Marilyn to pay the entrance fee to enter the kingdom though.

It must be costing the adults an absolute fortune in admission charges alone, Nona had thought to herself as they all quickly followed their now familiar path through the zoo to that night's targeted animal for rescue - the Rondo Dwarf Bush Babies.

But as they approached the cage where the animals were normally kept, Nona felt the fear rising in her throat as she suddenly noticed that not only was the cage door still locked but Doyley was not in

position to help them as had been agreed the previous weekend.
"Sorry I'm late," a voice called from behind the group.
Nona felt an overwhelming sense of relief and confusion as they all turned to see Hayley Maguire approach, her face flushed and sweaty as she power-walked toward them, pulling a large bundle of keys from her pocket as she did so.
"This entrance is so ancient and old-school," Maguire muttered as she began to try several different keys into the antique lock that was fitted on the door.
"That's OK," Nona replied, "Where's Doyley though? He was supposed to meet us here."
"He's on a call to your brother," Maguire mumbled absentmindedly, her attention fixed firmly on opening the lock before her.
"Why?" Nona asked nervously.
"Something to do with the animals they've have already secretly sold," answered Maguire, still trying to twist the key before adding, "Doyley has to go along with it still even though he hates what they're doing…There - that's done it..."
Nona and the others breathed a collective sigh of relief as the small iron gate swung open before them, groaning as it did so.
"I'll stay back and keep a lookout," Marilyn whispered, casually leaning on one of the gate posts, keenly watching as the children, led by Luca, followed Hayley Maguire into the cage, quickly making their way over to a small hutch at the end of it.
The vet then reached in through a small door at the side and rummaged around for a moment or two before pulling out a curled up little brown creature, it no bigger than a squirrel, which sleepily looked up at the children, before quickly falling fast asleep again.
"Aw - it's so cute!" Keeley clapped as Maguire turned towards her, the bush baby now gently wrapped in her hands.
"Turn around then," Maguire whispered.
Keeley immediately did as she was asked, allowing the vet to carefully slip the sleeping bush baby into her hood.
"Next," the vet declared as Keeley carefully made her way back towards the entrance to the cage as Paige then took her place in the line.
Having repeated the process with each of the children, all receiving a sleepy bushbaby of their own to look after, Marilyn then the children them back through the kingdom, stopping briefly

whenever a member of the zoo staff passed by them.

Once they'd returned to the minibus, Nona breathed a huge sigh of relief before they made their way back to school to deposit their latest nocturnal guests in their new, top-secret surroundings…

That night, Nona had found it hard to sleep when she returned home, knowing that the following day brought with it her great-grandmother's debut as a fully-fledged member of the Zooper Troopers. She needn't have worried though as Mim proved to be more than capable of organising and executing her part in proceedings…

Believing it important to mix up the timings for each visit to the Kingdom so as to not raise any alarms or suspicions, Mim had persuaded her friends Valerie, Betty and Mo from the bingo hall to abandon their normal Wednesday afternoon matinee session and make their way to the zoo with her instead. Not that her friends needed much persuading. Valerie, in particular, being extremely excited to be doing something a little more dangerous than wielding a permanent marker pen to cross off the numbers on her bingo card

So it was that the self-proclaimed *Blue-Rinse Bunch* rode into Kingston's Kingdom on their mobility scooters that afternoon, proudly led by Mim, all wearing neck-scarves to cover their mouths as well as the clip-on sunglasses which were attached to their normal prescription glasses.

"Senior citizens, dear," Mim declared, flashing her bus pass at the ticket office like a television detective, "right then - free entry for me and my pensioner crew…"

Doyley had to suppress the laughter he felt bubbling up inside him as he heard the electrical hum of the OAPs' scooter engines slowly grow louder as they rounded the corner which led to their intended destination that day.

Mim slowly brought her disability scooter to a stop and raised a hand so that her friends would do likewise behind her.

"What's occurring, Mr Doyle?" Mim grinned.

Doyley put his hand to his mouth to conceal his own smile as he simply replied "Sloths."

"Ah, well, we'd best be getting on with it then," Mim nodded as she moved her scooter beside the enclosure door and raised the lid of the grocery box which was mounted on the front of the vehicle. Doyley nodded and looked around to make sure that they weren't being watched. When he was satisfied the coast was clear, he carefully made his way into the enclosure to gather up a small bundle of material before quickly returning to where Mim was sat waiting.

"Normally dey hang from trees," the Irishman whispered as he placed the material inside the basket, "but dese guys really like to snuggle into baby papooses instead..."

Mim looked into her basket, her rheumy eyes meeting the small, sleepy, beady brown eyes of one of the sloths her great granddaughter had unsuccessfully attempted to rescue before.

"There's lovely," Mim cooed as she lowered the lid of her grocery basket and moved forward to allow the rest of the blue-rinse brigade to each collect their own precious cargo...

Clive Tilley was dozing on the stool he'd positioned himself on whilst waiting for the latest unofficial delivery to arrive at the school that day. Normally he'd have edgily paced backwards and forwards, anxiously looking for any sign of his aunt, but today he could relax a little as Miss Bridges was attending a headteacher's conference on the other side of the Thames and wasn't due back in school until the following day.

But having nearly dropped off to sleep twice, he checked himself and anxiously looked at his watch...3.10 pm.

Where are they...? he thought to himself.

Clive was about to lock the gates to the rear entrance to the school when he caught sight of a flash of purple making its way towards him and sighed with relief as he slowly began to make out the unmistakable and instantly recognisable figure of Mel's grandmother leisurely driving towards him, closely followed by the three similar vehicles that were trundling behind her.

Finally, after what seemed to be an eternity in doing so, the Blue-Rinse Bunch slowly drove through the school gates, Clive quickly closing them behind them.

"Sorry to keep you, *cariad*," Mim declared, "but these blessed things go at no speed at all, see."

Clive shook his head and smiled as Mim continued.

"Not only that, but we had to keep stopping and take it in turns to answer the call of nature..." she tutted, "the damned vibrations riding these infernal scooters along the pavements around here don't half play havoc with your bladder, let me tell you..."

Chapter 15 – Monkeying Around

Thursday proved to be the most daring rescue attempt yet, led by as it was by Mel and Marilyn, neither of whom worked Thursday afternoons, much to Nona's disgust when she was told that she couldn't skip school to help. Her unhappiness was further compounded when she then realised it was also Mr Light's PPA afternoon – the time he had set aside for him when he'd normally be out of class planning, preparing and assessing the lessons he'd taught that week. This fact wasn't lost on both Mel and Marilyn either when they again asked for his help that day...

"I guess that means that you need me to drive the minibus again then, yeah?" he'd asked during the Zooper Troopers planning meeting.

Mel looked at Marilyn and shook her head.

"No, it'll be too risky taking it out during school hours," Mel replied, "Marilyn has her car and Sue is going to meet us at the car park as she's lending us some equipment that we'll need, so they'll be her car as well."

Lawrence looked slightly bemused, lightly scratching the stubble on his chin. "Okay, so what do you need from me then?"

Mel smiled with more than a hint of mischief in her eyes. "I don't suppose you've a dressing gown, scarf and hat you could bring with you, do you…?

So it was that Lawrence Light had arrived, by foot, at the car park straight after morning lessons had ended that Thursday afternoon, carrying a large backpack. He was relieved to see that Mel and Marilyn had already arrived and were struggling to open and assemble some strange, four-wheeled contraption they'd just removed from the back of Marilyn's hatchback.

"Need a hand?" Lawrence called, dropping his backpack by the back wheel of Marilyn's car.

"Yes please," Mel replied, "often it takes brute force and ignorance to get this damned thing open."

Lawrence pulled open the two padded arms of the object easily, the metal at the back of it snapping shut, instantly revealing it to be a collapsible wheelchair. He quizzically looked at Mel.

"It's my gran's," she said before adding, "Mim said we could use it today. Did you bring the clothes we need as asked?"

"Not quite," Lawrence replied, reaching down for his backpack, "I couldn't find my dressing gown and I think I left my cowboy hat at my previous school, but…"

Before he completed his sentence, Lawrence pulled a long, brown hooded gown with huge sleeves out of his backpack and held it proudly up in front of him.

"Ta-dah!" he smiled.

Mel and Marilyn stared at the gown, then at one another.

"What's that when it's at home?" Mel asked.

Lawrence sighed and shook his head. "Can't you tell? It's a wizard's robe!"

"Why do you have a wizard's robe?" Marilyn asked, "Do you secretly cast spells to make the kids like you or something?"

Lawrence sighed once again. "No, of course not. I use it for cosplaying..."

"I'm so sorry, I had no idea…" Marilyn replied innocently, "you poor man - is it serious?"

"Yes, it is – not in the way you think though!" Lawrence laughed I go to Sci-fi and Fantasy conventions in my spare time and -"

Upon seeing the perplexed looks on the women's faces, Lawrence decided to quickly change the subject. "Anyway, I thought that it might come in handy today instead. I also bought a face and neck mask, just like the assassins wear in those video games too!"

"I take it you're a bit of a geek then, Lawrence," Marilyn laughed.

"Yes, I am," Lawrence grinned, "and proud of it!"

"Well, I suppose it's better than nothing," Mel sighed before adding, "you'd better put it on before you sit in the wheelchair though.

"You want me to wear it," Lawrence said, looking bemused, "and then in that?"

"Of course - why else do you think we asked you here?" Mel replied.

But before Lawrence could begin to reply, a large blue people carrier came screeching into the car park, pulling into the space next to where they were parked.

"Sue's here," Marilyn smiled, "right on time as usual."

Sue Brightside turned the car engine off and opened the car door, having to stretch out her legs so that her feet could find the tarmacked surface of the car park as she climbed out the driver's seat.

"Afternoon," Sue smiled as she made her way round to the back of the vehicle, "Mr Light, would you mind giving me a hand to get this down from the back please..."

If Lawrence had been surprised to see Mim's wheelchair when he first arrived that day, he was now even more perplexed as he pulled out the double pushchair from the back of Sue's people carrier.

"I'm sorry, I think I might've missed something last weekend's meeting," he said, "what exactly are we doing again today? What are we doing again today?"

"We're improvising...get dressed and jump into the wheelchair, Lawrence," Mel grinned, wrapping a headscarf around her head before slipping on a large pair of dark sunglasses, "will soon be revealed...!"

Leaving Sue behind in her car, Mel pushed Lawrence across the car park in the wheelchair, the young teacher now covered from head to foot by his hooded gown and face mask.

Marilyn followed about twenty metres behind them, wearing a large pair of sunglasses, her hair tucked in under a big, floppy blue and white hat, its rim hiding her eyes from the sun. In the double buggy she was pushing sat two lifelike dolls, a plastic see-through rain cover pulled over the front of the buggy helping to conceal them from unwanted or prying eyes.

"Now let me do all the talking," Mel whispered as they approached the ticket office window.

"OK, but hurry - I'm sweltering under all this!" Lawrence moaned.

The woman who served Mel almost did a double take as she looked at the strange, hooded figure who was sat in the wheelchair chair below her window.

"It's all right," Mel said in a false, high-pitched voice, "my poor husband suffers from Polymorphous Light Eruption Syndrome."

"Polly-wolly doodle what?" the woman replied, straining to get a better look under the hood of the gown Lawrence wore low down over his face.

"He's allergic to sunlight," Mel replied, taking the end of one of the sleeves, "his skin quickly breaks out into pus-filled blisters and boils as soon as it's exposed to the sun. Would you like to see...?"

"No, no, it's quite all right, thank you - there!" the woman said, almost throwing Mel's tickets at her.

Such was the fluster she'd got herself in that as Mel pushed Lawrence away from the window, the ticket office attendant didn't even give Marilyn and the double buggy a second look when she asked for her own tickets shortly after...

"How much longer?" Lawrence moaned a few minutes later as Mel struggled to push him up the path, past the cartoon figure of Diana the Monkey which now pointed the way.

"Not much longer," Mel grunted, "just through those entrance gates up ahead, then off to the right."

Lawrence looked up at the large welcoming banner which hung over the entrance.

"'Realm of the Apes'... seriously?" he muttered as they trundled through the gates, "I'm supposed to be marking poor grammar and bad punctuation this afternoon, not stealing ruddy primates!"

"Wrong on both counts!" Mel laughed as they slowly made their way into the sheltered area, several vines and creepers hanging from its ceiling to help it resemble a jungle, where several different species of apes and monkeys were housed.

She then stopped and pointed at a small sign which read *'Louie the Orangutan.'*

"You and I are rescuing him, Lawrence!" Mel grinned...

Lawrence's shock and disbelief had barely faded away by the time Marilyn and her buggy had joined them outside Louie's cage where the orange ape sat quietly watching proceedings.

"Surely you're not being serious?" Lawrence protested, pulling his mask from his face before lowering his hood, "How the hell are we supposed to get him out of here? I mean, look at the size of him...and what if he's dangerous?"

Mel laid a reassuring hand on Lawrence's shoulder. "Don't worry, Louie's a gentle giant - Nona and I've walked around the zoo with him, holding his hand, many times. He's just a big softie really, nothing at all like his dad, Ken..."

"Ken, seriously?" Lawrence replied, "there's orangutan called Ken?"

"Yep - he lived at San Diego Zoo, where Louie was born," Mel nodded, "Ken used to escape on a regular basis though, every way from unscrewing the bolts to his cage to reaching around to steal his keeper's keys from his belt. He even climbed up and over the zoo walls to get out once!"

Mel turned, smiled and waved at the orangutan who raised a hairless palm and waved back at her. "Louie's completely different to his infamous father..."

"I couldn't agree more," a voice called out from inside the cage. Lawrence did an immediate double take as he stared at Louie, who was still sat quietly looking back at him. He was about to ask if Louie could speak too when Hayley Maguire stepped out from behind the orangutan and stroked his long, hairy, orange arm. "Come in - the door's open," the vet smiled.

Mel helped Lawrence, who gathered up his robe, out of the wheelchair before they made their way through the door, Marilyn standing guard whilst they did so.

"I've just given him his food, so he's quite happy and content at the moment. Are those the clothes you want Louie to wear?" Maguire asked, pointing at Lawrence.

Lawrence looked at Mel before suddenly realising just why he'd been asked to dress up in the first place. Mel nodded as he slid the robe and mask off his head, shaking it in disbelief as he did so. Mel and Hayley Maguire then took the clothes from him before carefully placing them over Louie's head, the orangutan tilting it slightly as they first slipped the hood over him, then put one arm, then the other, through the sleeves of the robe. The two women then gently pulled Louie's arms to make him stand up before tying the robe together at the waist before finally raising the hood to help to conceal the orangutan's face.

"This way, Louie," Mel said gently as she and the vet led the orangutan towards the wheelchair.

"Won't they notice him missing though?" Lawrence asked as Louie sat down on the seat, Mel lowering the footplates to place his feet on them.

"We've already thought of ways to cover that," Maguire said, shaking her head, "he'll either be napping, walking around the zoo, or visiting one of the other monkey enclosures if anyone asks - Doyley and I will see to that..."

Mel stood waiting, her hands on the wheelchair handles, ready to set off as Maguire closed the door behind her. She then looked over to where Marilyn was patiently stood waiting and nodded.

"Wait there whilst I get Jimmy and Barbra," Maguire said, "I've

143

made up a couple of bottles of milk for them. That should keep them quiet until you get out of the Kingdom..."
"Jimmy and Barbra?" Lawrence asked, "Who the hell are they?"
"Two young proboscis monkeys who are also coming with us," Marilyn replied, lifting the rain cover up from the front of the double buggy...

Around ten minutes later, having said goodbye to Hayley Maguire, the three of them slowly began to make their way back towards the zoo exit, Marilyn, with her two charges, now dressed in baby-grows and sucking from milk bottles safely secured in the buggy, taking the lead. Mel followed behind close, struggling to push the sizeable orangutan, with Lawrence nervously bringing up the rear. Lawrence had offered to push the wheelchair, but Mel had politely declined, saying it would have looked even more suspicious if the person pushing the wheelchair had somehow changed if spotted by the ticket attendant when they eventually exited the zoo.
As they neared the exit gates, an elderly man and woman slowly approached Marilyn and the double buggy.
"I bet you have your work cut out with the two of them," the woman said kindly, pointing at the front of the pushchair.
Marilyn smiled nervously and nodded as the woman shakily approached it.
"How old are they?" the woman asked as she bent down to peer through the rain cover.
"Er, eighteen months," Marilyn lied as the woman pushed her glasses up onto the bridge of her nose to squint through the plastic at the long, pink noses which hung over the bottles Jimmy and Barbra were now drinking from.
The old woman sadly shook her head.
"My eyes aren't what they used to be, I'm sure they're quite lovely, but..." the woman frowned as she started to unclip the rain cover, "let's have a closer look, shall we...?"
Marilyn was about to swing the buggy around and dash away when, fortunately, the woman's husband intervened.
"Come along now, Audra, leave them be..." he said gently.
"Yes, it's best to do so when they're feeding- they can be quite grumpy if their mealtimes are disturbed, I'm afraid... Marilyn replied, beginning to quickly walk away as Mel began to approach

the elderly couple, Lawrence trailing a little further behind her. As they passed the old woman, Louie pulled the mask down from his face and stuck out his tongue her.

"I really ought to get my eyes re-tested, George," the woman sighed, "they really are beginning to play tricks on me nowadays…"

Unexpectedly, a small queue had begun to form at the exit gates as Marilyn, Mel and Lawrence approached them. At the front of the queue was one of the zoo's employees, handing out leaflets whilst talking to each departing visitor as they passed him. Mel instantly recognised the man from when she'd been summoned to collect Nona from Lewis' office.

"It's that weasel, Clarke," she muttered to herself as they slowly made their way towards the exit.

Marilyn had now moved a little way ahead of her and the wheelchair, a woman and her child now standing between her and Mel as they joined the growing queue of people waiting to exit the zoo. Mel could feel the sweat begin to coat her forehead as she watched Clarke slimily talking to a woman at the front of the line.

"Be sure to come again soon," Clarke smarmily said, handing a small leaflet to the woman, "50% discount if you return by the end of the month."

"Thank you," the woman replied uneasily, taking the paperwork from him.

"It'll be more if you ask for me personally," he winked, causing the woman to quickly draw away from him as she raced towards the exit.

Nervously, Mel adjusted her headscarf, pushing her sunglasses further up her nose as she lowered her head whilst the line before her began to shorten. In no time at all, it was Marilyn's turn to pass Clarke. Luckily, he hardly gave her a second glance, his eyes now fixed on a pretty, young woman stood with her daughter behind her. Mel watched as Marilyn quickly left the zoo, glancing back as Clarke moved closer toward the young mother, who was now stood just in front of Mel and the wheelchair containing Louie the orangutan.

"Hello there, gorgeous," Clarke greasily said, running a hand over his receding hairline, "How'd you like an extra discount on top of the one I'm offering today?"

"Would that apply to children's parties too?" the young woman asked, bending over to talk to her daughter, unaware that Clarke's eyes were looking her up and down as she did so.

"Sofie, would you like your friends to come visit the animals for your birthday?" the woman asked her daughter, who nodded her head excitedly.

"Urgh!" Mel quietly spat as she watched Clarke continue to leer at the woman.

Unfortunately, her disgust was loud enough for him to hear, causing Clarke to look directly at Mel. At first, he wore a look of disdain and disgust, but then a hint of recognition began to cross his face. Fortunately, Louie inadvertently came to Mel's rescue as Clarke took a small step towards her.

Despite being hugely different to his legendary father, Louie still had the touch of the devil about him, sharing Ken's impish and mischievous nature, finding it almost impossible to ever resist the sight of a bottom bent before him…

Slowly, a long, furry orange arm reached out from the sleeve of the gown to gently pinch the young woman's bottom whilst Clarke stood between the two women, staring closely at Mel.

Shrieking loudly, the woman stood bolt upright and turned around sharply, causing Clarke to immediately turn to face her.

"How dare you! You dirty, old man!" she snapped, slapping Clarke squarely across the face, causing him to stagger back slightly as the woman quickly marched off, dragging her daughter behind her.

Mel saw her chance to rapidly follow, using all of her strength to propel Louie and the wheelchair past the startled and shocked zoo employee.

"But…but…" Clarke loudly protested, rubbing his face as Lawrence quickly passed him too.

"Yes, it was her butt, mate," Lawrence laughed, "only it's hers to touch - not yours!"

Nona chuckled loudly, remembering how her mother had retold her the events that afternoon during dinner the night before. She then yawned, stretched and looked up from her textbook and back out of the classroom window, back at all of the young cricketers running across the field. Nona grinned as she watched one of the young girls bend down to field a ball, only to turn and run after it as it squirmed and squirted through her legs. However, Nona's grin soon disappeared as her eyes fell onto the figure of Miss Bridges striding across the playground directly in front of the field, closely followed by her mother, Mr Light, Mrs Henderson and Mrs Brightside.

The shock of seeing them had barely begun to register with her when, suddenly, there was a loud knock on the classroom door, quickly followed by a humourless and official voice which said "Nona Lancaster - Miss Bridges would like to see you in her office…Now!"

Whilst Nona made her way from her class, her mother Mel, Lawrence, Marilyn and Sue walked quietly behind Miss Bridges, anxiously looking at one another as the headteacher strode silently before them.

Just a few minutes earlier, they'd all been sat in the staff room with two other members of the school staff discussing the details of an upcoming sports trip. However, the relaxed mood and friendly atmosphere around them was soon shattered by Miss Bridges' booming tones.

"Mr Light, Miss Lancaster, Mrs Henderson and Mrs Brightside. My office – now please…"

When the door to Miss Bridges' office swung open, the four of them were met by the sight of Clive Tilley stood next to her desk waiting. Clive silently mouthed 'Sorry' at them as Miss Bridges made her way around the desk and promptly sat in her chair.

"Close the door behind you," she barked at Sue, who instantly did as she was told.

Miss Bridges then pointed to the other chairs and small sofa which filled her office. "Sit!"

As Mel, Lawrence, Marilyn and Sue manoeuvered themselves into their different seating positions around the room, there came a quiet knock on the door.

"Enter!" Miss Bridges barked again.

Nona opened the door and slowly poked her head around it.

You wanted to see me, Miss?" she asked nervously.

Miss Bridges' tone softened slightly as she answered her. "Yes Nona, I did. Please do come in."

Nervously, Nona stepped inside and closed the door behind her, looking directly at the imposing figure of her headteacher, trying

desperately hard to ignore the other adults in the room.
Miss Bridges then stood at her desk, now looking even more formidable than ever before.
"Right, now that we're all here together," Miss Bridges said sternly, "would somebody please care to explain to me why the hell I've got an orangutan, some bush babies and sloths swinging from the equipment in the old gymnasium…"

Chapter 16 – The Game's Up?

Few things in life ever phased Miss Bridges…
She'd liked to think to herself that after nearly six decades on this weird and wonderful planet that she'd seen and done everything there was to do - so full and varied her life had been until this point in time. Sheila Bridges had travelled the world, done things you couldn't imagine and seen many hundreds of things you wouldn't have believed.
But nothing she'd ever previously experienced had prepared her for the sight of a gym full of animals when she peered through one of the small glass panels on the gymnasium door whilst carrying out an impromptu tour of Trinity's unoccupied buildings and facilities in readiness of next headteacher's report for governors.
At first, she'd thought her eyes to be deceiving her when she saw a huge, orange orangutan swinging from the ropes which hung from the ceiling in the disused gymnasium. Imagining the school to be in immediate danger from a mass zoo escape, she quickly sought out Clive Tilley, the school site manager, to order him to evacuate the school and call the police. What she didn't expect to find was her nephew casually and cheerfully throwing raw fish into the swimming pool for a group of penguins who were now occupying it. In truth, it was hard to decide who was the more surprised – Miss Bridges, Clive Tilley or the penguins themselves as the furious headteacher immediately ordered her nephew to stop what he was doing and to explain himself.
At first, Clive was reluctant to go into much detail as to why the unused school buildings were slowly beginning to turn into a wildlife sanctuary. But when faced with the full wrath of his favourite but formidable auntie, he'd no choice but to recount all the circumstances the events which had led to today's shocking discoveries that had been unexpectedly made by the headteacher…
That was almost two hours ago…
Now, Miss Bridges sat stoney-faced, impassively listening to those she'd summoned to her office detail their part in recent proceedings whilst they desperately tried to explain themselves, often adding to each other's conversation, or interrupting their co-

conspirators to add context or elaborate upon what had already been said to defend their unauthorised and illegal actions.

However, as the tales her school staff and young student told became increasingly more daring and outlandish, Miss Bridges began to shake her head more and more often in a mixture of surprise, disbelief and amazement.

Finally, when Mel Lancaster explained how they'd had to persuade Louie the orangutan to get out of Sue Brightside's car to go into the school by making monkey noises whilst waving two bunches of bananas at him, this proved to be the final straw for Miss Bridges as she could contain herself no more, bursting out into riotous laughter, a torrent of tears streaming down her face.

Unnerved, Nona first looked at her mother, then Clive, not quite understanding what was happening – a feeling shared by the other members of the escape committee who were sat with her that day.

"Miss Bridges," Nona asked as her headteacher raised her tortoiseshell-rimmed glasses from her and dabbed at her eyes with a tissue, "are you all right?"

Heaving heavily as though trying to catch her breath, Miss Bridges slowly began to compose herself again, gently wiping her nostrils before pulling her chair in so that she now sat straight and upright at her desk.

"Am I all right?" she began to reply, looking at the adults who anxiously stood around her, "No, not really as I'm surrounded by staff, family and friends who have lied to and deceived me. What a poor example to set you, young lady."

"But Miss Bridges, it's all my fault," Nona argued, "they were only trying to help me."

"Be that as it may - they are the adults here and should know a damned sight better. Animals in a school indeed...the only wild things that should be kept here are the children!"

"We'd no choice, Auntie Sheila," Clive replied, forgetting himself and where he was for a moment, "we had to help Nona. Lewis Kingston can't be allowed to treat her nor the animals this way. The poor creatures had to go somewhere where they would be safe."

"There's always a choice, Clive," answered Miss Bridges, continuing, "and you made a poor one at that. You should have consulted with me first before deciding anything."

"Please, don't blame Clive, Miss Bridges," Mel said quietly, "if someone has to take the fall for this, then it should be me...I was the one who organised all this, therefore it's only right I take full responsibility."

But before Miss Bridges could begin to reply, Marilyn and Sue both stood in unison.

"That's not true, Miss Bridges," Marilyn argued, "we didn't need much persuading when Mel told us about what had happened to poor little Nona."

"And what type of people would we be if we let a horrid and deceitful little bully like Lewis Kingston get his own way?" Sue Brightside added, "I'm as guilty as anyone in all this."

"All for one and all that malarkey..." Clive said cheerily, looking for a sign from his aunt that her anger may have been lessened by his vain attempt at finding the humour in the current situation.

Finding none to be visible on her stern and stoney-looking face, Clive quickly stopped talking as an uncomfortable silence soon fell across the room.

Miss Bridges sat quietly looking from person to person as though deciding what her next course of action were to be for what seemed to be an eternity before her eyes finally fell upon Lawrence Light, who had said very little during the discussions which had just taken place.

"And what about you, Mr Light?" Miss Bridges asked, leaning on her desk as she peered at the young teacher over the top of her glasses, "What have you got to say for yourself?"

Lawrence tugged at his shirt collar with an index finger and cleared his throat before replying.

"I know what we've done is wrong," he began, shifting uncomfortably in his seat, "using school property inappropriately, taking animals from the zoo without the owner's permission -"

"But they're my animals too!" Nona interrupted, quickly falling silent at the look her mother shot her.

"As I was saying," Lawrence continued, "we took the animals from the zoo and then hid them here from you without your knowledge or permission. For that, I am truly sorry, Miss Bridges."

"And so you should be, Mr Light," the headteacher replied.

"However," Lawrence continued, suddenly seeming to grow in stature and confidence as he spoke again, "I'm not sorry for helping Nona. Although the way that we've gone about all this is totally wrong, the reasons for us doing so aren't. We constantly teach our children at Trinity to stand up and fight for what they believe in, I can't now turn my back on Nona nor my friends for doing exactly that now, can I?"

Lawrence looked at Nona and smiled before turning back to look at Miss Bridges, whose head was now turned towards a picture which crookedly hung on her office wall. After a moment or two, she slowly stood and walked over to it, righting it before reading aloud the motto the picture frame contained.

"Sometimes it is difficult to decide what's right or wrong," Miss Bridges read, continuing, *"the only thing to do is follow your heart and hope that it all works out in the end."*

Nona noticed Miss Bridges lower her head and sigh a little before turning back to face them all again.

"I want you all to go and gather your things please," Miss Bridges said quietly, "that includes you, Nona."

Startled, everyone looked at one another with a mixture of shock and disbelief on their faces.

"Are we all to be suspended, sacked or expelled, Miss Bridges?" Lawrence eventually asked, expressing what everyone else was secretly thinking.

Miss Bridges opened the bottom drawer to her desk and took a handbag out of it.

"What? Oh, don't be so dramatic, Mr Light!" the headteacher tutted, "As I said before, the only wild animals who should be in Trinity are the pupils…Now, go get your things and meet me in the car park. There's something I'd like for all of you to see…"

Whilst Nona and the others were piling into Sue Brightside's people carrier, Miss Bridges jumping into the front passenger seat, ready to give directions as to where they were all heading next, Lewis Kingston sat in his office, desperately trying to conclude the phone call he'd spent an awkward and difficult hour of so on.

"Like I said, Aleksander," he sighed, trying hard to keep the growing frustration he was feeling out of his voice, "we've overcome a lot of the hurdles that were put before us so there's no need to worry - we're still schedule to close the zoo and complete the sale of the land to you by the end of September as promised."

"For your sake, I hope that you do," a gruff and heavily accented voice replied from the other end of the line, "my investors will be most unhappy if you are unable to meet our deadline, especially after the generous cash advance that we have already given you… Until we speak again, *Dos Vedanya,* Comrade Kingston."

Lewis waited for a moment to make sure the line had gone dead before speaking.

"Freakin' Ruskies!" he muttered, popping an indigestion tablet in his mouth hoping to quell the fire which seemed to be burning his throat.

He rested his head on his desk and closed his eyes enjoying the blissful peace after the lengthy and often heated discussions with his Russian investor. But the silence was soon abruptly ended by the frenetic sound of knocking on his office door.

"Give me a minute, gentlemen," he wearily called without lifting his head from the cool surface.

Let's hope my next conversation goes a whole lot better than the last, he thought to himself as he slowly sat up and readjusted his tie.

"Enter."

The door opened slowly and in walked John Stafford closely followed by Doctor Au, his medical whites covered with dirt and grime. They both sat across the desk from Lewis, Stafford placing the folder he carried with him on his lap whilst Au brushed at a large crease in his trousers.

"You've brought an up-to-date account of all our transactions so far as asked, I hope?" Lewis said, dispensing with the need for any pointless small talk.

"Yes, Mr Kingston," Stafford replied, patting the cover of his folder, "all the completed outgoing transactions are detailed in here."

Stafford opened the folder and passed it across the desk to Lewis Kingston, who immediately began to flick through its pages.

"There is a summary at the back to save you having to read through each document in detail," the accountant continued.

"Good, good," mumbled Lewis, turning to the very last page, "and I trust our *'transactions'* have all been given the necessary documentation to not arouse any further suspicion or inspection?"

Doctor Au leant forward and rested his elbows on the edge of the desk.

"Fake death for the animals' certificates have been raised by yours truly and then been countersigned by young Miss Maguire," Doctor Au drawled, "confirming that natural causes were behind the *'deaths'* of all the animals who have now sadly left us for a much better place…"

"Excellent news, gentlemen - well done!" Lewis smiled, "Now let's see what these tragic *'losses'* for Kingston's Kingdom have done for my personal bank balance."

Lewis began to read the list of animals who had been secretly sold to private collectors and zoos around the world.

Date	Species	Quantity	Buyer	Fee Paid
May 1st	Iberian Lynx	1	L.Garcia	£20,000
May 3rd	Sumatran Rhino	1	Java Zoo	£75,000
May 4th	Philippine Crocodile	1	M.Dundee	£50,000
May 4th	Northern Bald Ibis	1	Noah Ararat	£25,000
May 6th	White Antelope	1	Toto Reserve	£50,000
May 7th	Amur Leopard	1	G.Stojadinovic	£20,000
N/A	Rondo Bush Baby	2	John Morris	-------
May 10th	Black-Eyed Frogs	3	Pascal Zoo	£12,000
May 15th	Giant Garter Snakes	2	Monte Python	£22,000
N/A	Borneo Orangutan	1	Eastwood Zoo	-------

"As you can see, we've managed to bring in £274,000 without arousing suspicion so far," Stafford smiled as he watched his boss scan the figures, he'd carefully prepared for him before continuing, "We've also had strong interest in several other animals and think that we've had come up with a fail-safe way to increase the reduction in -"

"Why've we received no money for the orangutan or the bush babies yet?" Lewis interrupted.

Stafford and Au looked at one another sheepishly, neither one wishing to offer a reply first.

"Well?" Lewis urged.

"Well," Stafford nervously began to answer, "as you can see, we've a firm interest in both animals, but…"

"But what?" Lewis pressed.

"But we couldn't find either species when we came to arrange for their sad '*demise*'," Doctor Au replied, Stafford eagerly nodding in agreement.

The veins in Lewis Kingston's temples started to budge, his face growing redder and redder as he stood at his desk.

"What do you mean, *couldn't find them*?" he growled.

The atmosphere in the room suddenly seemed to grow a whole lot warmer as the two men sat opposite Lewis Kingston looked at one another again, waiting for the other to speak first.

"As you've both seemed to have lost the power of speech, I'll ask you one more time to explain," Lewis said quietly but the anger he felt was evident in his voice, "why couldn't you find them…"

It was Au who eventually replied. "When I went to their enclosures, I was unable to collect either of the two-species listed from them."

Lewis looked at Au, arms outstretched before him, lips tightly pressed together as he moved his head forwards slightly as though waiting for the doctor to continue.

"And why was that?" he asked.

"I was told by Miss Maguire that the orangutan was quarantined and kept in isolation due to a high fever it has developed. As it can become extremely aggressive if disturbed, I have not attempted to inspect it again as yet - but I will," Au insisted.

Lewis picked up his phone and jabbed three numbers on its keypad. He rapped the fingers of his free hand along the surface of his desk as he waited for the reply from the other end.

"Hello? Doyle? My office. Now!" Lewis shouted before slamming the phone receiver back into its cradle to look up, back at Au. "What about the bush babies?"

"They're nowhere to be found," Au said, continuing, "despite the best efforts of Clarke and myself to find them, Clarke could offer no reason as to why they should not be there in their enclosure."

"Something ain't right here," snarled Lewis, "animals don't just disappear into thin air - there's something fishy going on here…"

Just then there came a loud knock at the door and in strode Doyley in what appeared to be a muddy pair of dungarees.

However, the smell the dungarees emitted were so strong that the three other men in the office could almost taste the stench of it on their tongues.

"Yer wanted to see me Mr Kingston?" the friendly Irishman said, wiping both his hands on the front of his chest.

Lewis raised the back of his hand to his nose as he spoke.

"Can you please explain to me why some of my animals are missing," he spluttered.

Doyley stared in surprise, first at Lewis, then at Stafford and Au.

"Missing animals. Yer must be mistaken, Mr Kingston," the Irishman cooly replied, "all der animals are exactly where dey are meant to be, Mr Kingston."

"Is that so?" Lewis replied before thrusting the inventory sheet into Doyley's face. "Where are the orangutan and bush babies then?"

Doyley drew his head back away from the paper to better focus on it.

"Ah, well, yer sees, Miss Maguire believes dat der reason for der orangutan's illness is depression, so she's arranged for him to spend a few days in a monkey spa in Bristol, so she has," he calmly replied, "he should be as right as rain in a week or two."

Lewis glared at Doyley in disbelief.

"A monkey spa? She sent it there without my permission?" he growled, "The cost of that will come out of her wages!"

"It's costing yer nutink, Mr Kingston," Doyley cheerfully replied, "a good friend of hers runs it - owes Maguire a favour or two, so she does…"

"What about the bush babies," Au interrupted, "I went in there the other day and couldn't find hide nor hair of the critters."

"To be totally honest wit' yer, Doc, yer could spend a month in dere and yer still wouldn't find dem!" Doyley said, shaking his head, "Oi can count on der fingers of me left-hand der amount on times Oive seen dem since Oive been at dis zoo. Dey are possibly der most reclusive creatures dat we've ever had here in der kingdom."

Lewis sat back down in his chair, dropping the sheet he was holding back onto the desk.

"Mr Doyle," he began, "if I find out that you're up to something, behind my back -"

"Like what, Mr Kingston?" Doyley replied, now looking more than a little perplexed by the conversation.

"Like removing the animals from my zoo without my authority," Lewis Kingston growled.

"Now, whatever makes yer tink dat Oi would ever do a ting like dat?" the tall Irishman asked, leaning down on the desk to stare directly into the face of his employer. "Do yer honestly tink Oi would bite der hand dat feeds me? Oi was loyal to yer grandfather, Mr Kingston, and Oi remains as loyal to yer."

For all his arrogance, bluster and bravado, Lewis now felt more than a little intimated by the sight of the tall Irishman staring him down. However, after a moment or two of uncomfortable silence, Lewis Kingston eventually smiled.

"I've no doubt about that, Mr Doyle…" he said before adding, "However, I've a hunch Nona Lancaster and her mother have not taken my previous warning seriously enough…"

Lewis stood up from his chair and walked around to where Doyley stood, reaching up so his hand just about rested on the shoulder of the tall zookeeper as he gently guided him back towards the office door.

"I'm not sure what they've done or how they've done it but I'm certain that there's something going on right under our noses in this zoo," Lewis said quietly, "do I have your word, Mr Doyle, that you'll keep your eyes and ears peeled, reporting anything you see or hear directly back to me?"

Doyley stood up straight in the doorway and raised his dirty hand to his pale forehead in a mock salute.

"Rest assured, Mr Kingston, Oil make sure dat yer get all dat yer deserve for yer animals. No more animals will disappear in dis zoo without me knowing about it!" Doyley winked as he turned and walked out through the office door, leaving Lewis, Stafford and Au to sit staring at each other in silence for a moment or two.

"Either he's an excellent liar, or is just incredibly stupid," Stafford said as they listened to Doyley's heavy boots clunk down the wooden staircase.

Probably the latter - he is Irish after all…" Lewis sneered as he sat on the edge of his desk. "Still, we need to keep a close eye on him and the girl Maguire - I can't afford to have any more animals go missing on me."

"Why not?" Au asked, "Surely the quicker you get rid of the animals, the sooner you can close the zoo and sell it to our Russian friends."

"In theory, yes," Lewis replied, adding, "however, I need all the money I can get in the meantime. Not only did my grandfather leave me without a penny, but he's also halved my share of the zoo by giving a 50% share of it to that damned half-sister of mine. Therefore, saying that the animals are dead whilst secretly flogging them to the highest bidder means that I keep all the cash raised without Nona knowing nor getting her grubby little mitts on any it!"

Lewis grinned confidently at Doctor Au as he marvelled at his own cunning and ingenuity before continuing.

"But, if Alistair Leadbetter finds that out there are other animals missing and unaccounted for, he'll say that I'll have to forfeit the zoo and she'll get the whole damned lot!" he growled, "So, from now on, we make doubly certain that an animal only leaves this zoo when I expressly say it does!"

"Do you honestly think your sister's had something to do with both the missing orangutan and the bush babies?" John Stafford asked.

Lewis shrugged his shoulders as he walked over to the office window to look at the people who were walking in and around the zoo grounds.

"Seems a bit coincidental that we caught her trying to smuggle out a sloth and then, just a few weeks later there are other animals supposedly missing, don't he think?" he replied.

"But an orangutan's a whole lot bigger than a sloth to get out in your school bag!" Doctor Au laughed.

"True, but look," Lewis said, pointing to the exit, "the public can practically come and go as they please so short of putting more security guards or gates in place at more expense that I can ill-afford, I can't just stop people from coming to the zoo now, can I? And I can't just close it as that would break another term and condition of my grandfather's will…"

"Oh, but you can, Mr Kingston…" Au replied, a smile beginning to flicker across his lips.

"Can what?"

"Close the zoo," the doctor grinned, "and legally too…"
Lewis turned from the window and looked at Stafford, who shrugged his shoulders, before turning to stare directly at the doctor.

"Tell me, Doctor Au - how might we do that exactly…?"

Chapter 17 – Islands and Bridges

Hardly anyone spoke as Sue Brightside drove her reluctant passengers to their unknown destination as she closely followed the directions being given to her by Miss Bridges, who was sat in the passenger seat beside her.

Nona was at the rear of the vehicle in one of the two seats there, sat directly opposite her mother, the two of them drawing the short straw by being the smallest passengers who could fit in the additional space saving seats. In front of them, Marilyn was wedged between Lawrence and Clive, '*a rose between two thorns*,' she'd joked as they climbed aboard.

But no one had dared to laugh, such was the nervous tension coming from the six of them as Miss Bridges brusquely informed Sue that they would be driving out of Ventham down towards the neighbouring county of Kent.

When pressed as to why they were going there, Miss Bridges had sharply replied '*Wait and see,*' cranking up the *tension-ometer* inside the packed vehicle just a few notches more.

The journey had already taken over forty minutes, going from the bustling roads around Ventham onto the busier dual carriageway which snaked away from the Thames before they'd eventually left the built-up surroundings of the city and begun to drive through the English countryside, passing through several villages and small towns, all far removed from the streets of London Nona had grown up in.

As she quietly sat looking out the rear window of Sue Brightside's car, Nona began to imagine several worst-case scenarios in her head whilst trying to figure out where on Earth Miss Bridges was now taking them. She'd looked at her mum for reassurance early on their journey, but Mel's face was as grey as granite giving her no comfort at all.

"The next exit please, Sue," Miss Bridges suddenly said, pointing toward a large sign beside the dual carriageway, "Head towards the one which says, '*Dockyards and St. Margaret's Island*'…"

Sue silently nodded her understanding and flicked her indicator, its ticking sound hypnotising Nona momentarily as they all waited and watched for the exit to appear. Eventually, the road began to fork in two different directions as Sue guided the car down the left exit road which led to a large roundabout.

"You'll need to take the third exit onto the bridge over there," Miss Bridges said, pointing to a road that appeared to rise up ahead of them.

As the people carrier made its way around the roundabout, Nona noticed that they were now driving alongside a river which flowed to the left of the car.

"Is that still the River Thames, Miss Bridges?" she asked.

"No, my dear, that's the Medway," Miss Bridges replied without turning to look at Nona.

"I didn't think it was - it's a lot smaller and not quite as grey as the Thames," Nona replied.

"It is here, my dear, but just you wait and see..."

There it was again - that small phrase Miss Bridges had said earlier, almost like a veiled threat...

Wait and see...

Nona now felt even more worried as to where they were going as the ticking of the indicator signalled their exit as the people carrier headed up and over the bridge which now took them high above the river below. Now Nona started to understand exactly what Miss Bridges had meant as they slowly drove down the other side of the bridge.

In the far distance, just a little way of them, Nona could now see a much wider expanse of water, with various clumps of land dotted within it.

"Not much further now - about ten minutes or so," Miss Bridges said as Sue continued to drive them along the road which now followed the banks of the River Medway.

The headteacher glanced down at her watch and nodded.

"Good, we ought to get there just in time..." she said, a faint smile now creasing her pursed lips.

Nona watched as the sun suddenly broke through the clouds and glistened on the water in between the various buildings and industrial parks that populated the waterline before they soon reached a stretch of desolate land.

"It's the next turn on the left, Sue," Miss Bridges said abruptly.

"What - here?" Sue queried as they approached an open gate which led to an old dirt track that wove down toward the shores of the river.

"Yes, Sue – here…" Miss Bridges firmly instructed.

Sue Brightside slowly turned the steering wheel as the large vehicle squeezed between the two weather-worn fence posts which marked the entrance to the turning.

"You'll need to go slower now," Miss Bridges said, "there's quite a lot of deep potholes which will do some serious damage to your car if you're not careful..."

You're not lying, Nona thought as the people carrier bumped up and down on the natural roller-coaster of a road, the occasional splash of muddy water spraying up against the front and sides of the people carrier as it hit the numerous rain-filled potholes the single-track road had, Nona's window soon becoming completely covered by the sandy, brown silt water from up by the wheels of the vehicle.

Now unable to see out of it any further, Nona turned and leant forwards to try to peer between the heads of the adults sitting in front of her and out through the front windscreen beyond them.

"Say when you want me to stop, Miss Bridges," Sue said as the car slowly drew closer to the riverbank which fell slightly ahead of her vehicle, a large crop of land, with what appeared to be a large, stone building stood on it now clearly visible in the near distance.

"I will," Miss Bridges replied, "just keep driving slowly over the causeway towards that island over there."

Sue peered over the steering wheel.

"Island? Causeway? What causeway? I can only see the riv-" she said anxiously, "Wait - there! I think I see it now!"

There, beneath the surface of the water, Sue could just about make out a single-track road, no wider than her people carrier.

"You want me to drive over that?" she asked, "I mean, is it safe?"

"Perfectly, Sue," Miss Bridges smiled, "it's been here since the Roman era after all. Also, it's low tide, meaning we've a good few hours before the island is totally cut off from the mainland once again."

"Auntie Sheila, what are we doing here?" Clive suddenly piped up.

"Wait and see, dear boy..." came the now familiar and foreboding reply, "wait and see..."

The crossing from the mainland to the island took another ten minutes as Sue Brightside carefully drove her people carrier along the narrow, stone road, her wheels only just managing to stay within the width of it. If her vehicle had been another six inches or so wider, it would almost certainly have slid off the road and down towards the muddy riverbed which was now slowly becoming more exposed by the river ebbing away from it. Eventually, the causeway began to rise again towards what looked to be an old fort, its entrance protected by a huge pair of heavy wooden gates, a large sign which read *'Private property, keep out!'* displayed before it.

"Stop here," Miss Bridges commanded as the people carrier slowly approached the entrance.

Sue immediately slowed the car to a complete stop, allowing Miss Bridges to get out and stride toward the gates.

"What are we doing here, Clive?" Mel whispered as she leant close to the ear of the man sat in front of her.

"Beats me," Clive replied, shaking his head. I've absolutely no idea as to what the old girl is up to now…"

All the passengers sat in the people carrier watched as Miss Bridges lifted a small black flap on one of the gates to reveal an electronic keypad. Carefully she tapped it six times and closed the flap again before turning to make her way back to the vehicle.

"There," Miss Bridges proudly declared, "it'll only be a moment or two for the gates to - ah, there they go now…"

Nona watched as the two gates opened before them, like arms waiting to embrace them as Sue immediately dropped the handbrake and eased the car slowly towards the entrance.

"Auntie Sheila, where the hell are we?" Clive asked.

"Home, dear." came the reply as the wheels crunched across the gravel path that led into a courtyard of the fort.

"But you live on the Thames on your riverboat…" Clive replied before adding, "don't you?"

"Not my *weekday* home, dear," Miss Bridges said, turning and smiling, "my *weekend* home!"

"I never knew you had a second home, Auntie Sheila," Clive frowned.

"Dear boy - there's a lot about your Auntie Sheila you don't know…" Miss Bridges winked as the security gates closed behind them.

Nona gently blew the steam which now rose from her cup of hot chocolate - it had been quite an afternoon...

Now, sat in Miss Bridges' old, stone kitchen, she could hardly believe she was actually sat in a fortress on an island, less than thirty miles from home as the crow flies.

"How long have you lived here?" Mel asked, swigging from her own mug of tea.

Miss Bridges pulled up a stool and sat down at the farmhouse table where everyone else were now sitting, drinking their respective teas, coffees or hot chocolates.

"Nearly twenty years, give or take, it's been a long-term passion project of mine," Miss Bridges smiles, "the fortress had been deserted for nearly seventy years and left to wrack and ruin. I had my work cut out though when I first got it. It's slowly getting there, thanks in no small part to the friends I have who've given up their time and expertise to try and help me restore it to its former glory."

"It was a Roman fort then," Marilyn said, wiping the coffee froth from her lips.

"Yes, originally," Miss Bridges nodded, "but then, back in the 1850s, Queen Victoria ordered it to be fortified as a secret stronghold for her to escape to and hide in should England ever be invaded again by the French again."

"England - invaded by the French during Victorian times?" Lawrence replied, nearly spitting his coffee out. That seems a rather far-fetched idea!"

"You'd think so, on the face of it, yes, but tensions were running high at that time between England and France for a number of different reasons," Miss Bridges smiled, "hence the Queen's instruction to build her a secret fortress here. It was close enough to London for Victoria to escape to if needed whilst still being in close enough to speak with her government. All very hush-hush and top secret, hence no official records of that period remain..."

Miss Bridges paused for a moment to take a long sip from her mug before continuing.

"Of course, Victoria never needed use of it, so after her death in 1901, it reverted to the Ministry of Defence," Miss Bridges explained, "they used it up until the Second World War for top-secret meetings involving several important political figures as well as high-ranking military personnel. Eventually, it was shut down and abandoned, that's how it remained until the Ministry of

Defence decided to sell it off and how I bought it on the cheap."

"How'd you come by it?" Marilyn asked, spying a particularly appealing chocolate-chip cookie on the plate before her.

"A dear friend of mine was working for the Ministry of Defence at that time and tipped me off," Miss Bridges replied, taking another sip from her mug, "he put a good word in on my behalf when they finally agreed to sell it to me, for services I'd given to my country supposedly, so I got it for an absolute steal!"

"But you've lived on the Thames ever since I was a kid," Clive protested, "Why've you never told me about this place?"

"Clive, dear, the riverboat is *Auntie* Sheila's place. This is where Sheila Bridges, international athlete, national hero and celebrity entertains," Miss Bridges explained, "Can you imagine me inviting the rich and the powerful to stay on my tatty, old riverboat? However, this place is perfect for wining and dining the great and the good, as well as all of the other secret squirrel stuff I like to get up to in my spare time…"

"What sort of 'secret squirrel stuff'?" Clive asked pressed.

"If I told you that, I'd have to kill you, dear!" Miss Bridges laughed, though Nona wasn't certain whether she was being serious or not.

"How big is this place?" Mel asked, changing the subject as she cast her eye around the room.

"The island itself is 140 acres and the fortress has fourteen large rooms in total. Plenty room enough for all," Miss Bridges replied, "there also used to be a working farm here too. Sadly, that went the way of the rest of it, though the outbuildings and fences are still in place, albeit a little the worse for wear…"

Clive walked to the window at the back of the kitchen and stared out at the deserted land which stretched outside of it.

"Who owns the rest of the island?" he asked.

"I do," Miss Bridges replied in between sips, "I own Hoon Island, as well as its two sister islands."

"Three islands…" Nona gulped, "You own three islands, Miss Bridges?"

"Yes - would you like to see?" Miss Bridges grinned, standing from the table before making her way towards the kitchen door.

"We need to keep an eye on the time though," the headteacher added, looking up at the clock on the wall, "the tide turns quickly here, and the causeway soon covers over again, trapping people if they're not too careful...."

The seven of them walked through the kitchen door and into the courtyard before passing through a small gate in the rear, outer wall where the sight before them caused Nona and the others to gasp out aloud in awe and wonder. There, directly before them, as far as the eye could see, were open fields, crisscrossed by numerous fences, with several buildings dotted here and there. Nona felt as though she'd stepped back in time, so old and remote did this small, English island feel to her.

"See there, over to the left..." Miss Bridges said, pointing towards another island, one perhaps a third of the size of the one that they all now stood on. "that's Burnt Oak Island - it can only be reached by boat either from here or the mainland. In the late 1700s and early 1800s, it was a popular haunt for smugglers. So that they avoided paying any duty tax, things like tea, alcohol and even owls were smuggled from over there. It's totally deserted now, bar a few sheep and the local birdlife, of course..."

"What about that one?" Nona asked, pointing to a smaller island to the far right of where they were stood, "It looks like it has a causeway running to it from here."

"It does - well spotted, my dear, though it only becomes visible every now and then during very low tides, like today," Miss Bridges smiled, "that's my favourite of the three islands, mainly due to its dark, sinister and macabre history…"

"Which isle is that then, Miss Bridges?" Sue Brightside asked as she squinted at the island which had now begun to be partially covered by the mist which was now starting to roll in.

"That, Mrs Brightside is Deadman's Rock," Miss Bridges said gravely.

Lawrence again started to cough loudly on his coffee as he turned and looked at the headteacher who was still stood gazing across at the now more eerie and mysterious looking island.

"Did you seriously say it's called Deadman's Rock, Miss Bridges?" he eventually asked once he'd caught his breath again.

"Indeed, I did, Mr Light," Miss Bridges proudly declared, "it's had quite a colourful and chequered history mind, it being the only island directly connected to Hoon. The Romans started it all off, using it to imprison difficult Celtic tribe chiefs on. They'd got quite a bloody nose with Boudicca's rebellion and death, so decided it best to torture their enemies and then keep them alive

instead of executing them to help prevent another uprising...."
Miss Bridges drained her mug, wiping her lips before continuing. "In later years, it's had several uses, housing captured pirates as well as French prisoners during the Napoleonic Wars. High-ranking German POWs from both World Wars have been imprisoned on it too, though you'd never have known it...Some say it's haunted and that you might be able to see both supernatural devil dogs and headless soldiers who allegedly roam the island, restlessly looking for their missing bonces late at night..."
Miss Bridges slowly turned to look at the others who were now stood, opened mouthed behind her. Suddenly, she roared with laughter, instantly causing Sue, Marilyn and Lawrence to jump.
"Stuff and nonsense, really," Miss Bridges chuckled, "however, the island's infamous name and its urban legends were deliberately created to keep nosey parkers such as the press away from whoever was kept there at various times by both our government and the secret service. Now, it's just a load of abandoned old buildings you can only reach by boat or by the causeway which leads from here. The island has a natural, rocky coastline which protects it from unwelcome visitors, making it almost impossible to reach if you don't know the way onto it."
Nona breathed a sigh of relief as Miss Bridges began to walk back towards them.
"Come on, we'd best head back," the headteacher said, "I'll just go lock up, then we can begin to make our way back to the mainland."
Miss Bridges began to march back towards the gate, leaving Nona and the others trailing behind her, feeling slightly bemused by their visit that afternoon. It was Mel who finally plucked up the courage and asked what everyone else was thinking.
"It's been lovely seeing all this and learning about the history of the islands, Miss Bridges," Nona's mother said, "but I don't see why you wanted to bring us all the way out here just to give us local history and geography lesson."
"Because," Miss Bridges said as she opened the gate which led back into the courtyard, "I wanted to show you that there's a much better place than the school to bring your rescued animals to..."

Chapter 18 – One Step Forward…

On the face of it, there wasn't much difference between their journeys to and from Miss Bridges' fortress home on Hoon Island. Like before, Sue Brightside drove whilst Miss Bridges gave her travel directions while the rest of the passengers in the people carrier sat in silence.

However, where the first journey they took together filled Nona, Mel and their friends with a mixture of dread and trepidation, their feelings and emotions returning home were a happy cocktail of relief, hope and excitement, all shaken and stirred up by the incredible offer Miss Bridges had made to them before they finally left the fortress that day...

"The animals can all live out their lives naturally – rent free - on any of the islands I own," Miss Bridges had declared "the only condition I have is that you all have to foot the cost of, or make the necessary repairs to, any fencing, buildings or enclosures needed to keep them safe and secure."

Clive had, of course, instantly volunteered to take charge of inspecting all of the structures which were already built on the island. He was then told by his aunt to come up with a rough plan as to how all the animals they'd rescued - plus the others still waiting to be saved, could be housed across the three islands belonging to Miss Bridges.

"So, any suggestions I make, and we all agree to, regarding building work," he asked as Sue's people carrier pulled back into the Trinity Staff car park, "will be completely acceptable to you, Auntie Sheila?"

Miss Bridges nodded, unfastening her seat belt as the people carrier slowed to a stop.

"Yes, but within reason of course…" the headteacher replied before continuing, "for example, no animals can be housed too close to the fortress - can't have any important or influential visitors to Hoon scared off by the sight, smell or sound of our exotic wild tenants now, can I…?"

Now, having hugged, then thanked, then hugged Miss Bridges again before saying goodbyes to the others, Nona tiredly sat in the back of Marilyn's car next to her mother as Marilyn drove them home, almost unable to take in all the day's events. They'd been joined on the journey by Lawrence Light, who'd gratefully accepted Marilyn's offer of a lift home.

Despite the fact that it was out of her way, Marilyn had other reasons for offering to drive the young teacher home, the matchmaking teaching assistant hoping that her single-mother friend Mel might see an opportunity to get to know Lawrence just a letter better.

"You could always have tea at ours if you're not in any real rush to get home," Mel had asked as Lawrence placed his fold-up bicycle in the boot of Marilyn's car.

"No, I mean, I've no real plans," Nona's teacher had eagerly replied, "that would be lovely, thank you. But are you absolutely sure? It's been a long day and I don't want to put you out."

"Yes, she's sure, and no, you aren't!" Marilyn said firmly, bundling Lawrence into the front seat of her car, "Whoever heard of anyone turning down good company and a free meal?"

Marilyn looked in her rearview mirror and winked at Mel knowingly, causing Nona's mother to blush slightly, aware too aware of her friend's motives and intentions that night…

Nona was still pinching herself at the fact that her teacher was now sitting across the table as her mother brought out a large, steaming bowl of bolognese, placing it sown on the table between the three of them. Ordinarily, there wouldn't have been enough food to go round had Mim joined them for dinner like she normally did.

However, when told what tea was to be that night as had been planned when Mel had prepared the bolognese earlier, ready for when she and Nona returned home, Mim had soon declared that she wasn't going to eat any of '*that foreign muck'*, adding that she'd go to the bingo hall earlier than usual to '*have kebab and chips with Betty and the girls there'* instead!

After she'd disappeared in a haze of blue rinse, the conversation around the table was a bit awkward at first, Lawrence saying that the bolognese was lovely and tasted '*cleaner and meatier than any I've had before.'*

Mel had thanked him and explained that her secret was that she '*strained the mince off first to get rid of all the excess grease'* whilst Nona just sat there, silently trying to suck up each strand of spaghetti on her plate.

"Did you know the name for a single, individual strand of spaghetti is *spaghetto*," Lawrence suddenly declared, expertly twisting his fork into his food before putting the perfectly pasta-wrapped piece of cutlery into his mouth.

"Really? How interesting!" Mel had replied, mirroring the young teacher's actions.

God! How can two people who are normally so funny, intelligent and interesting talk such rubbish to one another? Nona thought as she slurped up another piece of spaghetti – correction - *spaghetto*...

Fortunately, before Nona felt the need to turn her spaghetti into a makeshift noose to end the two adults' obvious suffering, the conversation quickly turned to Miss Bridges' generous offer earlier that day. Suddenly, the air was instantly charged with excited laughter and chatter as the three of them recalled and repeated everything the headteacher had said to them and the conditions she'd attached to her offer of sanctuary to the animals.

"Do you think it's possible?" Nona asked, pushing her now empty plate away from her.

"I think so," Mel nodded, "it's gonna take a lot of hard work and effort, but there's no reason we couldn't eventually create a new home for the animals we rescue from Kingston's Kingdom."

"However," added Lawrence, who seemed to relax more with every passing moment in their company, "for it to be successful, we'd need to make sure certain species are kept away from each other and that each area is safe and secure for both animal and human alike."

Nona frowned and quietly thought for a moment before smiling.

"Deadman's Rock sounds like the perfect place for the penguins," she grinned, "they could easily live on the rocks."

"True," Mel smiled, "but we'd still have to make sure that they had a regular supply of food provided to them whilst they get used to hunting for fish themselves."

"You must remember, Nona," Lawrence said, subconsciously adopting a teacher tone with her despite himself, "that a lot of the animals in the zoo were born in captivity and have known nothing else. We'll have to make sure we do whatever we can to make sure any new home for them is suitable for their needs."

Nona's face must have shown the disappointment she now felt, something her teacher immediately picked up on.

"However, it'll be great fun learning as we go along, won't it Mel?" Lawrence added cheerfully.

Nona's mother eagerly nodded back at him, causing her daughter to smile knowingly to herself.

"Definitely, Lawrence," Mel replied, "now that we have somewhere we can move the animals to, we can start to think about taking larger numbers out of the zoo at any one time, rather than just a few here and there."

"And how would you propose we do that then, Miss Lancaster?" Lawrence asked, almost playfully.

"Why, my dear Mr Light, I thought you'd never ask!" Mel teasingly replied.

God, I don't know what's worse, Nona thought, *the two of them talking gibberish like before or flirting with each other like this! Urgh!*

Despite feeling slightly awkward initially, by the end of the evening Nona quite liked the way her mother and Mr Light seemed to be getting along with one another.

Added to that, they'd all managed to come up with a quite brilliant and audacious plan which they intended to put into place the following week, once they'd spoken to the others.

Nona had said goodnight to her teacher and then secretly watched from the kitchen door as Mr Light stood at the front of the house, holding the handlebars of his bicycle, talking to her mother. Nona couldn't quite make out what they'd said to one another but the kiss on the cheek Mr Light gave Mel spoke more than a thousand words ever could…

Whilst her mother slowly closed the front door, Nona scurried back to sit at the kitchen table, waiting for her mother to eventually join her.

"It's turned out to be a good day after all, hasn't it Mum?" Nona said as she took a huge mouthful of the jelly which was left over from tea.

"Very," Mel replied, grinning broadly.

When she turned in much later that night after the two of them had booked and printed off four adult and thirty children's entry tickets for Kingston's Kingdom the following week, Nona couldn't help but wonder just what *that* kiss on the cheek would mean for them all in future…

Usually, Nona didn't want the weekend to ever end, it normally being filled with various football matches, sporting events or times just chilling with friends or family but, for once, she was delighted to be back at school the following Monday.

The escape plan her mother and Mr Light had concocted together was so audacious that she couldn't wait to hand pick the other twenty-nine accomplices needed for the following Friday.

The first two names obviously picked themselves – Luca and Keeley, her BFFs and partners-in-crime. These were closely followed by Kirsten, Amy, Kylie, Mya and Paige who had all proven themselves to be more than willing and able to help, as well as being totally trustworthy with the secrets shared with them whenever called upon before. Selecting the other twenty-two friends could have proved problematic to invite to any ordinary twelve-year old's birthday party, let alone them becoming part of a secret zoo escape party but it was one Nona had relished and gratefully accepted when the plan was first mooted.

So it was that she wholeheartedly set about her task as soon as she'd settled into school again that hazy Monday morning. Little did she then realise but Nona had probably been given the most difficult task as the rest of the Zooper Troopers met in the staff room to be briefed by Mel and Lawrence as to the plan, support and resources needed for their rescue attempt later that week. ...

Once all were assembled and present, roles were then distributed based on the skills and expertise needed. It was also decided that Lawrence would lead the *raid* on Kingston's Kingdom this time, being the group leader for what would appear to all to be just another everyday school visit to the zoo, Mel, Marilyn and Sue assisting him, each being a designated leader to a small group of ten children, those who'd been handpicked by Nona.

Clive Tilley would oversee logistics, arranging for a *friendly* coach company to provide them with transport to and from the zoo, as well as then finding suitable temporary accommodation for the non-human refugees they'd planned to successfully return to the school with.

Even Miss Bridges had played a small part in the deception this time, helping to raise and organise all of the necessary risk assessments and documentation needed for the local authority to approve the visit, especially as it was arranged at such short notice. The headteacher spent ages talking on the phone with the council's officer for school trips and visits, explaining how the opportunity had *'suddenly arisen'* and that it would be *'a life-changing experience,'* which would *'greatly enhance the lives'* of her *'disadvantaged children,'* some of whom had never seen *'the open green countryside,'* let alone gazed upon *'wild and exotic creatures such as those in Kingston's Kingdom...'*

Eventually, the officer had agreed to speedily push through the approved paperwork, though it was debatable whether Miss Bridges' words had actually persuaded him or simply beaten him into submission so that by Thursday morning, everything needed for the trip was in comfortably in place. Permission slips had been received from every parent of the child Nona had specially selected and sworn to secrecy.

The coach was booked, first aid boxes gathered up and packed lunches for those needing them arranged with the kitchen. Lawrence had given Mel, Marilyn and Sue their groups, along with the names of the ten children they'd be responsible for clearly highlighted whilst Nona had carefully vetted her final selection, making sure that none of the other twenty-nine team members chosen had allergies which would be affected by their close proximity to the creatures they'd willingly offered to help free from the evil clutches of her brother.

Sue had then spent most of her evenings that week cutting, sewing and sticking together the materials needed to make a secret pocket which would then be slipped inside the clothing of the thirty children prior to their visit to Kingston's Kingdom, adding Velcro fasteners for extra security.

Finally, Friday arrived, kicking and screaming as it dragged its heels to reach the weekend. Nona was, of course, the first of the children to be at the bus stop just outside of the school that day, along with Luca and Keeley. All three of them were dressed in mufti clothes so as to not reveal the school they were from once at Kingston's Kingdom, Mel having booked their entry tickets in the fictitious name of Attenborough Secondary.

It was all the adults who arrived next, Marilyn and Mel having travelled together as Sue rolled up in her people carrier, whilst Lawrence furiously cycled in, hardly breaking a sweat in the process.

"You'd three had best get on the coach when the rest of the parents arrive as we need to make the trip look as ordinary as possible,"

Mel had whispered as the first car drove into the car park beside the school as Mr Light stood, clipboard in hand, ready to sign in the students who'd been specially picked to help that day with the zoo raid.

It wasn't long before the coach was full, the chattering excitement of the children only matched by the concerned expressions on the parents' faces stood on the pavement outside, trying to catch the eye of their offspring prior to their departure. None though were forthcoming, the children, some of whom had still yet to become fully fledged Zooper Troopers, being eager for the coach to get underway.

Marilyn stood at the front of the coach, taking the register, whilst Mel and Sue checked that all the pupils had everything they needed for the morning, as well as dishing out the secret pockets to the children, instructing them how to attach them to the inside of their jackets, shirts or hoodies so that they were invisible from the outside.

Lawrence anxiously looked at his watch.

"It's nearly 9 o'clock," he called from the foot of the coach stairs, "time to give a final briefing as to how the morning will play out. Have the children got everything they need?"

Mel nodded and moved to the front of the coach, picking up a clipboard from her seat as Sue Brightside took the seat behind her.

"Oh - I've forgotten the sick bucket!" Marilyn cried, dashing down the aisle towards the exit.

"Will the children really need it, Mrs Henderson?" Lawrence asked as Marilyn made her way past him, "It's only a short journey across the city."

"It's not them – it's for me!" Marilyn called as she ran towards the school, "I hate travelling by coach!"

Mel smiled and shook her head, before turning back to address the children.

"Right, everybody," she grinned, "you all know why we're here today…"

"To steal some goddamn pesky little critters!" a voice with a terrible American accent called out from the back, causing everyone to erupt into riotous laughter.

"Yes, thank you, Luca!" Mel smiled, instantly recognising Luca's poorly disguised voice immediately, "As Master Bonnetti so eloquently put it, we're going to help to rescue some more animals from Kingston's Kingdom. Usually, we tell you that it's wrong to take something which doesn't belong to you, but as the animals are co-owned by Nona -"

A huge cheer now filled the coach, causing Nona to blush heavily, gesturing to her mother to hurry up to save her from any further embarrassment.

"As I was saying, what we are doing isn't technically stealing," Mel continued, "we are simply rescuing the creatures from an uncertain future, saving them from someone who is more interested in the money he can make from them rather than their health, safety and welfare..."

Silence had fallen over the coach as the children listened intently to what Mel was now saying.

"So, if anyone has any doubts or concerns about what we are doing today and wants to get off the coach," she added, "then do so now...I promise that it won't be held against you..."

Nona waited with bated breath, half-expecting some of the more reluctant recruits to change their minds and leave the coach. After a few moments though, she breathed a heavy sigh of relief as all the children remained in their seats, each wearing a more determined look on their face than before.

However, a single hand rose up in the centre of the coach as a head popped out from behind a seat to look at Mel.

"Miss Lancaster, I have a question?" Kirsten asked, her baseball hat turned the wrong way on her head around as usual.

"Yes, Kirsten, what is it?"

"Nona said that we are going to be gathering up some exotic minibeasts, as many as we can carry in fact," Kirsten continued, "she said that she chose all of us because we aren't particularly squeamish but was a bit vague as to exactly what type of minibeasts we'd be rescuing today."

Mel shot Nona a look as if to say *'thanks, pal,'* then flicked over the pages of the clipboard she held before answering the bleached blonde-haired girl was now chewing and popping pink bubblegum bubbles in front of her.

"Dependent on your level of yuckiness, you may be asked to carry one of the following..." Mel announced, "Slender stone grasshoppers, Tansy Beetles, Columbia River Tiger Beetles, Violet Click Beetles, Seychelles Palm Crickets, Winged Stick Insects, Ladybird or Great Raft Spiders..."

"Spiders! No one told me there'd be spiders!" a high-pitched voice shrieked.

Slowly, Mel looked up from her clipboard to see which child had called out, only to see a dozen hands all pointing in the direction of the door to where Mr Light now stood, his face pale and his eyes as wide as saucers.

"Seriously, Mr Light?" Mel asked as the colour slowly began to return to Lawrence's face.

The teacher nodded sheepishly as the rest of the coach - Nona, Sue and the coach driver included - tried to stifle their laughter whilst Mr Light shakily took his seat.

"It's all right, we can go now - I've found the sick bucket!" Marilyn panted after finally returning to the coach.

"Just as well you did," Mel laughed, nodding her head towards the young teacher at the front, "looks like someone else might be needing it more than you do…"

The coach journey that morning took longer than it normally should have done due to temporary traffic lights allowing only two or three vehicles to pass through a particularly busy stretch of road between the school and the zoo.

Mel decided to use the time to good effect, using the coach's microphone to outline each step of the morning once, from their arrival at the zoo, their planned journey around each part of it, the timings of their snack and loo breaks before their visit to the Bug House. There, the children would each be handed their minibeast, to slip and seal into their secret pockets, before finally paying a visit to the gift shop, just as any normal school trip would do so as to not arouse any suspicion. They were then to return to the coach and place their minibeasts in the cages and tanks which were hidden in the luggage compartment in the belly of the vehicle.

When Mel was confident that everyone knew the itinerary and their role that day, she replaced the microphone and sat back down in her seat, smiling confidently for the remainder of the journey.

It wasn't long before the coach swung through the gates of the kingdom's visitors' car park and pulled up in one of the coach bays close to the main entrance.

Having regained some of his lost composure, Lawrence Light stood and faced the children.

"Right, kids, you know the drill…I'll go ahead and check that they're ready for our arrival…" he said, waving the e-tickets he was carrying above his head, "whilst you're waiting for my return, check under your seats and overhead lockers to make sure that you have all of your belongings with you. We can't afford any slip-ups today, OK?"

With the cries of *'Yes, Sir,'* still ringing in his ears, Lawrence made his way off the coach as Mel, Marilyn and Sue began to go up and down the aisle, giving the children their final instructions. Mel paused when she reached her daughter and Keeley.

"Are you ready for this, sweetheart?" she smiled.

"Totally!" Nona beamed, Keeley nodding eagerly beside her. Mel grinned back at the two girls, only for her smile to soon disappear as she glanced out of the coach window, noticing that Lawrence was now rapidly running back towards the vehicle.

She'd hardly been able to move away from Nona and Keeley's seats by the time the young teacher had made his way back up the stairs, breathing heavily as he did so.

"Sue, can you stay on the coach with the children whilst I speak to Mel and Marilyn?" he gasped.

Sue nodded as the two other women hurriedly followed Lawrence off the coach again.

"Whatever's the matter, Lawrence?" Mel asked anxiously the moment her feet hit the ground, Marilyn closely following behind her.

"I'm sorry Mel, but I think it's over," Lawrence said sadly, "they've only gone and shut the zoo…"

Chapter 19 – As One Door Closes…

Back inside the coach, Nona anxiously continued to look out of the back window to where her mother was stood, her back towards Nona, her hands waving and gesturing wildly as she spoke with Marilyn and Mr Light.

Although she was unable to hear their conversation, Nona could tell by the way her mother was standing, her hands now on hips, head tilted slightly to the side, that something serious had happened. She'd seen her mother stand like this before on many separate occasions… for example, when the washing machine had packed up mid-wash, or when Mim had caused the microwave to explode by covering her dinner with tin foil being two such instances.

Now, Nona could imagine the fed up look on her mum's face as she grappled with a solution to whatever the problem was that they'd encountered upon arrival this morning.

She could feel the tension begin to build inside the coach as all of its occupants now watched as Mr Light, Miss Lancaster and Mrs Henderson began to march off together, back in the direction of the zoo entrance.

"I don't like this," Nona muttered, jumping up out of her seat and headed towards the exit door, "I don't like this one bit…"

"Where do you think you're go -" Sue Brightside began to say, only for her sentence to be cut off by the look Nona immediately shot her, Sue soon realising that it wasn't just any pupil getting off the coach, but Nona herself. She nodded her approval as Nona jumped from the steps of the coach and sped after the others, who were now a little way ahead of her.

When she finally reached them, Nona found all three of them stood, peering at a sandwich board which had been hastily positioned in front of the now barred and padlocked entrance to the main zoo.

"What's going on, Mum?" Nona asked, pushing herself between Marilyn and her mother, "Why aren't we -"

But Nona stopped speaking, mid-sentence, upon reading the message which was written on the large sandwich board in front of the four of them. Capitalised and printed in large bold writing, a single paragraph on the sign struck her silent.

It read...

WE REGRET TO INFORM ALL CUSTOMERS AND VISITORS THAT DUE TO A HIGHLY SERIOUS AND CONTAGIOUS SUSPECTED ZOONOTIC DISEASE OUTBREAK, KINGSTON KINGDOM WILL BE CLOSED TO THE PUBLIC FOR THE FORESEEABLE FUTURE.

PLEASE VISIT OUR WEBSITE FOR MORE DETAILS AND FURTHER INFORMATION OVER THE COMING DAYS.

WE APOLOGISE FOR ANY INCONVENIENCE CAUSED.

"This is some kind of sick joke, right?" Nona asked, looking pleadingly at her mother, "A zoonotic disease sounds so fake and made up, doesn't it, Mum...? Mum?"
Mel didn't answer, instead she gently placed a hand on her daughter's shoulder.
Despairingly, Nona turned to her teacher, who was vigorously scrolling up and down on his mobile phone screen.
"It's a line, ain't it? It can't be real, can it Mr Light?" she begged.
Mr Light frowned, pursing his thin lips together tightly
"I'm afraid it is, Nona," he sadly replied, handing Nona his phone.
Nona numbly scrolled through the information displayed on it, scarcely believing her eyes as she read the information...

'A Zoonotic disease is an infection which can pass between animals and humans. These diseases are incredibly diverse and difficult to identify where they spread from. Some are fast acting and can cause serious illness, some progress slowly and may not cause any serious harm, showing no symptoms. While these diseases can affect anyone, they are most likely to cause serious illness in children, women and adults over 65...'

"It seems pretty genuine to me, Nona," Mr Light said quietly, "and there's no way of knowing what the threat is unless your brother chooses to reveal it, which I suspect he won't do... There's no more detail on the zoo's about it website either."
Nona's head dropped at the crushing news, her hopes and dreams shattered by the sudden realisation that this really was the end. They'd been lucky that it had been relatively easy to get the animals in and out of the zoo up until this point in time.

Now Lewis Kingston had finally got the better of her as Nona fought back the tears which were desperately trying to escape her eyes.

"What I don't understand is why Doyley didn't tell you any of this when you spoke to him about the raid today, Marilyn?" Mel finally said, turning to her friend.

"I'm sorry, what?" Marilyn asked, seemingly surprised by the news, "Was I meant to call him?"

"Yes! Like you agreed to!" Lawrence replied, shaking his head.

"Oops – sorry, must have slipped my mind..." Marilyn replied sheepishly.

Mel shook her head sadly, knowing that she should have known better than to have expected her absent-minded friend to have remembered to do such a simple task without the need to check up on her. Marilyn was a good friend, but sometimes the little things often escaped her memory...

For example, the time when Mel's sandwiches, which Marilyn had offered to take put in the fridge for, had disappeared for months, Marilyn having totally forgotten where she'd put them, having stopped to chit-chat with several other members of staff whilst en route to the school staffroom that day ...

"I'll call him now," Lawrence said, tapping the screen of his phone.

Mel put her arms around Nona and Marilyn, unable to stay angry with her friend as Lawrence stood, phone pressed to his ear, waiting for the call to connect.

"Dis be Doyley, who be dat?" the loud voice of the zookeeper said on the other end of the line.

"It's Lawrence Light, Doyley. I'm stood at the entrance to Kingston's Kingdom..."

"Hang on a sec..." Doyley said, the phone line going silent for a moment of two, "Dat's better - fewer ears around. Whys are yer dere? The zoo's closed likes Oi told yer!"

"Told us?" Lawrence said loudly, looking at Mel in amazement, switching his phone to hands-free mode so that the others could also hear the conversation, "When exactly did you tell us?"

"Well, it weren't anys of yer, exactly - Oi phoned Mel's house on Sunday," the Irishman replied, "tried her mobile first, but it kept going to voicemail and Oi hate those tings. So, Oi calls der house instead and the phone's bin answered by dis weird woman..."

"Mim..." Nona sighed under her breath.

"So, Oi asks her if Mel or Nona were dere and she sez *'Oi wouldn't be answering der phone now if dey were, would Oi,'* all sarcastic like," Doyley continued, "So, Oi den asks her if she would give yer a message and she's like *'can't yers just call back, yers are making me miss der wrestling!'* So, Oi sez dat it's important and tells her dat der zoo's been closed and dat Lewis is keeping a very close eye on me and Maguire as dat he suspects yers all have been up to no good. She goes, "*Is dat it? Are you done now?'* all angry like and Oi tells her to let Mel know Oid let her know if anytink changes and to call me if yers all need me. She den goes *'Right!'* and hangs up, just like dat - didn't even say goodbye, mad old bat..."

There was silence on the other end of the phone as Mel and the others stood and stared at one another in disbelief, Marilyn now feeling more than just a little relieved that somebody else had dropped a bigger ball than her in this sorry chapter.

"Yers did get me message now, din't yer?" Doyley asked, his Irish burr suddenly breaking the silence.

Just as Lawrence was about to answer him, Mel's phone began to ring loudly in her pocket.

"We'll call you back later, Doyley," Mel shouted as she pulled out her mobile and answered it, not recognising the number at first, "Hello?"

"Ah, Mel - I thought it was you and Nona...I see you've brought some friends too..." said a familiar but unfriendly voice from the other end of the phone line.

Mel suddenly spun around, now realising that Lewis Kingston was spying on them from somewhere nearby, goading her as he did so.

"What do you want, Lewis?" she asked, causing Nona and her friends to look on in shock.

"Oh, you know, just thought I'd call and say *Hi!*" the smug and slimy voice replied, "especially as you've all taken the time and trouble to come and visit me... Unfortunately, as you can see though, we're closed and will be until further notice..."

"You won't get away with this!" Nona shouted over Mel's shoulder, loud enough for her brother to hear.

"Is that my darling sis- sorry - half-sister? Tell her I don't quite follow?" Lewis asked, "Get away with what exactly? I've only closed the zoo to protect the public from a particularly nasty and highly infectious disease…can't be too careful, especially after Covid. That's no crime, is it? I mean, it's not like I've *stolen* something now, does it? Now, that a crime…"

Mel could tell by the way he said the word *'stolen'* that Lewis suspected something but chose not to react or acknowledge it.

"What do you want, Lewis?" she repeated, still trying to work out where he was spying on them from.

From the back seat of John Stafford's car parked on the street about two hundred metres away, Lewis Kingston smiled as he watched where Mel - and those with her - stood fidgeting and squirming in the zoo car park. He was enjoying this.

"What I want is for you all to keep your noses out of my business. Stay away from the kingdom," he growled, "It's not a lot to ask. In fact, I'll make it a whole lot easier…the offer for Nona's share in the zoo is still on the table, just take it…We can then we shake hands, say our *'Goodbyes'* and have nothing more to do with one another ever again. Sounds perfectly fair and reasonable, don't you think?"

"No," Mel replied, not even bothering Nona's opinion, already knowing her daughter's likely reply, "You won't get rid of us that easily. By law, half the zoo's Nona's. This ain't over by a long way, Lewis…"

"Oh, I think, Mel…" Lewis replied, his voice now adopting a more serious menacing tone, "I warned you before when your daughter tried to steal from me that I'd get the law involved so you'd might also like to know that I've promoted my man Clarke – put him in charge of zoo security, especially as he already knows your faces. I'm certain you already know the whereabouts of some of my missing property, so if you don't back off and keep away from the kingdom, I'll have no alternative but to report you and your friends to the police. Do you understand?"

"Perfectly," Mel replied, trying to conceal the anger she felt, "but don't try to fob us off with your miserly offers though - we know the zoo is worth a whole lot more than you've offered us were you to close it and sell off the land…"

Mel's words seemed to take Lewis slightly aback.

"Is that so…? he sneered before continuing, "You're not as dumb as you look, Mel, are you? But, as I said, if you don't back off and I prove Nona took just one of the animals illegally from the zoo

against the terms of my grandfather's zoo, then she'll lose her share of the will, meaning she'll get half of nothing…"
Lewis smiled when Mel failed to answer, so smugly continued. "As it happens, I've already a buyer lined up stay away from me and the kingdom until this *terrible* disease has run its course…" he said seriously, "I'll then make sure you get your fair share of the proceeds of the sale. No, why don't you and Nona toddle off back to your council estate like good little girls, Mel. Laters…"
Before Mel could even begin to reply, the phone line suddenly went dead.
"Why that no good, slimy, little…little…sh-" she angrily stuttered
"Mel - language!" Marilyn shouted to remind her that Nona was still listening.
"It's all right, Marilyn, I've heard Mum say a whole lot worse…" Nona smiled weakly.
"What did he have to say for himself then, Mel," Lawrence asked. However, the look Mel now wore on her face showed him Mel had already all but admitted defeat.
"You were right, Lawrence, it's all over," Mel sadly replied, "I'll tell you all everything on our way back to the coach. Sue will be wondering where we are, plus we need to get those kids safely back to school…"

Lewis sat smugly watching his four very unwelcome visitors turn and make their way back to the visitors' car park, Mel Lancaster now having wrapped an arm around her daughter to comfort her.
"Ah, poor little diddums…you don't think I've upset them, John, do you?" he laughed.
Stafford turned around in the driver's seat to look at his boss.
"I'd say so, Mr Kingston," he smiled, "in fact, I think it's fair to say that you've well and truly knocked the stuffing out of them!"
"Good, let's get going then," Lewis replied.
"Of course," Stafford said, starting the engine to the car, "may I ask one question though?"
"Shoot!" Lewis replied cheerily.
"You said they'd get their fair share of the proceeds from the sale of Kingston's Kingdom to Aleksander Kashlotov," the accountant said before adding, "did you honestly mean to say that?"
"That I did, John. However, I happen to know an extremely good accountant who's going to use most of the money made from the

sale, to pay off my poor grandfather's *secret and extensive hidden debts* which have only come to light since his sudden and unexpected death," Lewis winked, slapping Stafford on the shoulder, "if you know what I mean…?"

"Oh, I think I do," Stafford laughed as they drove off, his car now joining the busy traffic as they headed away from the zoo.

"Like I said, Nona Lancaster and that mother of hers will get exactly what's coming to them," Lewis grinned, sinking deeper into his car seat, "just you mark my words…"

There was a much more sombre mood on the coach on the return to Trinity after Mel had revealed the full extent of her telephone conversation with Lewis Kingston. It had been further dampened by the call that Mel had then made to Alistair Leadbetter to see if there was anything he would be able to do to stop Lewis Kingston's plans and have the zoo quickly re-opened.

"I spoke with Mr Kingston and Doctor Au earlier this week, Miss Lancaster," the old solicitor replied, continuing, "although visitors are unable to enter it currently, the zoo still continues to function in every other way, meaning that it still meets the obligations set out in Roger Kingston's will. However, the welfare of the public must be the prime concern in instances such as these especially since the pandemic, so I wholeheartedly agree with Mr Kingston's actions as they seem most prudent to me..."

Mel had sighed and shaken her head as Leadbetter continued. "Once again, many thanks for raising your concerns as to Mr Kingston's motives with me but let me assure you that Doctor Au is a world-renowned zoological medical specialist, so the danger they face must be very real," the solicitor said gently, "But rest assured - I'm due to do a full inspection and audit of the kingdom, its contents and its animals soon, so if there are any irregularities then, these will be highlighted and addressed then."

Mel had almost blurted out exactly what Lewis planned to do with the animals but stopped short, all too aware of the fact that they could end up in trouble themselves if Leadbetter suspected what the escape committee had been doing in the meantime.

Instead, she thanked the solicitor for his time and said *'Goodbye,'* now fully resigned to the fact their one last hope of stopping Lewis Kingston and his plans had ended along with the phone conversation.

Now, as the coach passed through Trinity's gates, all they had left to show for their concerted rescue efforts were the few animals who still resided in the old school buildings…

Hearing the hum of the coach's engine idling, Miss Bridges swivelled the chair from her desk and looked out through the blinds of her office window.

Odd, Miss Bridges thought to herself as she looked at her watch, *they shouldn't be back until early this afternoon.* She quickly got up from her chair and began to make her way through the school to meet and greet them.

By the time, the headteacher had reached the coach, most of the children had already been signed off and released to go back to lessons, leaving only Nona, Luca, Paige and Keeley still standing there with the remaining school staff.

"I didn't expect to see you back from your trip so early!" Miss Bridges cheerfully said as she approached them.

However, by the glum and despondent faces which met her arrival, the headteacher instantly knew the trip must have been reluctantly and unexpectedly cut short.

"Run along to class now, children," Miss Bridges said brusquely. "I need to talk to Mr Light and the rest of the staff in private."

"But Miss Bridges," Nona began to protest until her headteacher shot her a look as if to say, *'Are you still here?'*

"Yes, Miss," Nona said glumly as she trudged off, her friends silently walking behind her.

Miss Bridges watched and waited until the four children were safely out of earshot and had entered the school building before she turned back to where Mel and the others stood.

"So - tell me what happened…?"

By the time Mel, Lawrence, Sue and Marion had retold the day's sorry events, Clive Tilley had returned in the school minibus, completely covered from head-to-foot in dirt and grime, having spent yet another morning carrying out the essential work needed to house Nona's animals.

"What have I missed?" he asked as he slowly climbed out of the school vehicle.

"Plenty," Sue said, sadly, "but, basically, it's over…. we've been rumbled and the zoo's been closed. There's no way we'll be able to get any more animals out, especially as Lewis Kingston will report us to the police if he can prove what we've already been up to."

Clive looked at Mel who nodded.

"That pretty much sums it all up, Clive," she sighed sadly.

"But me and the guys from the rugby club have been working on day and night this past week getting things ready to start moving the animals onto the island," he protested, "you're seriously telling me that we've spent all that time and effort for nothing?"

"I'm so sorry, Clive, but I'm afraid it is," Mel replied, "we've got no choice…"

"Oh, there's always another choice," Miss Bridges boomed, "you just don't know what it is yet… Tell you what, to help us re-group and re-focus our energies and efforts, as well as cheering us all up, let's meet at the Woolwich Warren Golf Club first thing tomorrow. We can play a spot of golf and have brunch together - my treat!"

Mel frowned at Lawrence and the others.

"With all due respect, Miss Bridges, but I'm not sure how a game of golf will help lift our spirits," she eventually said.

"Plus, none of us play golf either," Lawrence added.

"Oh -we do!" Marilyn and Sue answered in unison, causing Mel the others to look at them in surprise.

"Right - that settles it then!" Miss Bridges declared, "Mel, you and Lawrence can take it in turns to caddy for Sue and Marilyn. We can say it's an approved sporting event so Nona can attend too – they can be a bit funny about children playing at the club sometimes… Clive, you'll drive my buggy and carry my clubs! It'll be just like old times, won't it dear?"

"Great!" Clive muttered, bitterly recalling the countless times when, as a child, he'd carried his aunt's golf clubs, which were much larger than himself, around dozens of golf courses up and down the country.

"Miss Bridges, I really appreciate the gesture, but I don't know how chasing a small, white ball around a golf course will help raise our spirits with the situation as it is," Mel said glumly.

"You'll be surprised just how much a brisk early morning walk around the Woolwich Warren will help clear the mind and give you hope for the future," Miss Bridges grinned, "just you wait and see…"

Chapter 20 – In the Bunker

Getting her daughter out of bed on a Saturday morning was usually hard enough normally if she was due to play for her beloved Ventham FC that day. However, trying to wake her up an hour and a half earlier than usual was proving even more difficult for Mel as she wrestled with Nona and the duvet.

If that wasn't bad enough, Nona's foul mood since returning home the previous night, immediately taking herself off to her room, hadn't improved so the prospect of reluctantly taking her to the golf course was growing less and less appealing that morning.

Ordinarily, when meeting with such stubborn resistance, Mel would've given up and left her daughter there, knowing that Nona would eventually rush to get herself ready at the last minute, desperate not to miss a single minute of her game.

But there was no match today so much less reason for her to emerge from her polyester chrysalis, that was until Mel had told her that Miss Bridges herself had insisted Nona come to the golf course as well. Only then did Nona flop out of bed, throw on the nearest crumpled clothes she could find before finally slumping into the back of Sue's people carrier, resting her feet on the two golf bags she now shared the journey with in protest.

It was only when they pulled into the Woolwich Warren Golf Club car park, that she grunted her first words of the morning.

"Why am I here?" Nona asked moodily,

Mel looked at her daughter in the back of the vehicle and smiled wanly.

"Like I said, Miss Bridges' invited all of us to play here today," sighed, "thought that it might cheer us all up. I'm not so sure myself, but it's a lovely gesture nonetheless..."

Mel turned back to smile at Lawrence who was sat next to her. The young teacher smiled back, tugging at the collar of the ill-fitting polo shirt he wore that day, along with some tan chinos.

"You look very nice, Lawrence," Mel said, not noticing Marilyn winking at Sue in the front of the car.

"Er, thank you, Mel, but I hate wearing this sort of stuff though - give me a T-shirt and a pair of jeans any day of the week!" Lawrence replied.

"I bet you look good in anything you wear," Mel replied before suddenly catching herself, blushing as she continued, "Er, what I meant was that you always look smart no matter how you dress…"

Nona pretended to stick a finger down her throat, the gesture only seen in the rear-view mirror by Sue Brightside, who grinned and pulled on the handbrake of her car.

"There's Clive and Miss Bridges over there," Sue said, pointing towards the imposing clubhouse which stood a little way ahead of them.

Miss Bridges, who was beautifully turned out in immaculate matching golf wear, saw them arrive and waved enthusiastically as they all began to climb out of the people carrier. Clive Tilley, on the other hand, looked like he'd just raided a local charity shop wearing a pair of ill-fitting cotton trousers and a tight, pink short-sleeved shirt covered by a sleeveless checked pullover. Over one of his shoulders was slung a huge golf bag with an array of expensive clubs sticking out of it. To cap Clive's golf-tramp look off, he wore a woolly bobble hat, it perching on the top of his head, like an abandoned tea-cosy.

Mel thought that Clive looked as happy to be there as her daughter was, which made her feel a little better about dragging Nona to the golf course that day.

"Morning chaps and chappesses!" Miss Bridges called as Sue and Marion walked around to the back of the people carrier, "What a glorious day! I've already paid our green fees, so we can get started just as soon as Marilyn and Sue are ready to tee off."

"Did Miss Bridges just swear, Mum?!" Nona gasped.

"No sweetheart, you tee off to start a round of golf." Mel smiled. As Sue and Marilyn got their clubs out of the back of the car, Miss Bridges walked over to Nona.

"I'm sorry to hear about what happened yesterday my dear," the headteacher said sympathetically, "however, your brother was bound to find out sooner or later - it was only a matter of time before he eventually stopped you coming and going so freely."

"I know, Miss Bridges," Nona nodded, "but it was the only way to rescue all the animals. Now he's closed the zoo, we've no chance of saving any more of them."

"If there's one thing that I've learned in all my years on this planet," Miss Bridges smiled gently, "it's that there are more ways than one way to skin a cat…"

Nona looked horrified at the suggestion as Miss Bridges laughed loudly before winking at her.

"Don't worry, Nona," she smiled, "It's just an old saying meaning that there are other ways to go about things."

However, before Nona could ask the headteacher exactly what she meant, Miss Bridges had marched off in the direction of the golf buggies that were parked just before the path which led to the first tee, Clive scampering behind, desperately trying to keep up with his aunt.

"Come along then, troopers," Miss Bridges bellowed, "we'll do the back nine holes first so that we beat the morning rush of golfers..."

"I love Miss Bridges, Mum," Nona said as they followed behind Miss Bridges and her nephew to get a buggy with Marilyn, "but sometimes I think she's as mad as a box of frogs!"

"All the very best teachers are, Nona!" Mr Light called from behind the two of them as he carried Sue's golf bag for her on his shoulder.

It wasn't long before the seven of them were gently making their way across the course in their golf buggies, Miss Bridges leading the pedestrian charge, closely followed by Marilyn and Sue's golf buggies respectively, Mel and Lawrence grappling to control the electric vehicles which seemed to have developed minds of their own. Mel's driving was especially impressive given the fact that she'd never passed her driving test, something Marilyn had totally forgotten when asking for her friend to drive.

Behind the two women, Nona hung on to the side of the golf buggy for dear life, remembering the only time she'd ridden in the back of Clive's car during on one of her mother's few attempts at learning to drive. It was a painful and traumatic experience they'd all desperately tried hard to forget...

Eventually, the three golf buggies reached the wooden bridge which separated the front nine holes from the back nine, it crossing a backwater especially created to be a water hazard which flowed from the Thames into an artificial lake in the centre of the course. Clive made to drive over the bridge but stopped when his aunt suddenly raised a hand.

"Wait here please, dear, so that the others can catch us up," Miss Bridges quietly asked.

A short while later, the whirring electric motors of Marilyn and

Sue's golf buggies finally announced their arrival.

"You see that large mound over there everyone?" Miss Bridges shouted, pointing between a row of trees which grew together, their branches tangled together, making them look as though they were doing a leafy guard of honour, "That's the raised green to the most difficult hole on the course - the tenth - the Great Bunker... 600 yards long and an absolute beast of a hole."

"Why's it called that, Miss Bridges," Nona asked, leaning forward in her buggy.

"The hole from tee to green is surrounded by several large sand bunkers of varying sizes, shapes and depths," Clive said, recalling the number of occasions he'd had to rake over the sand whenever his aunt's golf ball had landed in one in the past.

"However, the largest and most treacherous sand trap is right in front of the green itself, either side of a small, crooked bridge you must clear just to reach it," he added, "you put your ball in there and you're in real trouble - hence the name *the Great Bunker.*"

"All very true, Clive," Miss Bridges nodded in agreement, "but that's not the only reason they call it that…"

The headteacher slowly began to turn Clive's steering wheel to the left and pointed at the trees.

"That way please, dear," Miss Bridges winked, "I've something I'd like you all to see...."

Clive looked at his aunt suspiciously but knew better than to question her as he dropped the handbrake on the golf buggy and began to head in the direction he'd been asked to go, the other two buggies soon following.

As they passed through the archway of trees which had knitted their branches together like hands joined in prayer, Nona noticed that the foliage was so thickly entwined that even the sun could scarcely pass through them, causing eerie shadows to be thrown everywhere.

Clive flicked on the buggy's headlights to light the way as they slowly made their way through the trees.

"Auntie Sheila, I don't understand…" he began to say before his aunt cut him short.

"Not much farther now, dear boy - trust me…" Miss Bridges smiled, resting her hand gently on his thigh, "Here – stop here!"

Clive immediately slammed on the brakes as the buggy came to an abrupt and shuddering stop.

189

Mel and Lawrence slowly brought their buggies alongside and did the same, the headlights from all three falling on a wall of earth and grass ahead of them, a gnarled ivy-covered old tree standing just to the right of it.

"Dead end," Clive sighed as his aunt turned and began to reach into the side of her golf bag, unzipping the front pocket as she did so. The headteacher then pulled out a large flashlight from it, switching it on as she stepped out of the golf buggy.

"Follow me, troopers!" Miss Bridges cried as she marched towards the tree ahead of her.

"Told you, Mum…" Nona said, shaking her head, "mad as a box of frogs…"

For once, Mel didn't disagree as they quickly followed Clive and Miss Bridges, Marilyn, Sue and Lawrence following suit, closely bringing up the rear.

Up ahead of them, Miss Bridges had stopped just in front of the tree and was peering at it intently, moving the flashlight back and forth across the leafy and moss-covered tree-trunk.

"I think she's finally lost the plot," Lawrence whispered to no one in particular as the headteacher place her hand on the tree.

Suddenly, she began to frantically claw at the trunk, tearing large clumps of moss and ivy away from the bark. After a few moments, Miss Bridges stopped and reached for her neck, slowly pulling out a chain with a large key attached to it.

"Hold this for a minute, dear," she said, handing the flashlight to Clive as she now used both free hands to slip the chain up over her head. Miss Bridges then inserted the key into a hole in one of the now exposed knots in the tree trunk, first turning the key one way before then turning it the other.

Suddenly, a branch sprung out from the tree as Miss Bridges took the flashlight back from Clive before pushing the branch down hard against the trunk. Instantly, the air was filled with a loud whooshing sound as though a seal had been broken on a giant bottle of fizzy drink.

Miss Bridges turned and smiled at the others, who were all now stood open-mouthed behind her, staring on in amazement.

"Welcome to the *real* Great Bunker…" she declared as she slowly slid open a hidden door which had been concealed in the tree.

Once fully open, Miss Bridges slipped the chain with the key back around her neck and poked her head through the opening she'd just revealed them all.

"What the -" Clive gasped as he watched his aunt step through the door, her flashlight shining the way before her as she began to disappear down into the tree trunk.

"Come on then, troopers!" Miss Bridges shouted, her voice echoing in the hollow chamber she was now descending into, "Where's your sense of adventure?"

"Where the hell is she going?" Mel asked as she began to follow Nona, who hadn't hesitated in following her headteacher into the tree trunk.

"I've absolutely no idea!" replied Clive, squeezing his heavy frame through the secret doorway, "I'm now seeing a whole new side to my aunt I never knew existed…"

It wasn't long before the six of them were all carefully negotiating their way down a narrow stone stairwell following the torchlit pathway Miss Bridges was creating ahead of them, their journey being made all the more difficult by the wet moss which grew on the edges of some of the steps.

"I don't like this one bit…" Sue moaned as she inched her way down, pressing her back against the stone wall that followed one side of the stairway, feeling droplets of water find their way between the collar of her golf shirt and skin of her neck.

"Not much further," Miss Bridges called as she pressed on ahead, "if memory serves me right…"

"That's reassuring – not!" Lawrence muttered as he followed closely behind Mel, "Sounds like Miss Bridges hasn't been in here - wherever *here* is - for some time herself…"

Eventually, they all saw the beam of the flashlight level out as Miss Bridges reached the bottom of the stairs before moving straight ahead in front of them.

As the last of them reached the end of the stairwell, they heard a large *clank* then a faint *buzz* which soon grew into a loud *hum* as several fluorescent lights slowly lit up, illuminating the walls of the huge underground structure they were now standing in.

"Whoa…" Nona gasped, craning her head around to take in all that she could now see.

"As I was saying," Miss Bridges said, turning her flashlight off before rejoining the rest of the group, "this is *the* Great Bunker!"

"This is incredible…" Marilyn gasped as she tried to take in the sheer size and scale of the room they were now standing in, "What exactly is it though?"

"It's an underground bunker," Miss Bridges said, "it does exactly what it says on the tin - just like the old TV advert used to say…"

"A bunker for what?" Marilyn asked, causing her friends to shake their heads in dismay.

"It's a shelter to protect people from an enemy attack," Nona said, adding, "Was this one built to save people from the Blitz during World War II, Miss Bridges?"

"Initially, yes," Miss Bridges nodded, "but when the Americans dropped the first two atomic bombs on Hiroshima and Nagasaki in 1945, the government decided to fortify it even more so that it could withstand a nuclear blast from our Cold War enemies at the time, such as the Soviet Union."

Miss Bridges patted one of the walls proudly before continuing. "The walls are now four and a half feet of steel and concrete thick, the idea for the mound of earth and grass growing on top the bunker coming from the way Anderson Shelters were constructed in the 1940s," the headteacher smiled before continuing, "it was only later when the golf course was built that they, unwittingly, turned the top of the bunker into a green instead!"

"Is it still used then?" Nona asked, fascinated by this unexpected history lesson from her headteacher.

"No, dear," Miss Bridges said, shaking her head, "at least, not officially, not since it was sealed up back in 1987 just before the land was sold off to the owners of the golf course. All incredibly low key and hush-hush, of course…"

"Then how do you know about it, Auntie Sheila?" Clive asked, not quite certain as to whether he actually wanted to know the answer to the question or not.

"All former members of the British Secret Service are given a key to the Great Bunker as a *Thank You* when they leave," Miss Bridges sniffed, "in recognition of all they've done for their country and in case of any future national emergency…"

"When were you in the secret service?" Clive asked in disbelief.

"Oh, it wasn't for long, dear," Miss Bridges said, matter of factly, "I did a little bit of undercover work for them during the Moscow Olympics, back in the day..."

"I never knew you spied for your country, Auntie Sheila?" Clive gasped.

"There's quite a lot you don't know about me, my dear…" Miss

Bridges replied, causing Nona to laugh loudly - much to her headteacher's obvious approval and amusement.

"It's all very impressive, Miss Bridges," Mel interrupted, "but I still don't see how bringing us to a secret bunker under a golf course is going to help us feel better about Lewis Kingston and the zoo."

Miss Bridges chuckled as she turned and slowly walked over to the far wall of the room, shining her flashlight against it. With her free hand, she slipped the chain up over her head again and inserted the key into another hole in the wall, this time turning it clockwise.

"Because," Miss Bridges said loudly over the mechanical sound of the cogs and gears that were now clanking in front of her as another door slid open before her, "there's more than one way in and out of the Great Bunker…"

Nona and the others crowded around Miss Bridges as she shone her light down another dark corridor the sliding door had now revealed to them.

"What is it?" Lawrence asked, standing on tiptoe to look over the heads of those gathered before him.

"A tunnel," Miss Bridges said before adding, "one of several that link a series of underground rooms and chambers together which were first used by the Armoury, then the Ministry of Defence before the British Secret Service finally, took control of Woolwich Warren…"

"And they all run underneath the golf course?" Nona asked, trying desperately hard to resist the urge to go exploring.

"Yes," Miss Bridges nodded, "well, half of them do, to be precise."

"Half of them, Auntie Sheila?" Clive asked, "What about the other half?"

"Oh those…well, they run underneath the other half of the land the Ministry of Defence previously sold off…" the headteacher grinned mischievously.

"And where might that be exactly?" Marilyn asked but Clive smiled and had already replied before Miss Bridges could even begin to answer.

"Kingston's Kingdom," he said, grinning, "the zoo's built on top of the rest of the old armoury site, isn't it, Auntie Sheila…?"

Chapter 21 – A New Hope

The silence which met Clive's announcement was made eerier by the quietness of the tunnel which stood before them as everyone tried to take in his sudden revelation.

"You're telling us Kingston's Kingdom is built on top of a network of hidden tunnels?" Lawrence finally said, "Why didn't you tell us about them when you first found out about what we were doing, Miss Bridges?"

"Which bit of the title British *Secret* Service do you think is the most important, dear boy?" Miss Bridges replied, giving her teacher a withering look, "Do you think I go around telling everybody I meet that there's a *secret* nuclear bunker hidden under a golf course in London every day? I'm breaking the Official Secrets Act by telling you now as it is!"

Lawrence Light shuffled his foot across the floor in front of him like a naughty schoolboy being scolded as Miss Bridges continued.

"There are some things that ordinary members of the public never need know, especially what goes on behind closed doors in order to keep them safe in their beds at night," the headteacher sniffed.

"Why tell us now then, Auntie Sheila?" Clive asked, more than a little miffed his favourite aunt had never once taken him into her confidence before today.

"I've spent my life fighting for the underdog in one way or the other," Miss Bridges sighed, "always saw a little of them in myself before good luck and fortune kindly smiled on me. Nona's grandfather left her his zoo for one reason and one reason alone – he knew that she'd take care of all the animals who are unable to defend or look after themselves."

Nona wasn't altogether sure, but for a moment or two she thought her steely headteacher's eyes had misted up as Miss Bridges continued to explain herself.

"When you returned from the zoo yesterday, I felt the same sense of injustice I had when I chased that horrible little official who messed up my only chance of a gold medal at the Los Angeles Olympics all those years ago," Miss Bridges continued, "I quit running there and then because I believed I'd never get the chance to win gold ever again. It's a decision I've regretted ever since…

There was no way I was going to let you all quit when I knew there might be another way for you to save your animals. All I ask in return is that you do not discuss or share what you've learned here today with anyone other than those you absolutely trust with your lives. Will you please do that for me at least?"

"I promise," Nona immediately replied, looking at the others all gathered around her who also nodded their heads in agreement.

"Thank you," said Miss Bridges, placing her hand against Nona's cheek.

"We should be thanking you, Miss Bridges," Mel said cheerfully, stepping forwards to hug her headteacher.

"Oh, stoppit!" Miss Bridges half-heartedly protested, "Anyone would do exactly the same as I were they to be in my shoes today."

"I'm not sure they would…" Mel replied, her eyes now following the beam of the flashlight down the tunnel, "I do have another question though - other than members of the government and the British Secret Service, who else knows of this bunker?"

"No one," Miss Bridges smiled, "one of the safeguards the Ministry of Defence put in place and insisted upon before they sold off the old armoury, first to Roger Kingston and then the golf club, was that they wouldn't reveal to either buyer what was *under* both sites."

"How far underground are we exactly?" Lawrence asked.

"Thirty feet, give or take…" Miss Bridges smiled, "more than deep enough to not be accidentally discovered!"

"If you don't mind me asking, Miss Bridges," Sue began to say, "but what was there to stop either Kingston or the golf club owners from digging underground themselves anyway?"

"Shells…" Miss Bridges replied.

"Like at the seaside?" Sue asked.

"No, Mrs Brightside," Miss Bridges laughed, "military shells. The Ministry of Defence gave Roger Kingston and the golf club a map with certain no-go areas where they said old mortar shells from the armoury were buried, amongst other things which were best left undisturbed. It really was a *win-win* situation for all parties - the buyers got prime London locations to build upon which were much cheaper than their market value and the country got to keep its secrets secret!"

"And you're absolutely certain Lewis Kingston and his crooked cronies have no idea about the tunnels and rooms which run under the zoo?" Nona asked.

"I'm positive," Miss Bridges nodded again, "there was a second large entrance where the back wall to the car park is, but that was bricked up and concreted over to look just like the rest of the zoo's outer wall long before Lewis Kingston was born. They figured that one main entrance in and out would be enough due to the amount of tunnel exits there are already which could be used in a national emergency."

Nona squeezed between her mother and Miss Bridges and peered into the dark.

"How many tunnels are there altogether?" she asked.

Miss Bridges paused for a moment, her eyes looking up as though searching for the answer in the air.

"Last count, there were eight of them," she replied, "three running directly under the golf course, the remaining ones stretching out under the zoo."

"Five tunnels under Kingston's Kingdom?" Lawrence gasped loudly in disbelief.

"It's lucky I didn't employ you solely for your mathematical skills, Mr Light!" Miss Bridges laughed before continuing, "Yes, there are five tunnels beneath the zoo - fancy exploring them…?"

"Thought you'd never ask!" Nona grinned, grabbing the flashlight from her headteacher before striding into the dark, briefly stopping and looking at those still stood motionless behind her.

"You all coming or what?"

"It's a bit damp, dark and dingy down there," Marilyn said, Sue nodding her agreement beside her, "perhaps the two of us should stay here - in case of emergency…"

"What a jolly good idea," Miss Bridges replied, saving the two women's blushes and embarrassment.

"Well, I'm game," Mel said, looking at Lawrence and Clive who both nodded as she'd hoped and expected.

"Excellent!" Miss Bridges said, "Nona, if you run your left hand along the wall you should find a light switch which ought to help guide our way."

Nona continued to walk slowly along the cold, damp corridor, gingerly touching her fingers lightly against the rough surface of the walls, eventually being relieved to find a small, metal toggle switch brush against the tip of her index finger, which she immediately flicked up.

Slowly, but surely, the low-level lighting which was mounted high up on the rounded walls flickered into life, giving out just enough light for the travellers to safely find their way through the dark tunnel. As she stood waiting for the others to reach her, Nona extended her arms out towards both walls on either side of her, so narrow were the confines of the tunnel itself. She then looked up and reached above her head, standing on tiptoes to try to touch the top of the tunnel too.

Despite her best efforts though, Nona was unable to reach it, it just eluding her clutches. However, the tunnel was small enough for the likes of Miss Bridges and Clive Tilley – them both being around six feet in height - to have to bow their heads as they approached her. They were followed by the smaller statures of her mother, who was not much taller than Nona herself, and Mr Light, who despite being a few inches taller than Nona's mother could walk without any fear of hitting his head on the rough surface of the tunnel ceiling.

"It's a bit chilly in here," Mel said, her words now echoing slightly as she rubbed her hands against her arms as she joined her daughter.

"One of the downsides," Miss Bridges replied, "no heating systems were ever installed as it was only meant for emergencies. I suppose they figured it would be more than warm enough upstairs if the big bomb ever dropped…"

The five of them continued to slowly make their way along the tunnel for a few more minutes until it began to open up into a wider but much darker chamber.

"What now?" Clive asked as Miss Bridges took the flashlight from Nona and shone it around, staring intently ahead of her. Finally, the beam reflected off a wall, revealing a huge power switch which appeared to be made of iron jutting out from the brickwork.

"There it is!" she grinned, stepping forwards to grab its wooden handle before forcing it down with some considerable effort.

At first, there was nothing as Nona looked anxiously at her mother. Then, suddenly, light seemed to appear from all around them.

"Awesome!" Nona smiled as five different tunnels soon revealed themselves, each one heading off in a different direction to the others, looking like the outspread fingers of an open hand.

"Which way now, Miss Bridges?" Mel asked as she watched her daughter look on, completely in awe at what lay before her, a fact which had not been completely lost on the headteacher either.

"I think it only fair that we let Nona decide," Miss Bridges said before adding, "after all, it's her zoo under which we'll be travelling. It's only right and proper that she gets to choose which direction we go first…"

Nona felt the eyes of the adults fall on her, making her feel slightly uneasy and suddenly self-conscious.

"Well, what do you think, Nona?" Mel asked, smiling reassuringly at her daughter.

"I don't know, Mum…" Nona replied.

"Go with your gut, *Nones*," Clive said, grabbing hold of his amble stomach, "that's what I always do."

"I'm not sure," Nona said, biting her lip slightly as she tried to make up her mind.

"Can I make a simpler suggestion then?" Miss Bridges said, "Why don't we all split up and explore a tunnel each – after all, there are the five of us…"

They all looked at one another as they pondered Miss Bridges' suggestion.

"Nah, you're good Auntie Sheila," Clive said, the others eagerly nodding in agreement, "it's probably best we all stick together, just in case and all that. Right, Nona?"

In truth, Clive was mightily relieved to see Nona agree as the thought of exploring these tunnels not appealing to him in the slightest, a result of watching too many *'Look out it's behind you!'* horror films when he was much younger, more invincible and far mor invulnerable…

"Wuss!" Miss Bridges smiled.

"Too right!" Clive replied.

Lawrence Light bent down to talk to Nona, his eyes now level with hers as they looked towards the tunnels together.

"Try to apply some logic to the problem like we do in lessons, Nona," Nona's teacher began, "we know that we've travelled from the bunker entrance at the golf club, which itself is to the east of Ventham. So, we then must have been moving in a westerly to north-westerly direction for approximately 15 minutes or so to have reached the point we now find ourselves at. Therefore, were we to calculate which direction each tunnel will takes us should we choose it, we'll -"

"*Eeny, meeny, miny, moe...*" interrupted Nona, pointing to each of the tunnels in turn, "*catch a tiger by the toe. If he hollers, let him go, Eeny, meeny, miny, moe! O-U-T spells OUT!*"

Nona's finger finally ended up pointing in the direction of the second tunnel from her right.

"Not as quite as calculated a choice as you were suggesting, Lawrence," Clive laughed, "but an effective one none the less!"

"That one," Nona confirmed, "we go that way..."

Nona quickly set off in her chosen direction, the rest of the group immediately following behind her.

The journey they now took closely resembled the one they'd recently completed to get to the crossroads, the narrow tunnel still being dimly lit but stretching out a lot further than the one they'd travelled earlier.

"Will it never end?" Clive muttered after ten minutes of stooping whilst trailing the others - single file - at the back of the line.

"Patience, dear," Miss Bridges said just in front of him, "all will be revealed soon enough..."

The five of them continued a little further, Nona taking the lead before they came to a slight turn in the tunnel. As Nona rounded the corner, she was surprised to find a bar fixed to the wall before her with a metal ladder attached to it.

"We've made it - we've reached the end!" Nona shouted excitedly, as her mother joined her.

"It would seem so," Mel smiled as Nona looked up at the ladder which extended skyward, now knowing how Jack must have felt when stood at the foot of the beanstalk, a mixture of nerves and excitement competing with one another for her full attention.

"Unfortunately, there isn't enough room for us all to stand looking up into the crawlspace to admire it," Miss Bridges called from behind them.

The headteacher was right - the area around the ladder was only just wide enough for one person to climb it at a time.

"I'll go first!" Nona said, placing her foot on the bottom rung.

"No, Nona - let me go first. We don't know what condition the ladder is in after all these years," Lawrence said, adding, "plus we're not exactly sure where it'll open into. It'll be safer if I go and check it out first."

Nona turned to look at her mother, who looked at Lawrence and nodded.

"Mr Light is right, sweetheart," she whispered.

"OK, Mum," Nona sighed as Lawrence carefully squeezed past Mel to swap places with Nona.

"Be careful, Lawrence," Mel said as he slowly began to climb the ladder, the metal rungs loudly clanging with each step he took.

"I will," Nona's teacher replied as he carefully made his way up the narrow crawlspace which led to the surface.

Below him, Mel and Nona watched nervously, relaying Lawrence's progress to the others who were patiently waiting behind. They both gasped as a foot slipped off one of the rungs but, fortunately, he had a good enough grip to quickly adjust himself so not to fall.

"I'm all right," Lawrence called as much to reassure himself as those below him, "not far now…I think I can see the end of the ladder…"

He was right as after a few seconds, Lawrence reached the top of the ladder where a round metal door - much like the hatch you'd find on top of a submarine - stood between him and the outside world. On the inside of the hatch was a metal locking wheel. Lawrence placed his hands on the wheel and tried to turn it, as though unscrewing the lid of a stubborn jar but it refused to budge.

"What's happening, Mr Light?" Nona distantly called from below.

"Not a lot…" Lawrence grunted as he struggled with the wheel, "There's a hatch but it's a little stiff from its lack of use…if…I just…could…get it…to…budge…"

Suddenly, the wheel moved about an inch, catching Lawrence off guard, causing him to almost lose his balance. He quickly regained it though and braced his back against the wall of the crawlspace, allowing him the chance to dry his sweaty hands on his shirt.

"Nearly there," Lawrence called as he gripped the wheel once more, gritting his teeth as he used all his strength to slowly, but surely, twist the hatch lock round.

At the bottom of the ladder, Nona and Mel covered their ears at the shrieking sound the door hatch made - metal grating against metal – echoed through the tunnel as Lawrence continued to turn the wheel lock.

"Almost there," the young teacher said as he felt the lock become easier between his hands it now spinning more freely with every rotation it made. Eventually, the wheel would spin no more as Lawrence grabbed hold of the large locking plate which was clipped to one side of the hatch and slowly pulled it down.

Here goes nothing, he said to himself as he carefully pushed at the hatch.

At first, it refused to budge, Lawrence fearing that he hadn't unlocked it enough after all but when he placed the top of his shoulder against it and pushed harder, the hatch began to inch open. As it lifted up though, straw and soil fell in from the open entrance it made, Lawrence having to brush it from his eyes and lips as it fell past his face as he eased his head up so that his eyes could see through the narrow gap he'd just created.

"There's no sign of anyone," Lawrence called to Nona and Mel, continuing, "it appears that they've covered over this manhole cover meaning that it must open up into one of the animal enclosures -"

However, the sight of a huge animal suddenly charging towards him from nowhere caused Lawrence to quickly drop the hatch back into place as he heard the creature's feet clang on the metal surface just above his head.

"What is it, Lawrence?" Mel asked anxiously.

"I'm not altogether sure," Lawrence panted, frightened by the sound of claws furiously scraping the hatch above him, "it looked like a giant cat though – a white one with stripes…didn't hang about to find out exactly what it was mind!"

"Sounds like Benji. He's a rare white Bengal Tiger but a bit of a pussycat really!" Nona shouted, "You must have come up in the big cat enclosure."

Overhearing Nona, Miss Bridges called up from behind her.

"Secure the hatch and come back down Mr Light," the headteacher said firmly, "we'd better check where the other four tunnels lead instead as I don't think we'll have a lot of luck getting in and out of that one with all our limbs intact, let alone with any of the animals who live in there…"

By the time they'd all emerged out of the bunker entrance they'd entered several hours earlier, the sunny brightness of the morning had been replaced by a cloud-filled afternoon sky. However, despite their tired minds and aching bodies, their spirits remained high. Having waved goodbye to Clive and Miss Bridges, Nona again now sat in the back of Sue's people carrier as they headed home. In her hands she now held a sheet of scrap paper with a rough map scrawled on it - drawn by Clive Tilley - after they'd all explored the rest of the tunnel and chamber network hidden beneath Kingston's Kingdom. It was Nona who'd suggested they named each tunnel, just like the British prisoners had done in Mim's favourite war film *The Great Escape*. Nona smiled as she looked at the nicknames that they'd given to each tunnel...

Tunnel 1 – Kong *(As it led directly into the home of the Bonobo Monkeys at the furthest part of Kingston's Kingdom, close to the Thames).*

Tunnel 2 – Wildcat – *(Named for obvious reasons by Mr Light).*

Tunnel 3 – Lulu *(The tunnel being hidden behind the restaurant's toilets near Elsie's enclosure, in the centre of the zoo. A good, secluded area from where they could explore the rest of the zoo).*

Tunnel 4 – Monty *(The entrance to it opening near the snake and reptile houses).*

Tunnel 5 – Hammy *(The final tunnel which led them into the rodents' area of Kingston's Kingdom.*

Smiling happily, Nona felt a new sense of hope, optimism and a far greater excitement as to what now lay ahead of them.
This had been greatly added to by Clive Tilley and Miss Bridges having invited everyone over to the fortress for Sunday lunch when they'd finally left one another that afternoon. There, they could then discuss the best way forward, Miss Bridges had explained, as well as them all being able to see first-hand the progress that had been made in getting the islands ready for the animals to move to. Nona yawned, feeling her eyes growing heavier, sleep being encouraged to take her away from consciousness by the quiet humming of Sue's car engine, the wheels rolling monotonously on the road beneath her.
As she stepped into her dreams, Nona imagined she was standing, looking over the new island home for the animals her grandfather

had entrusted her with.

"I'm so proud of you, Nona," her grandfather had then said, coming to stand behind her, wrapping his arms around her, shoulders, squeezing her tightly to him.

"Thank you, Grandpa," Nona sleepily whispered as she wrapped her arms around his and nuzzled her head into the headrest, letting sleep carry her home...

Chapter 22 – Home from Home

For once, Nona was up way before her mother that Sunday, so keen was she to go and see the progress Clive and his friends had made in preparing the islands for the planned arrival of its new permanent residents.

She'd twice shocked Mel by making her a cup of tea that morning too. Firstly, because she never, ever, made her mother a cuppa in bed and, secondly, because in her haste, Nona had forgotten to add a teabag, Mel pretending to enjoy her cup of hot water and milk as Nona chattered incessantly beside her.

So loud and enthusiastic was Nona that Mim had poked her head around the bedroom door demanding that she *'put a sock in it'* as she was nursing the *'mother and father of all hangovers'* after having too many ginger beers at the bingo hall the night before...

By the time Sue Brightside had tooted her car horn later that morning, Mel was relieved there were others in the people carrier who her daughter could bounce off the walls of the car with. She smiled as Nona bounded into the back of Sue's vehicle and began to bend Lawrence's ear as to how excited she was that morning and what she thought they should do to get the rest of the animals out of the zoo.

Mel felt a warm glow as she watched Lawrence patiently smile and listen as Nona spoke, ten-to-the-dozen, to her teacher, her arms waving around her head as though she was directing traffic. *I bet he'd be a fabulous father*, Mel caught herself thinking before abruptly turning away from him, suddenly realising that she was going all gooey looking at the teacher...

Fortunately, the journey to the Hoon Island Fortress was much smoother and quicker than previously thanks to the absence of traffic that morning, apart from the usual *'Sunday drivers'* who managed to inflict road-rage upon the normally placid Sue Brightside by failing to indicate which way they were going or suddenly pulling out in front of her or ignoring her right of way. So frequent were these occurrences that Marilyn ended up sitting with her hand permanently rested on Sue's knee, gently telling her to *'keep calm and carry-on regardless'* despite the fear and terror she felt as Sue wove in and out of the traffic, cursing loudly as she did so.

Eventually, much to Marilyn's obvious relief, they safely turned into the approach to Hoon Island, the people carrier slowing to negotiate the potholed dirt track which looked more like the surface of the moon than an old industrial park in London once more.

As they neared the water's edge, Nona was surprised to see the backs of two people in full bike leathers and helmets just ahead of them - one being very tall whilst the other stood a good foot shorter. They were stood beside an old motorcycle and sidecar staring out toward the fortress, the causeway being totally covered by water lapping against the shore.

Sue slowly pulled her car up to the left of the couple before cutting its engine.

"Who'd you think they are?" she asked as the two mysterious figures slowly turned to look at them.

"Dunno," Mel replied, adding, "but they ain't half giving me the creeps!"

Just then, the two strangers began to walk towards the car, the sun wildly glinting off their mirrored crash helmets, now causing them to look even more sinister and menacing as they approached.

"I don't like this...I don't like this one bit..." Sue whispered, locking the car from the inside as the taller figure drew closer, it's mini-me twin hanging back a little way behind.

The tall figure then drew a long, gloved finger from its side and tapped heavily on the rear window on the driver's side of the car, causing Mel to move back across herself seat until she firmly pinned Lawrence between her and his door.

"Owaya?" a muffled voice said, its heavy accent instantly giving its owner away to all nervously sat in the vehicle.

"Doyley!" Nona shouted in relief as the zookeeper raised the visor to his helmet.

Sue wound her car window down for the Irishman to lean on the door.

"What are you doing here?" she asked, her heart now returning to its normal rhythm.

"Mc and Maguire," he said, waving a thumb over his shoulder at the smaller figure now waving frantically behind him, "were over at der school dis morning, giving der animals a once-over, as well as a few little titbits when we bumped into yer man Clive and his auntie. She introduced herselfs and invited us over for a bit of grub as well as checking over der work dats been done so far."

Doyley looked back across the causeway to the fortress before continuing. "However, we've been here for about fifteen minutes and dere's not been much sign of life as yet."

"That's probably because the tide's in," Sue replied, "have you called either of them by any chance?"

"Ain't got dere numbers," Doyley replied, shaking his head.

"I'll give Clive a call," Mel said, fumbling in her pocket, Nona noticing that her mother was still leaning against Mr Light and smiled to herself knowingly.

But before Mel had even managed to unlock her phone, Hayley Maguire had begun to jump up and down, waving manically as she did so.

"Over there! Over there!" she repeated as a couple of small boats with outboard motors attached to their rears appeared from behind Hoon Island and began to motor towards them.

Nona and the others got out of the people carrier and stood alongside Doyley and Maguire as the two boats gradually drew closer to the banks of the river, the sound of their engines becoming much louder the nearer they got to the shoreline.

"It's Clive and Miss Bridges," Nona said excitedly, bouncing on the spot as the unmistakable figures of their two friends became clearer and more recognisable the closer they got to them.

Clive Tilley was the first to approach them, the site manager slowing his boat as he neared the land.

"Here - catch hold of this!" he shouted, unsteadily standing up in his boat as he threw a long rope towards Lawrence, who dropped it initially before quickly bending to pick it again.

"Tie it to that post there," Clive instructed, pointing to a weather-worn stump which stood between the two men.

Lawrence duly obliged, allowing Clive, once convinced the rope was secure, to cut his engine and pull himself and the boat into the shore.

Miss Bridges patiently waited until her nephew had stepped off his boat and was safely on dry land before she threw her rope in Doyley's direction, giving him instructions to do the same as Lawrence had.

"Good morning, troopers!" she said cheerily, "As you can see, the Tide's in at present, so the only way to make it across the Medway to the fortress is by boat. I hope you're all hungry as I've prepared a brunch banquet fit for a queen…"

Miss Bridges smiled as the voices assembled before her chattered excitedly, confirming that they were either *'ravenous'* or could *'eat a horse'* or that they felt like they'd hadn't eaten *"in forever…"*

"Excellent!" Miss Bridges smiled, turning to look and nod at her nephew.

"But before we go to the fortress," Clive grinned, "we've a little surprise for you all so climb aboard…"

However, trying to board the boats proved to be more problematic to some than helping wild animals escape from the zoo, the vessels pitching from side to side on the choppy water as each person gingerly stepped into them.

Eventually though, Nona, Mel, Lawrence and Doyley all were safely sat in the boat captained by Clive, whilst Miss Bridges had welcomed Sue, Marilyn and Hayley Maguire into hers.

"It's a good job dat yers two have such wee legs!" Doyley laughed as he stretched his long, skinny limbs towards Mel and Nona, "otherwise Oid never have had enough room in dis ting meself!"

"Hang on to your hats, folks," Clive said as he uncoiled the rope from the tree stump and pushed the boat away from shore, moving to the rear of it to sit next to its outboard motor, "it could be a bumpy ride…"

The site manager pulled hard on the ripcord and the engine immediately sprung to life, causing its passengers to lurch back in their seats as the boat buzzed into life.

Soon it was briskly skipping over the water, carving a white-water path on the river to the right of Hoon Island for Mrs Bridges and her boat's inhabitants' to follow, gaining speed on them as it passed the jetty, rounded the fortress and straightened up as it headed in the direction of Deadman's Rock.

"What's the big surprise then, Uncle Clive?" Nona shouted, struggling to keep her eyes completely open, the spray off the river glistening on her cheeks where it hit her face, dampening her fringe too.

"You'll see soon enough, sweetheart," Clive smiled as the smallest of the three islands began to grow larger as their boat approached it.

Nona peered as hard as she could at the rocky outcrop, realising that what they'd said about the island was true…there was definitely something sinister about it, the edges of Deadman's Rock being completely covered by sharp, jagged rocks, snarling at them, as though warning them to stay away from its shores and its secrets…

"I can see why they used the island as a prison…Look! Over there!" Nona suddenly screamed as she stood up in the boat, pointing towards the island.

"Nona - sit down!" Mel shouted, grabbing her daughter's arm to pull her back down into her seat, "You'll have us all in the water if you're not careful!"

"Did you see them, Mum?" Nona asked excitedly.

"See what?"

"The penguins…they're already on the island…Look!" Nona said, jabbing her finger in the direction of one of the rock-filled bays.

Sure enough, as Mel and Lawrence squinted in the general direction Nona had indicated, a solitary Humboldt Penguin confidently skipped across the jagged surface, looking like it had always lived there. Soon it was joined by two more penguins who casually appeared from behind a large, moss-covered group of rocks higher up on the face of the small cliff ahead of them.

"How wonderful!" Mel said as Clive cut the engine, the boat now gently bobbing up and down on the water about twenty feet away from where the penguins were all stood, acting like they didn't have a care in the world.

"How long have they been here?" Lawrence asked as another penguin suddenly flew out of the water, awkwardly landing next to its friends.

Clive looked over at Doyley. "How long would you say it's been?"

The Irishman looked at his watch and shrugged. "Probably tree-or-four hours, give or take."

Nona looked quizzically at him, wondering how he could know that exactly.

"Sorry little lady, Oi forgot to say dat me and Maguire have already been here once today, helping to get these little fellas settled in before yer got here," he winked, "me and yer man Clive dere tought it would be a nice surprise for yer. Yer like?"

"I like!" Nona beamed as she watched the animals hop backwards and forwards across the rocks, now joined by several more penguins who suddenly appeared from in and around them.

"Hang on a minute," Nona said frowning, "we only managed to get six of them out before - there's got to be at least ten there now! How's that possible?"

"Dere's twelve to be precise," Doyley corrected, "me and Maguire tought that as deres an epidemic at der zoo dat Mr Kingston wouldn't notice a few more missing animals, so we brought dem with us dis morning."

"How did you ever manage to do that?" Mel asked.

"Simples, we put dem in a large, industrial cool box, walked right past der man Clarke and told him dat we were off to der fish market to get some grub for dem," Doyley smiled, "he never tought to check us once - not der sharpest tool in der shed, dat one…"

"Just as well," Mel replied, "you've got to be really careful though, Doyley, especially if Lewis Kingston is watching you."

"Oh, Oi will be, dontcha worry about dat!" Doyley winked.

Just then, Miss Bridges called across from her boat which had stopped just a short distance away from them.

"Hope that you've all enjoyed your little pre-brunch treat!" she laughed, "Time to head back now - we've still much to see and discuss this morning. 'd rather not do it on an empty stomach though..."

The food Miss Bridges had slaved away over to prepare for that morning didn't last long, the eight people who sat around the large dining table devouring its contents in no time at all as a feast containing two cooked chickens, a joint of ham, cheese, salad, fresh bread, coleslaw and potato salad, amongst other things, disappeared in a frenzy of feeding her guests the fruit of the kindly headteacher's culinary labours.

Miss Bridges sat at the head of the table and smiled as she watched those around it eat, drink and chat happily to one another, delighted to be bringing this caring group of people ever closer together. As the fervour with which people ate reduced, so conversations began to return to the small matter of Kingston's Kingdom and the impact the newly found tunnel complex beneath it would make to the rest of their rescue plans.

"Given this most fortunate and quite unexpected turn of events,"

Sue Brightside announced whilst trying to prize a particularly stubborn and stringy piece of pork from the gap between her two front teeth, "I think we should just go for it and get as many animals as possible out of the Kingdom before Nona's brother profits any more from them."

"Dat's all fine and dandy in theory," Doyley replied, leaning back in his chair, his metal-toed cowboy boots resting on the table, "but Oi tink dat he'll notice yer taking out his most valuable animals and will be all over yer like a bad rash."

"What do you propose then, Mr Doyle?" Miss Bridges enquired, shooting the Irishman a fierce glance, leaving him in no doubt as to her opinion of his inappropriate table manners.

Doyley quickly dropped his feet to the floor and promptly sat up. "Well, Oi tink dat we should concentrate on der little fellas who aren't as valuable to him," he replied, "dat way we can move a lot more animals out without raising too much suspicion."

Mel looked at Nona, who shrugged her shoulders, showing her disagreement.

"But the rarer animals need our help just as much, Doyley," Mel replied, "what he's doing isn't right – Lewis Kingston shouldn't be able to get away with it."

Nona smiled at her mother, happy that she'd expressed what she was thinking so well but hadn't wanted to say for fear of upsetting the zookeeper who'd helped and looked after her so often in the past.

"I totally understand," Hayley Maguire said quietly, shocking those who'd hardly heard her speak during brunch, "but surely, it's better to get as many animals as possible out whilst we can? With the best will in the world, you're not going to be able to get a Sumatran Tiger or Amur Leopard in the back of a school minibus now, are you? And as to Elsie…"

"There's no way he's selling Elsie!" Nona suddenly said, springing out of her chair, "She was Grandpa's favourite - we've got to get her out!"

Mel rested her hand on Nona's arm, totally sympathising with her daughter's anger and frustration.

"Oi tink dat der grand old lady is safe for now," replied Doyley, "ain't dat right, Maguire?"

"Yes - he's only interested in moving on the high-value animals at present," the young vet agreed, "selling Elsie, or claiming she'd died as a result of this unknow *disease* would work against him. She's so famous and iconic that it would bring a whole host of unwanted attention and scrutiny on him and the kingdom… No, he wants to make as much money as he can from his most prized assets. Fortunately, Elsie isn't that valuable to him – yet…"

"May I ask, Miss Maguire," Lawrence asked, leaning closer to the young vet, causing Mel to feel a sudden, unexplainable burst of jealousy, "are you able to explain exactly what this zoonotic disease is and how deadly it may be?"

"Hayley," replied Hayley Maguire, "please call me Hayley. As to the disease, no one really knows for sure. Doctor Au claims that it is highly contagious and can from pass species to species. No one will challenge him as he's so highly renowned that people daren't question what he says, especially after Covid, but…"

"But what?" Lawrence asked.

"But I wouldn't trust a single word he says," Maguire sniffed, "especially as he has no qualms in helping Lewis Kingston to drug the animals and say that they're dead, to ship them out of the zoo to private owners all around the planet."

"If you're so outraged by all this, *Miss* Maguire, then why haven't you already quit?" Mel asked, ignoring the vet's earlier request to be called Hayley whilst feeling an inexplicable anger suddenly rise within her. It was now Nona's turn to place a calming hand on her mother's arm.

"I live at home with my disabled mother who I'm the primary carer for," Hayley said sadly, "were it not for that, I'd have told Lewis Kingston exactly where to shove his job by now…"

Mel felt a sudden pang of guilt as the young vet pulled a tissue from her pocket and gently blew her nose into it.

"Anyway," Marilyn said, sensing the need to swiftly change the subject and move the conversation on, "all that doesn't matter now - the only thing which does is the fact we now have a way to give both of those horrible little men so much more than a bloody nose."

"Exactly!" Sue agreed, adding, "the way I see it is that we split into two teams moving forwards. One team works during the week on animal rescue with the other working here on the island to help build, prepare and repair. That way, we can all help to move the animals from the school to the islands before helping them settle into their new island homes."

"A capital idea!" Miss Bridges said, happily clapping her hands.
"Well, it makes sense then that we continue to get the animals in and out as before," Nona said, happy to be involved in the conversation once more after having to listen to the adults twittering on. "Me and my friends could go after school when its less busy and there's not as many eyes on us then, especially as there won't be any visitors in the zoo at the moment."

"A wise idea," Doyley nodded, "just say der word and Oi will make sure Oim about to help with tings."

"I'm more than happy to work here on the island with my mates during the week, Auntie Sheila, if that's OK?" Clive asked, already knowing what the reply would be.

"Of course, we can all pitch in to cover what you would normally do at school," Miss Bridges replied, pushing her chair from the table and standing.

"Cool," Clive replied, "it'll mainly be things like opening and closing the school, as well as checking that the computer suite and servers are running smoothly."

"Plus feeding the animals!" Nona laughed as she followed the others, who'd all risen from their chairs and were now walking behind Miss Bridges and her nephew through the hall which led towards the front of the fortress.

Clive opened the front door and looked out at a sky which was now full of dark clouds, the wind having bitterly picked up around the fortress, the waters around Burnt Oak Island and Deadman's Rock now beginning to darken and grow choppier.

"Don't like the look of those…" he said pointing up, "it's probably best that we make our way back to the mainland before things start to get a little hairier around here..."

"Aw," Nona said, hanging her head slightly in disappointment, "I thought we were going to see more of what you've done, Uncle Clive."

The site manager smiled and wrapped his arm around Nona as they made their way back out across the courtyard to the gate and pathway which led down to the jetty.

"To be honest with you, you've seen the best of it so far with the penguins this morning," Clive whispered, "other than that, we've just mended fences, repaired roofs, fixed doors and installed some new electric fencing to keep any unwanted visitors away. Nothing too exciting really…Tell you what, Nones - I'll let you in on one more little secret if you'd like?"

Nona nodded excitedly as Clive pretended to look left and right, as though making sure he wasn't being overheard by the others. "I've hung a couple of tyres and a rope ladder from the old oak tree right in the centre of Burnt Oak Isle," he winked, "do you think Louis and the other monkeys will like that?"

Nona leapt up, flinging her arms around Clive's shoulders as he caught her and lifted her high into the air.

"I'm sure they will!" she laughed, "Oh, thank you, Uncle Clive - I love you so much!"

"I love you too, munchkins, but you're getting a little bit too big to be hanging from my shoulders nowadays!" Clive grinned, gently lowering Nona to the ground, before taking her hand to walk and join all the others all waiting on the jetty.

They were stood beside the boats which were moored there, the increasingly choppy waves causing them to rise and fall more angrily in the now murky-coloured waters of the Medway.

Miss Bridges, Marilyn and Sue had already set off on their way across the causeway by the time Clive and Nona had joined Mel, Lawrence, Doyley and Hayley in their boat.

The crossing back was a lot choppier than their first journey that morning. Nona wishing that she hadn't eaten that last piece of cheese as the small boat pitched up and down on the water, cutting through the waves which lapped at its bow like an Olympic breaststroke swimmer.

Despite feeling a putrid shade of green, Nona noticed that Mr Light sat with one arm around her, the other around her mother, as though trying to protect them from the elements. She had to admit she was growing ever fonder of her teacher and suspected that her mother was doing so too…

Eventually, they reached the banks of the shore, Doyley saving Hayley from a dunking by grabbing her hand and drawing her to him when it looked like she was about to plunge backwards into the water as they stepped off their boat.

Nona lost count of the hugs and goodbyes she was a party to before Miss Bridges and Clive set sail for Hoon Island, again, the fortress now cloaked in black clouds as though issuing a fierce warning to keep any unwanted visitors away from it…

They'd parted from Doyley and Hayley and had begun to walk back to Sue's car when Nona's mother stopped and looked over at the two figures who were walking back to their motorcycle and sidecar.

"You get in the car, I'll be back in a moment," Mel whispered to Nona as she turned and started to jog after Doyley and Maguire. "Hayley - wait a minute..." she called.

Nona stayed outside the people carrier as Sue, Marilyn and Lawrence climbed into the car, watching her mother as she closed in on the small figure of the young vet who was now stood waiting for her as Doyley climbed aboard his motorbike, kicking his starter pedal repeatedly.

"About earlier, Hayley," Mel began, "I'm really sorry if I came across all short and snappy."

"It's all right, Mel - water off a duck's back!" Maguire smiled.

"No, it was bang out of order," Mel replied, shaking her head, "We all really appreciate everything you've already done for us. I don't know what came over me..."

"Well, there's no harm done," Maguire grinned before adding, "anyway, gotta dash. Doyley has sorta invited me to watch a band down his local this evening. I'm classing that as a date, even if he doesn't know it himself yet! Keep your fingers crossed for me, won't you?"

"I'll keep everything crossed, Hayley!" Mel laughed as she hugged Maguire tight to her, "Have a great time!"

Nona watched as her mother walked back towards her whilst Hayley Maguire climbed into the sidecar, putting her crash helmet on as Doyley gunned the engine and sped off, waving as he did so.

"What was all that about?" Nona asked quietly once her mother had rejoined her.

"Nothing," Mel replied.

"Mum?"

"It's nothing, really - I just felt a bit bad earlier for speaking to Hayley the way I did earlier," Mel sighed, "or the life of me, I can't think why I suddenly felt so angry towards her..."

"I do!" Nona smiled knowingly, now feeling like the grown-up in their relationship for once.

"You do?" Mel replied, more than slightly taken aback, "Well then, smarty-pants, spit it out!

"It's because she was sat chatting to Mr Light and you were so jealous!" Nona winked.

214

"Me, jealous! Don't be so silly!" Mel replied, flushing slightly.

"Liar, liar, pants on fire!" teased Nona.

"Sometimes I wonder where you get your crazy ideas from!" Mel said as the two of them began to walk back to the people.

"*Mr Light and Mummy sitting in a tree…K-I-S-S-I-N-G!*" Nona sang quietly to herself as she skipped behind her mother, watching as Mr Light got out of the car to hold the door open for her and Mel.

And I definitely think he likes you too, Mum, Nona thought, smiling happily to herself…

Chapter 23 – Snakes and Ladders

Morning lessons had hardly ended that Monday by the time that Nona had begun to plan the next zoo breakout. She'd already run her initial idea first past her mother over breakfast, then by Mr Light during form time, both agreeing that it made sense what she was suggesting. However, Nona had to be certain before setting the wheels of her plan in motion that she'd have enough volunteers to help her given what their next target was to be – the snake and reptile house at Kingston's Kingdom…

In theory, it was the easiest location of all to reach from the Great Bunker – the one closest to Tunnel 4, code named Monty, it being a concealed tunnel that they could easily get many of the cold-blooded creatures housed there out of the zoo in one fell swoop.

The tunnel exit opened behind a maintenance door to the back of the building, meaning that Nona and whoever she could persuade to help her could enter and exit it at will without being seen from the front by any unexpected or unwanted visitors or zoo staff.

It was the perfect location for their next heist, except for one obvious fact – who'd be brave enough to Nona take these cold-blooded creatures out? So it was that Nona went to both of her usual *go-tos* first - Luca and Keeley - that break time...

"Snakes? Are you crazy?" Luca declared, squirming at the very thought of them, "They're creepy, slimy and dangerous! Just leave them there, Nona, and go for something much cuter and furrier instead."

Nona sighed and shook her head slowly.

"No, they're not and no I won't!" she replied determinedly, "It makes so much sense to do this next, especially given where the underground tunnel is - don't you agree, Keeley?"

"Hmm, I can see both your points of view," Keeley began as they walked together to their next lesson, "but I'm with Luca on this I'm afraid – aren't they just a little too dangerous to try to remove from the kingdom?"

Nona paused in the doorway of her next class as the bell rang, a throng of children passing the three of them as they scurried along the school corridor.

"None of them are dangerous at all," she whispered, "Grandpa had a real thing about snakes himself, so whilst saving them, he also made sure that the only ones he kept in the zoo were non-poisonous ones, like Louisiana Pinesnakes, Red Bellies and Diminutive Wood Boas, amongst others, as well as Conor, who's a larger boa, but he's been hand reared and is very tame."

"A boa constrictor…can't they crush you?" Luca asked, almost hiding behind Keeley at the very thought of the snake.

"Yes, they crush their prey, but let's face it, all we're going to do is pick them up, put them in a carry case and take them out of the zoo…" Nona smiled, "Where's the harm in that?"

Keeley looked at Luca who just shrugged his shoulders reluctantly.

"Count us in then. I'll have a word with scaredy cat here in our next lesson, he'll soon come to his senses…" Keeley winked, "Want me to have a chat with a few of the others to see who else would be up for it?"

"Yes please, I'll sound out a few of the guys in here too," Nona replied, "I'm thinking, all being well, that we'll do it sometime on Wednesday, I just need my mum and Mr Light to get back to me later today to confirm how we are going to do it. See you both after school…"

By the time the three of them met at the end of the school day, the final plans had been confirmed and were in place; Miss Bridges had arranged with the golf course that ten of her *'most talented pupils'* would play the last nine holes on Wednesday afternoon, those being Nona, Luca, Keeley, Charmayne Cunningham, her boyfriend Billy Pearce, Kirsten, Amy, Kylie, Mya and Paige.

Mr Light would then swap his afternoon lessons with another teacher so that he could drive the children to the course and back. Marilyn would help Mr Light, much to Mel's initial disapproval, but Miss Bridges had insisted as Marilyn was a qualified first aider and Mel wasn't.

Although she understood the reasons behind the decision, Mel admitted that she'd rather have been going instead of staying behind with Sue, ready to help relocate the animals to the old changing rooms at Trinity.

Therefore, Sue Brightside, not Marilyn, was given the task of phoning Doyley, which she did immediately, filling the Irishman in on the finer details of the planned rescue operation that day. Doyley in turn said that he'd make sure that there were travel carrying cages left out for them and that he'd put a *'Cleaning in progress'* sign outside the snake and reptile house to stop them from being disturbed. Nothing could be left to chance, especially with the zoo now being closed to all, bar a few employees and those working on Lewis Kingston and Doctor Au's behalf.

With everything carefully planned and firmly put into place, Nona felt a quiet confidence as she and her friends walked across the fairways which led to the back nine of the golf course that Wednesday, each of the ten children carrying their own half set of clubs in a bag far bigger than needed by a normal year 7 child who were taking part in a school sponsored taster session.

But this is no normal round of gold, Nona thought to herself as they followed Mr Light towards the now not-so-secret bunker Miss Bridges had revealed to them all just a few short days before. When they finally reached the ivy-covered surface to the bunker, Mr Light set down the small satchel he carried and took the key Miss Bridges had entrusted him with from his pocket.

"This is dead exciting," Luca whispered to Nona as Mr Light slid the key into the lock, "and absolutely terrifying!"

There were gasps from the children as the door slowly slid open as Mr Light opened the icebox and pulled out a torch which was attached to two straps. The teacher turned on the torch and slipped the straps over his head, adjusting the torch so that it sat snugly on his forehead before turning to the awaiting children, who had to shield their eyes from the brightness of the torch's beam.

"Sorry, kids..." Mr Light said, placing a hand over the flashlight, the skin between his fingers instantly turning pink as he covered it, "now, we all know how this is going to work don't we?"

"You lead us down the tunnel, Nona goes up the ladder at the end of it with Keeley and Luca, grabs a snake, chucks it into a travel container, passes it back down the ladder, with the rest of us acting like a human chain. The person at the back then takes it out, puts it in the zippy pouch at the front of their golf bag, passes the container back down the line again, back up the ladder. Then we repeat until we've all got a snake each..." Kirsten said, popping her bubble gum as she spoke, "Have I missed anything?"

"Nope, that pretty much sums it all up!" Mr Light smiled, "You OK to wait in the first chamber again, Mrs Henderson, in case of any emergency?"

"Just you try stopping me, Mr Light!" Marilyn replied, raising a thumb towards him.

"Right then, let's go..." Mr Light said, "make sure you all watch the first step though as there's a bit of a drop..."

The journey through the tunnel system seemed to be a lot quicker to Nona the second time she travelled it, the anticipation as to what was around each corner now replaced by the knowledge of having already safely navigated them before.

However, behind her, Nona's friends chatted nervously, each one trying to outbrave the other, hiding their fears of the dark and unknown, not wishing to appear any less confident than the rest of the group. Eventually, there was a collective sigh of relief as they all came to a juddering halt, the wall holding Monty's ladder in place preventing them from travelling any further forward.

Mr Light switched positions with Nona, Luca and Keeley.

"You all set?" he asked as Nona placed her hands on either side of the ladder.

"Yep, good to go," she replied, looking Keeley and Adam's nervous faces, who both wordlessly nodded behind her.

Slowly, Nona began to climb the ladder, Luca waiting until she was four rungs up it before beginning to follow, Keeley doing the same a few moments later.

"I'll climb up once you've made it to the top," Mr Light called, "that way, I'm right at hand in case you get into any difficulty. Good luck."

Nona took a hand off the ladder and gave a thumbs-up sign to her teacher without looking back in his direction as she continued to climb, occasionally looking up to see how far she'd still to travel. *Twenty-three, twenty-four, twenty-five*, Nona counted in her head, each rung drawing her a foot closer to the top as she looked up again, the round metal hatch which stood between her and the surface now almost in touching distance, meaning that she only had to climb a few rungs more.

Nona briefly looked down to check on Luca and Keeley's progress below where Luca was holding onto the ladder so tightly that his knuckles had lost all their colour, looking as white as the Sumatran Tiger Mr Light had had such a near miss with the previous weekend.

Keeley, on the contrary, looked like she was having a grand old time, easily moving like a cat behind him, encouraging him - geeing her friend up, something that seemed to have no effect on

Luca at all.

"Hold it there - I'm at the top," Nona called, causing her friends to stop and wait as she braced her back against the wall of the crawlspace as she'd seen her teacher do previously, feet squarely set on the ladder.

Nona was more than a little relieved to find that the hatch that Mr Light had loosened at the weekend spun freely in her hand before she unclipped the clasp which was helping to keep it securely in place.

Cautiously, Nona pushed at the hatch, slowly moving it as she climbed the final three rungs which took her to the surface. Once open, she sat on the lip of the hatch and looked around, relieved to find no sign of anyone else as Nona eased herself away from the edge, resting flat on her stomach to look back down at her friends.

"Come on," Nona whispered, "the coast is clear - up you both come…"

It wasn't long before the three of them stood by the maintenance door, scarcely breathing as Nona slowly turned the door handle. Thankfully, it opened easily, Nona now feeling slightly guilty for ever doubting Doyley as she, Luca and Keeley stepped inside the building, the indoor temperature far warmer than that they'd just left outside.

"Can you see a carrier anywhere?" Nona asked, looking around the room, "It ought to look like the sort of thing you normally take a pet to the vets in."

"Is this it?" Keeley asked, holding a large blue and white container up above her head.

"Perfect!" Nona smiled as Keeley walked across to join her whilst Luca stood next to the first snake tank.

"Which of these do we have to go for first?" Luca asked, a permanent look of horror and disdain now etched on his face as he watched the various snakes wriggling around in their tanks.

Nona lifted the lid of a tank labelled *Somali garter snakes*.

"This one…come here, my beauty," she said gently as she slipped her hands under its belly and lifted it from the tank.

The garter snake coiled up in her open palms as Nona turned with it to where Keeley was now stood, her carrier open, Luca recoiling back from her as she walked past him.

"I don't know why you even bothered coming," Keeley sighed as

Nona carefully placed the snake on the floor of the container.

"Moral support," Luca replied as Nona walked back to the tank to retrieve a second snake, "I thought we were all gonna just have one snake each?"

Nona stopped to look at her friend and then shook her head.

"Look at the size of them," she replied, "I'm sure that one of the guys down below will have no trouble fitting them both in their golf bag, unless you want to put it in your pocket, of course?"

"No chance!" Luca said, pulling a face of pure disgust as Nona looked at Keeley and smiled before gathering up the second snake to remove it from its tank.

"Look over there," Nona said, gesturing with her head to the far corner of the room, "Doyley's left another carrier out for us. Make yourself useful, Luca - go get it whilst we fasten this one up…"

By the time Luca had returned, both garter snakes were safely secured in the first carrier.

He handed the new container to Nona, who took it from him and offered him the full one in return. Luca looked at the blue and white carrier, then back at Nona.

"What do you want me to do with that?" he asked.

"Don't tempt me…" Nona laughed before continuing, "As we have a second container, can you take the full one back to the tunnel for Mr Light to pass down the line. Keeley and I can then fill this one up. It'll help speed up the process a bit."

Luca looked at the carrier again, then Nona, then the carrier.

"You want me to carry *that*?" he sniffed.

"That's why you're here, isn't it?" Nona replied.

"Well, yes, but now that I'm actually, physically next to them, I'm not sure I can do it," Luca said, shivering, "They're creeping the hell out of me!"

"Luca," Keeley sighed, "One, they're harmless, two, they're in a sealed container and you don't want to know what three is…"

"What's three?" Luca asked, despite himself.

"I'll tell Charmayne you fancy her…" threatened Keeley.

"Don't you dare!" Luca spluttered, looking at Nona who'd first gasped, then laughed in amazement.

"You fancy Charmayne Cunningham!" she asked.

"No, I mean yes, but you can't tell her…" Luca begged, his pale face now flushed with colour, "her boyfriend will kill me!"

"Then you'd better decide which is worse – carrying the snake in that container or Billy Pearce…?" Keeley said firmly.

Suddenly, Luca picked up the carrier and snatched open the door, muttering under his breath as he did so, before marching off, back in the direction of the tunnel.

Nona and Keeley waited until he was safely out of earshot before bursting into laughter.

"Charmayne Cunningham – I'd had no idea he had the hots for her!" Nona exclaimed.

"Ever since Foundation," Keeley chuckled, "got it really bad for her has our friend…"

The two of them were still giggling when Luca soon returned, the carrier still firmly held in his hands.

"Laugh it up, fuzzballs," he moaned before continuing, "you won't be laughing for much longer though…"

Nona and Keeley immediately stopped as they gazed at Luca's serious looking face, not quite sure as to whether he was winding them up or not. Finally, Keeley bit.

"What's wrong, Luca," she asked, "why've you still got the carrier and snake in your hand."

"Because," Luca replied, setting the container down on the ground again, "the damned thing won't fit through the tunnel hatch, that's why!"

"What do you mean it won't fit?" Nona asked.

"Hmm, let me see…the carrier is a large 3D cuboid shape whereas the tunnel hatch is a smaller 2d circular one - too biggy, no fitty!" Luca said, sarcastically, adding, "Or, to put it bluntly, you can't fit a square peg into a round hole!"

Nona raced towards Luca, snatching the carrier from him, and hurtled out the door, closely followed by Keeley, leaving Luca to just stand and sigh.

"Don't believe me then," he muttered, before following them both outside.

There he found Nona sat on the ground, just staring at the tunnel.

"You were right," she admitted without looking up at him.

Luca felt an overwhelming urge to say *I told you so* but soon thought better of it.

"So, what do we do now then?" he asked.

"It's quite simple really, Luca," Mr Light's voice called out from the tunnel below, "you'll just have to pass us the snakes and we'll send them down the line by hand, one by one, through the tunnel until we have filled up all the golf bags."

"Us...? Man-handle the snakes...?" Luca exclaimed, looking at his friends, "Are you mad? It's bad enough having to carry them in a sealed container, let alone then have hold one in the flesh!"

Keeley shook her head and sighed deeply.

"Well then, clever clogs, it's either that or we walk through the zoo with them and get caught by Lewis' cronies instead..." she huffed.

"Or we could just leave the snakes here, go home and rescue something else on another day," Luca countered, much to Nona's annoyance.

"There's a third option, Luca..." Nona said quietly.

"What's that Nona?"

"You can either pass the snakes down the line just like Mr Light's suggested, or..." Nona began to explain.

"Or what?" Adam asked nervously.

"Or you can smuggle them out of the zoo with them down your trousers instead!" Nona winked.

"I'll go first then, shall I?" Luca immediately replied, opening the carrier to take out one of the snakes, his eyes closed, and his nose screwed up in disgust.

Nona and Keeley smiled at each other as Luca slowly opened his eyes.

"Hey, this little guy isn't so slimy after all!" Luca said in disbelief, "I think I'll call him Lewis..."

"Told ya!" Nona said triumphantly as Luca leant over the edge of the tunnel hatch and passed the small serpent to Mr Light, who gently took it in his hands.

"Careful not to drop Lewis," Luca said, feeling a sudden protective warmth towards the small creature who now squirmed slightly in Mr Light's outstretched hands.

"I won't," the teacher replied, before he bent to pass the snake down into Charmayne's hands, Billy Pearce standing on the ladder below her, ready to do the same.

It wasn't long before the second garter snake was safely on its way to join its cousin in the first golf bag which was waiting at the very end of the rescue team's human chain.

"Come on," Nona said to Keeley and Luca, "there's plenty more where they came from..."

By the time Nona had put the empty carrier back inside, closed the hatch above her head and carried the last snake chosen down the tunnel with her, the afternoon raid had successfully yielded fifteen snakes rescued.

Initially, she'd suspected that the trickiest one to get down the tunnel would be Conor, the Boa Constrictor, the largest snake they'd planned to rescue that day. It was only right then that Nona carried him down last, draping his long muscular body over her shoulders as she made her way back down the ladder.

Although he'd been hand-reared and was as tame as any snake could ever be, Nona made sure that he was coiled first over her left arm, then across her shoulders, before his tail reached where her right arm met her body.

She breathed a huge sigh of relief when she eventually reached the bottom of the ladder, Mr Light carefully uncoiling Conor from her body before placing him carefully inside her golf bag.

Then, Nona whistled loudly, a sign for Paige, who was at the back of the line to turn and head off, leading them all back through the tunnels, back to where Mrs Henderson was patiently waiting for them in the first chamber of the bunker, ready to take the line of children out into the daylight again.

"Everything go all right?" Marilyn asked, having dropped back to walk alongside Nona as Mr Light led the rescue party across the fairways, their golf bags and slippery passengers slung over their shoulders.

"Apart from one little mishap, it all went as planned," Nona smiled, patting the side of her bag gently.

The two of them walked side by side as Nona watched her teacher and friends walk ahead of them, apparently enjoying their golfing afternoon, seemingly without a care in the world.

"All in all, a good day's work then, Nona," Marilyn smiled, draping an arm across Nona's shoulder.

"Yep! If we keep on having days like this, Marilyn, by the time that brother of mine realises what's been going on right under his nose, there won't be any animals for him to sell off!" Nona nodded happily, "I'd give anything to see his face then, especially as it'll then be too late for him to do anything about it…"

Little did Nona know then as she and the others left the golf course that day that that moment with her brother was coming sooner than she'd ever have hoped, or feared…

Chapter 24 – Santa Catarina, Baby!

Over the following two weeks, the number of raids on the zoo increased and intensified, as did the work on the animals' new sanctuary in the Medway, the Zooper Troopers becoming much bolder in their rescues, feeling safe and protected from the prying eyes of Lewis Kingston and his supporters by the tunnels which secretly ran beneath the kingdom.

During this time, various rescue parties and individuals had managed to help add to the ever-growing list of animals who'd been freed from the zoo and them holed up in Trinity whilst awaiting transportation to their new homes that were being specially built and prepared for them on the islands in the Medway.

The successful rescue missions were aided and abetted in no small part by the stealthy, undercover work carried out behind their enemy's lines by Doyley and Hayley Maguire who'd also managed to recruit additional help from a couple of other sympathetic zoo workers who'd been long-time, loyal employees of Roger Kingston and were disgusted by Lewis Kingston's' evil plans as well as being completely disgruntled by the way he was treating them the and animals at the kingdom. The list of animals rescued during that time period included, amongst others…

Four-Eyed Turtles x 3
Blue-Eyed Black Lemurs x 6
Ploughshare Tortoises x 4
Geometric Tortoises x 3
Sea Otters x 5
Baby Fishing Cats x 2
Vancouver Island Marmots x 5
Maned Sloths x 3
Black-Footed Ferrets x 5
Panamanian Golden Frogs x 6
Red-Crested Tree Rats x 7
Northern Hairy-Nosed Wombats x 2
Nelson's Small-Eared Shrews x 5
Tarzan's Chameleon x 1
Kaiser's Spotted Newts x 4

When these numbers were added to the other non-human guests

being housed in the old Trinity buildings, Nona's Ark of animals was swelling at a most dramatic rate.

So successful were the rescue missions proving to be it was now reaching the point that as each new set of animals were being ferried into the school, another load was having to be carefully transported across London by minibus, people carrier, car or boat to one of the islands Miss Bridges owned.

There, Clive Tilley and his expanding workforce of friends, rugby players, children and tradesmen tirelessly worked to make sure each newly completed pen, house or enclosure was suitable for its new tenant. They also had to make sure that each was also safe and secure enough for the animals not to inadvertently wander out of or for any unexpected visitor to accidentally creep into them.

Naturally, Nona had also worried about the weather conditions for some of the creatures who'd been transported from zoo to school to island, but Hayley Maguire had assured her that animals easily adapt but she'd help keep a close eye on them to make sure that they soon felt completely at home in their new surroundings and island habitat.

Of course, they'd had the added bonus of moving the animals in the summer months, but Nona soon voiced her concerns as to what would happen during the winter ones. It was Miss Bridges who'd told her not to worry as there were generators and solar panel on all three islands, adding that they'd worry about things like heating and lighting *'when it comes to it.'*

This had helped to reassure Nona but still, in the back of her mind, she knew the day was fast approaching when some of the animals would need to have more than hay or straw to keep them warm. However, what they'd do about it had yet to be resolved, so she focused on the here and now instead, deciding that she'd try not to think too much about the future - well, not that much anyway…

The successes they were achieving in rescuing animals on a daily basis helped to keep Nona positive and fully focused firmly on the present and on matters she *could* control.

Despite the tiredness felt by all, everyone pressed on, most now running on pure adrenalin with every visit to the kingdom or islands. Seeing the freed animals in their new surroundings gave them all the extra energy and motivation needed to press on before they either reached the point of discovery or had exhausted every escape avenue possible to them.

Due to the increased number of rescued animals being removed, additional measures had then been introduced by Doyley and Maguire to further delay the inevitable point when the animals' disappearances were eventually discovered. So it was that an even more elaborate system of misdirection was introduced, it being greatly increased by even more numbers of the kingdom's staff who shared their own disgust at what Lewis and co. planned to do with the zoo.

Rapidly, he ratio of animals rescued to animals sold rose to round 6:1, but this still required some clever use of manpower and resources to prevent the whole operation from collapsing around their ears. For example, Keeley had volunteered one afternoon to dress up in an orange monkey suit and sit with back turned, high up in a tree as Lewis Kingston made an unexpected and unscheduled visit to the zoo, prompted by the absence of the orangutan from his earlier sales sheet.

Satisfied all was well with the monkey, despite *its* reluctance to turn and face him when commanded, Lewis had then instructed Au and Clarke to arrange for the safe *disposal* of the orangutan when it was next on ground level, much to Keeley's quiet dismay. Fortunately, after a couple of fruitless hours, the two men had tired of waiting at the bottom of the tree and had gone home for the day.

Having climbed gingerly down on her jelly legs, Keeley gratefully changed places with the large, cuddly replica version of Louis the Orangutan that Janice (from the zoo gift shop) had taken out of the storeroom for Doyley. To help to further maintain the deceit, Doyley would scale the tree every night and move the fake Louis to a new location in the most dangerous parts of it to continue to keep Au and Clarke guessing.

However, it wasn't just Louis the Orangutan who they fooled their enemies with as dozens of soft toys, papier mache models and mannequins were bought, built and smuggled in to misdirect, fool and confuse those loyal to Lewis Kingston.

And misdirect, fool and confuse they did, but everyone knew that the time would eventually come when their luck and good fortune would finally run out, so it was vitally important that they concealed as much of what they were doing for as long as they possibly could, without leaving behind any evidence which could point to their guilt…

Luckily, throughout the whole of that golden period, the closest they ever got to being rumbled was during a mission to get the entire collection of Santa Catarina's Guinea pigs out of the kingdom in one fell swoop.

Having safely negotiated her way out from the exit of Tunnel 5 – the one codenamed Hammy - Nona had then made her way into the pen where all ten of the small, brown and friendly rodents were happily hopping around without a care in the world.

The escape plan was relatively straightforward – grab a guinea pig, run unseen back to the tunnel, pass it to Kylie who'd volunteered to act as back-up that day in Luca and Keeley's absence, before running back to the pen before repeating again the whole process again.

The first run had gone surprisingly well…

Sprint from tunnel to pen – *check*…

Grab guinea pig – *check*…

Run back to tunnel – *check*…

Pass to Kylie – *check*…

Return to pen – *check*….

However, when Nona turned again with the second guinea pig in her hands to leave the pen, she was met by the unwelcome sight of Clarke, now Lewis Kingston's most trusted zoo employee, head of security and chief snitch, who was purposely walking in her general direction.

Fortunately, Kylie, a tall, thin and incredibly agile girl, had spotted him and had disappeared back down the tunnel, sliding the hatch over the opening, concealing most of it.

Anxiously, Nona had herself jumped behind a small bush, the remaining guinea pigs who were hiding there being extremely excited to see Nona, climbing all climbed over her curled-up and motionless form.

Carefully, Nona peered through the foliage to look at the vile little man who was waddling ever nearer, clutching a large paper carrier bag in one hand. A short time later, Clarke passed the guinea pig pen and headed towards a bench, which was sheltered by the branches of a tree, that directly in between the pen and Tunnel 5. As he was about to sit down, Clarke pulled a crumpled newspaper from his back pocket and placed it on the bench beside him.

Then from the bag he carried, Clarke produced a huge baguette, stuffed to the brim with what appeared to be meatballs and melted mozzarella cheese, all covered by a thick, red tomato sauce.

Nona could barely begin to watch as Clarke opened his mouth, his lips wobbling beneath the tip of the huge nose which hung over it, and bit down deeply into one end of the baguette, the force of his jaws clamping on the bread caused the other end of the breadstick to open wide, emptying its contents into his lap, completely covering his beige chino trousers.

Gross... Nona thought as Clarke looked down for a moment then scooped up the escaped fillings in his hand before stuffing them back into his baguette before continuing to eat it again, seemingly unperturbed by the scarlet and messy grease stains which were left on his trousers.

Although it seemed like forever to Nona, in truth, it probably only took Clarke a little over ten minutes to devour his food, such was the immense size of the baguette. Finally, after pushing the final, large piece of soggy bread into his mouth with one, thick and pudgy finger, Clarke loudly smacked his lips together and sighed, a huge belch escaping his mouth as he did so.

From where she was still secretly sitting, Nona was almost convinced that she could smell the stench of his burp, meaning that it came as no surprise to her that suddenly, two happy and content guinea pigs lifted their heads and shrieked before scuttling away, seemingly disgusted by the pungent smell which now filled their delicate little nostrils....

Good, he's finished, he'll be going soon, Nona thought, safely tucked away in her hiding place still.

However, Clarke was still showing no apparent no signs of leaving, instead stretching his legs out before him and laced his fingers behind the back of his head before closing his eyes and tilting his head up towards the warm sun which was blazing down on the zoo that day.

After silently staring at him for almost twenty minutes, Nona was sorely tempted to pick up one of the little brown pellets which were dotted around the guinea pig pen and aim it at Clarke's mouth, which now gaped open, a small stream of drool limply hanging from it. She watched hypnotically as Clarke's barrel-chest rose and fell, the nasal rumble now vibrating in his throat a tell-tale sign that he'd fallen fast asleep, no doubt dreaming of yet another food substance to slovenly devour, or a weak and innocent person to bully or belittle...

Sensing her chance to finally escape, Nona slowly stood, her legs screaming from the effort after being forced to crouch for so long in the undergrowth as the zoo worker sat blissfully unaware of her presence not twenty feet away. Slowly she walked to the entrance of the pen, the sudden rush of blood to her now straightened legs causing the *pins and needles* in them to dramatically increase and intensify.

In fact, one of her feet had fallen so fast asleep that it was almost comatose, meaning that Nona had almost no feeling in it at all, her foot flip-flopping in front of her until its normal blood flow managed to reach it again. This caused an excruciating amount of pain for Nona with every step she gingerly took until the feeling began to eventually return to it.

Relieved to be fully mobile again, Nona looked through the glass door panel of the pen, past the slumbering Clarke to where Kylie now stood behind him, frantically waving both her arms her friend's direction.

Nona looked at Clarke, then Kylie before returning her gaze to the guinea pigs, who were making some sort of whistling/purring sound to show how happy and content they still were to be with her.

Perhaps I can grab two of three of them and leg it past Clarke, thought Nona, who then thought better of it, deciding to refrain from doing so for two reasons.

The first one was obvious – if Clarke woke whilst she was passing him and then saw her disappear down *Hammy* then the game would well and truly be up for them all.

Secondly and equally importantly, Nona knew that she'd be unable to decide which of the adorable little creatures she should take with and which to leave behind but as soon as one of the guinea pigs raised its head, wrinkled its nose and stared at her with its sorrowful brown eyes, Nona immediately made up her mind – it was all of them or none at all! She turned to look at Kylie and shook her head as she pointed at the slumbering figure of Clarke, who'd slid down the bench slightly, his head now tilted at an awkward and unnatural angle, causing the rattling sound in his throat to grow much louder as he twitched and squirmed about on the bench, like a bulldog who was having a bad dream.

Nodding slowly, Kylie grimly furrowed her brow, completely understanding what Nona meant and the dilemma she now faced.

Then, Kylie's eyes lit up like fireworks as she held up her right hand, now resembling Trinity's lollipop lady who stooped the school traffic for them every day on arriving at school. Nona nodded, instantly knowing that her friend was asking her to wait for a moment - not that Nona could go anywhere anyway - as Kylie disappeared back down into Tunnel 5.

During her friend's absence, Nona scratched her head as she wondered what Kylie was up to and sat on an overturned log, moving a plank which had come loose and fallen from the front of the observation window at the side of the pen.

Nona smiled naughtily to herself as she slowly realised what the pellets, she'd toyed with throwing at Clarke earlier were before looking up to see Kylie emerge from the tunnel again. She could also see that her friend was carrying something in her left hand as Kylie tiptoed away from the tunnel hatch, Mya's head now appearing from it as she rested her elbows on either side of the tunnel hatch to look at her two friends both stood above ground.

Slowly, Kylie walked forwards until she was about three feet away the hatch, closer to where Clarke still awkwardly slept on the zoo bench. Nona was still baffled as to what her friend was planning to do until she realised what Kylie was carrying in her hands…a well-worn pair of goalkeeper gloves.

Of course, Nona thought, *I should've known better…*

Not only was she a newly made friend that year but Kylie *'The Cat'* McGrath was also both Trinity Academy and Ventham FC's first-choice goalkeeper who never travelled anywhere without her trusty gloves.

Instantly, Nona understood what her friend wanted her to do – Kylie wanted her to throw the guinea pigs to her so that she could then catch them and pass to Mya and the human chain waiting below in the tunnel!

Nodding, Nona raised a thumb to confirm that she completely understood what Kylie wanted her to do as the goalkeeper slipped on her gloves and bounced up and down, kicking her legs out in all directions, as though waiting to save a crucial penalty in a world cup final rather than simply catching a Santa Catarina Guinea pig!

Whilst Kylie continued to limber up, Nona gently reached for the rodent closest to her and suddenly spotted an immediate and quite unexpected problem - despite its apparently smallish build, the

guinea pig was considerably heavier than it had first appeared…
Carefully, Nona picked it up with both hands and rested it against her shoulder, as it merrily chewed away on some recently found shrubbery.

Opposite her, Kylie danced back and forth behind the sleeping form of Clark, gesturing for Nona to hurry up and throw her the guinea pig, repeatedly slapping her gloved hands together, trying to reassure her friend that she'd catch the animal, but Nona was still not entirely convinced.

Not that she doubted Kylie's goalkeeping skills and agility, on the contrary, there were many a time in the past that the girls of Ventham FC had been grateful for the brilliance of their goalkeeper, either slapping her on the back or bundling on top of her in celebration or raising her high above their heads at the end of a match. Usually it was after Kylie had made a breath-taking stop or she'd saved a hotly disputed penalty or had come up for a corner in the dying minutes of a game and scored with an outrageous diving header.

Of course, most goalkeepers have to be a bit mad, much like Kylie herself, but Nona and the team trusted her with their lives…
Ordinarily…

No, the doubts Nona was having stemmed from doubting her own ability to throw the guinea pig to Kylie, figuring that she'd first have to throw it high enough to clear the two-metre wall in front of her. Not only that, then she'd also have to have enough upper body strength to propel the guinea pig yet another five to ten metres, over the loudly snoring zoo spy to even give Kylie a chance of safely catching it. If she failed in either of these areas, the remains of her disastrous attempt left on the grounds of the kingdom would easily resemble the dark brown and red stains from Clarke's baguette which were now crisply drying on the front of his chinos in the blazing hot sun.

Reluctantly, Nona shook her head at Kylie, before sitting down on the log again, the cooing guinea pig still in her hands. As she sadly stroked its soft coat in resignation, Nona jabbed her toes at the plank which was lying on the floor in front of her in pure frustration.

Suddenly, an idea immediately came to mind, causing her to speed to the front of the pen before raising an index figure as well as silently mouthing '*one minute*', in Kylie's direction. The young goalkeeper nodded and crouched slightly, still swaying side to side as she patiently waited for the first *piggy penalty* to hurtle towards her.

Meanwhile, Nona had gently placed the guinea pig on the ground beside her before lifting the discarded plank, eventually setting it down again on the upturned log she'd just been sitting on. Nona then pushed the log slightly and adjusted the plank so that it pointed more towards Kylie's general direction.

Once she was confident and satisfied at what she'd arranged, Nona raised her thumb, again, Kylie now mirroring the signal, and bent down to pick up the guinea pig, placing it on the end of the plank furthest away from the fence, causing the plank to gently tip down under the weight of the little rodent.

Fortunately, the guinea pig didn't appear to be in the slightest bit alarmed as it sat there still happily chewing away on whatever it had found earlier. Nona moved to the side at the opposite end of the plank and began to swing her arms back and forth, gently bobbing up and down on her feet as she summoned up the strength and courage needed to carry out her daring but quite bizarre escape idea.

Here goes nothing, she thought as she bent down and then pushed off with both feet, jumping high into the air before landing squarely on the other end of the plank, instantly propelling the little rodent skywards.

"Wheeeeeeeeeeeeeeeeeeeeeeeeeeeeeeeeeeeeeeeeeeee!" screamed the guinea pig as Nona watched the little brown projectile launch off into space, first safely clearing the fencing to the enclosure as well as the zoo pathway, before easily clearing Clarke's slumbering head as its arc began to decline towards where Kylie was stood, poised and ready to pounce...

Oh no, thought Nona as she watched her friend quickly re-adjust her feet to change her position, *I've overdone it - the guinea pig's going to fly way past her!*

But Nona's fears soon turned to welcome relief as she watched Kylie launch herself off the ground, raising both hands together, to catch the guinea pig high to her right before falling to the earth again, holding her catch tightly to her chest as she spectacularly rolled around on the ground.

Eventually, Kylie came to a stop and lay there for a moment, resting on her elbows, her head bowed down low, causing Nona to anxiously hold her breath. Then, Kylie slowly climbed to her feet, her hands still clutched to her chest before turning to raise her arms triumphantly towards Nona, the unharmed guinea pig happily munching away in her grasp.

Nona excitedly jumped up and down in delight as she watched Kylie walk to the tunnel hatch to carefully pass the guinea pig to Mya, who then disappeared into the tunnel briefly to safely pass the unharmed rodent on to the next person in the human chain hidden from view below ground.

By the time Mya's head re-emerged again, Kylie had resumed her goalkeeping stance as Nona hunted for the next guinea pig volunteer to take a trip into orbit...

Over the next twenty minutes, Nona launched a succession of guinea pigs high into the air, each flight mission following a similar path to her first successful attempt with the same positive outcomes as Kylie leapt, dived, caught and rolled each time, safely cradling all of the slightly bemused rodents who had returned to Earth almost immediately after being catapulted into the air by Nona from her makeshift launch pad at the Guinea pig Pen Mission Control Centre!

And every time, their nemesis Clarke slept, snored, grunted and repeatedly burped as each animal flew over his head, totally oblivious to proceedings.

However, as each guinea pig was successfully launched, caught and passed down the tunnel via Mya and the rest of the rescue team, Nona grew more tired, the height she jumped gradually reducing each time before she wearily landed on her end of the seesaw-catapult.

Fortunately, all the guinea pigs cleared the prone and slumbering figure of Clarke without waking him or causing any concern or suspicion with that remaining the case until mission ten and the final guinea-pigonaut...

On this occasion, Nona had taken slightly longer to find the last rodent, it obviously having watched all its furry cousins whilst they flew high up into the air, disappearing without warning, squealing wildly as they did so. This meant that the last rodent standing was now frantically doing its best to delay its own fate.

Nona desperately scurried around the pen, bending, lurching, swooping and diving for a good five minutes before she finally managed to hold the guinea pig in her hands, its beady little brown eyes bulging wildly, as though Nona was squeezing all the air from its body, trapping it all in its head.

Gently, Nona stroked the frightened rodent for a couple more minutes, feeling its tiny heart pulsing through its ribcage against her chest, before slowly walking over to gently place it on the end of the seesaw.

"Just wait you there," Nona whispered, slowly walking backwards to her end of the plank, expecting the final Santa Catarina guinea pig to make another desperate bolt for freedom as she did so.

Luckily, the poor animal looked to be so terrified as to what was going to happen to it that it remained firmly rooted to the spot, nervously watching Nona's every move as she backed further away from it.

"It'll all be over in a few seconds," Nona continued to reassure the rodent as she moved to stand opposite her side of the plank, her head turned so as not to lose eye contact with the guinea pig.

"Ready?" she asked, though more to herself than anyone else, before summoning up whatever energy she had left to leap up and land on the end of the plank one last time…

Now, if she'd been competing for the gold medal in Seesaw-Catapult Jumping at the Random and Pointless Olympics, then this would have given Nona Lancaster her lowest score of the day, possibly making her miss out on a medal position and a place on the podium.

However, her jump, such as it was given how tired Nona was, was still good enough for the guinea pig to easily clear the fence and sail upwards, over the pathway, over Clarke and into the safe hands of Kylie the Cat, causing Nona to wildly punch the air in celebration as she watched the little brown creatures grow smaller and smaller the further it flew away from her.

"Done it," she tiredly sighed as the guinea pig quickly began to descend, "and my brother and that vile little man over there know absolutely bog all about it…"

Unfortunately for Nona, these proved to be famous last words as what happened next instantly put the whole rescue mission totally at risk of failure and discovery….

Previously, with each launch Nona had carried out, each airborne guinea pig had squealed, "*Wheeeeeeeeeeeeeeeeeeeeee!*" without so much as a hint or a flicker of any recognition from the sleeping *unbeauty* who sat motionless beneath their flight path…And that had been the happy case until this one final time.

However, it wasn't the *"Wheeeeeeeeeeeeeeeeeeeee!"* from the guinea pig which woke Clarke up so unexpectedly – no, it was the *wee* of the terrified little creature instead, which flowed from its body as soon as it took off, high into the air…

That would've been bad enough, but worst was to follow as the wee left a wet trail along the ground before travelling up Clarke's trousers and shirt, briefly filling his mouth and coating his glasses as the guinea pig passed over his head which Clarke had thrown back whilst sleeping. Nona could only stand in shock, horror and disbelief as she watched Clarke suddenly leap from the bench, coughing, spluttering and spitting, frantically clawing at his mouth and chest, causing his glasses liquid-covered to tumble to the ground.

Luckily, Kylie had already caught the last rodent and rapidly disappeared into the tunnel with it, closing the hatch behind her by the time Clarke had turned and angrily squinted in her direction, blindly scanning the area for clues as to what had just happened to him.

Seeing nothing – literally - Clarke picked up his glasses before turning sharply back to the pen where Nona now hid deep in the undergrowth, desperately hoping to avoid detection and capture. Clarke reached into his pocket and pulled out a dirty handkerchief, trying hard to separate it from where it was stuck together by ancient snot as he first wiped his glasses dry before sticking out his tongue to wipe at it as the zoo worker cautiously began walking towards the guinea pig pen.

Inside the enclosure, Nona held her breath as Clarke approached, hardly daring to breathe as the zoo worker stopped and peered into the pen.

"Here, piggy-wiggies," he muttered, sniffing as he tapped on the glass of the door.

However, having initially seen no movement, Clarke then unclipped the large ring of keys which hung from his belt and began to rifle through them, frantically searching for the matching key for the pen's lock. Had he first thought to try the handle, he'd have found it unlocked - as Nona had done - but fortunately, Clarke hadn't, meaning that Nona a little more time to work out what her next move would be.

Anxiously, Nona started to chew the cuff of her school rugby top she'd worn for the day when an idea suddenly hit her. Pulling the long sleeve down so that it entirely covered her balled fist, Nona stuck part of her hand out of the side of the bush and began to move it between the leaves, making faint squeaking noises as she did so. This caused Clarke to look up through the smeared lenses of his glasses over to where Nona's guinea pig-puppet was scurrying in and out of the undergrowth, raising an arm to shield his eyes from the sun which was shining directly into them.

In horror, Nona suddenly realised that her shirt was black and that the guinea pigs were brown and felt the hope of escape drain from her as Clarke continued to look through his keys again.

But then, something completely inexplicable happened as the paper Clarke had laid next to him on the bench earlier suddenly lifted up behind him and violently flew against the side of the pen next to where he now stood, randomly opening on the racing pages, a thick red circle drawn in the left-hand corner of one of them which somehow caused Clarke to stop looking for his key, turning to closely look at the marked page instead. Nona watched as a look of realisation slowly seemed to appear on the zookeeper's face as Clarke peered at his watch.

"Blimey, it's almost time for the big race..." he shouted, grabbing the newspaper before rushing off, leaving Nona still undiscovered, a mixture of relief and confusion washing over her like a tsunami.

Silently, she waited for a couple more minutes until she was absolutely convinced that it was safe enough to leave the pen and walk back to the escape tunnel.

As she jogged across the pathway towards where the tunnel hatch now stood open again, Kylie waving at her to hurry, Nona stopped, raised her head and sniffed, immediately recognising the familiar smell of an aftershave which had suddenly wafter into the air, an aftershave unique to just one person she'd known...

"Thanks, Grandpa," she smiled as she began to climb down through the tunnel hatch, "that was a little too close for comfort. I never wanna go through that kinda stress ever again..." Little did Nona know then as she exhaustedly followed her friends back through the tunnel with their successful haul of rescued rodents, that worse much, much worse was to follow for them all less than forty-eight hours later....

237

Chapter 25 – The End is Nigh

Friday - the end of both the school and working week.
It also turned out to be the end of a tumultuous chapter in the lives of both of Roger Kingston's grandchildren, lives which had unhappily become entwined over the few months they'd known each other, having suddenly being thrown together by fate after the death of their grandfather.
But neither Nona Lancaster nor Lewis Kingston realised that morning that it also spelt the end of the secret activities they'd both been secretly committing and hiding from one another for entirely different reasons…
For Nona, Friday was meant to be another day of daring, excitement and adventure, making the most of the training day that had closed Trinity Free School…
For Lewis it was just another day to make as much money as he could from the zoo, bringing it closer to its permanent closure and the financial jackpot which awaited him at the end of his Russian property developer's rainbow…
Little did either of them know that, as events slowly began to unfold and plans began to unravel, over the course of the day that their lives as they knew them would never be the same again.
Nona's day had begun early that morning, briskly leaping out of bed, feeling more alive and refreshed having had a day's break from the hectic life she'd become so accustomed to recently, having had a full twenty-four hours of not raiding the kingdom.
After their close-call the previous Wednesday, everyone on the escape committee had agreed that it would be prudent not to immediately return to the zoo just in case Clarke had gone back to investigate the guinea pig pen further and found it to be completely empty - apart from some brown furry slippers which had been strategically placed in the undergrowth by Doyley and Hayley Maguire.
After Nona had shared her near-miss with her mother, Mel had then called Doyley to see whether Clarke had said anything to him or any of the other workers at the kingdom about the *wee* mishap he'd had…
Fortunately, Clarke hadn't - well, not that Doyley knew of anyway. Immediately, Mel had then rung around everyone,

postponing their next mission until the Friday as Miss Bridges had given permission for all the adults who worked at Trinity to be at *'an off-site training location'* that day - meaning that everyone would be able to work from home instead of school, a reward for all their hard work and efforts in getting Trinity up to speed in their first school year. This also meant that the Zooper Troopers would - for once - have their *A-team* together, all ready, willing and available for their next dramatic and daring rescue mission – removing the Bonobo Monkeys from the Kingston's Kingdom...
As she headed to the golf course in the school minibus with all those who'd so recently played such a major and important part in her secret life, Nona couldn't shift a feeling of impending doom which had suddenly appeared from nowhere.
Initially, she'd put it down to the fact that the list of animals they could realistically free easily from the zoo was now rapidly diminishing and, deep down, Nona knew that they'd struggle to rescue the larger creatures, animals such as the antelopes, rhinos or - worst of all - Elsie the elephant - especially Elsie...
She'd avoided thinking about the impending day when they could do no more for the last remaining animals but knew that it was drawing ever closer. Nona had tried hard to stay positive, concentrating on all the positives, whilst focusing on a day at a time. But even concentrating solely on the rescue they'd planned that day had done little to lift her spirits, her nagging sensation of unease refusing to go away, growing increasingly worse as they entered the car park at Woolwich Warren Golf Club.
Naturally, Mel had noticed Nona's sullen and sombre mood in the minibus that morning but had said nothing, putting it down to a combination of over-tiredness and the early start, coupled with the raging hormones of her soon-to-be teenage daughter. She'd hoped that Nona's mood would lift the closer they got to putting her plans into action, but, if anything, her daughter's mind was in a much darker place by the time they'd all climbed into their respective golf carts and were careering in convoy towards the Great Bunker once more...
"You all right?" Mel quietly asked.
"Yep!" came the terse reply.
"Anything bothering you?" Mel pressed.
"Nope."
"Want to talk about it?

"Nope."
"Can you say anything else which isn't *'Yep'* or *'Nope'*?" Mel asked, her patience now slightly strained by the lack of a response from her daughter.
"Maybe…"
So, Mel had thought it best to keep quiet for the rest of the journey, the silence punctuated only by the hum of the golf cart's electric motor, along with the occasional shout of *'Fore'* from the wayward golfers who were hacking their way around the busy fairways as the procession of golf carts passed by them…

Meanwhile, not too far away from them, Lewis Kingston had arrived at the entrance to Kingston's Kingdom bright and early himself that Friday, whistling cheerfully as he'd walked into the zoo, past the barricaded ticket office, the closed gift shop and the barred exit to the zoo, all devoid of any human life.
Today's going to be a good day, he thought to himself, smirking wildly as he'd strolled up the stairs which led into his office.
The day had indeed started well for him, having taken a brief early morning call from Aleksander Kashlotov confirming that the money promised him was now in place, ready to be transferred to his bank account as soon as Lewis gave him the word. In turn, Lewis had reassured the Russian that they were now well ahead of schedule and that - as things stood - the zoo would officially be closed with the month.
"Nothing can stop us now, Aleksander," Lewis had cheerily said before ending the long-distance conversation.
Now as he sat at his desk, Lewis had again looked at the small photograph in the frame which faced him, a photograph showing a much younger Roger Kingston proudly standing outside the gates to the kingdom.
"Must remember to have a photograph of me standing in front of this damned place whilst it's being bulldozed, Grandad," Lewis sneered as he picked up the frame and dropped it into the bin beside him before leaning back in his chair, swinging his legs up to rest his pointy, brown shoes on the desk.
Lewis then reached into an inside jacket pocket and removed a long, thick cigar from it.
"I think an early celebratory smoke is in order," he said to himself as he stuck the cigar between his badly nicotine-coated teeth as he

reached for his lighter.

But before he could even light the cigar, the telephone had rung loudly and violently, startling him slightly. He dropped his feet to the floor and quickly grabbed the receiver from its cradle.

"Yeah?" he asked curtly.

"Mr Kingston - it's John Stafford," came the nervous reply.

"Stafford - how good to hear from you. Funnily enough, I was just about to phone you. I've some positive news to share with you regarding our Eastern European friends…"

"That's good to hear, Mr Kingston," Stafford had replied unenthusiastically before continuing, "however, we have a far more pressing problem to address…"

Lewis' good cheer immediately evaporated.

"I don't do problems, Stafford, I do solutions - that's what you're for…" he replied curtly.

"Even I can't sort this one for you, Mr Kingston," Stafford replied sadly, "you see, Alistair Leadbetter has just called me as he wants to carry out a full audit and inspection of the zoo…"

"Is that all? Lewis laughed, "Go make the appointment. I'm pretty certain that between you, me, Doctor Au and my man Clarke, we'll be able to baffle, bewilder and bemuse the old codger when he eventually comes to see us!"

"It's not quite as simple as that Mr Kingston," Stafford sighed, "Alistair Leadbetter is already on his way here as we speak…and he's bringing an entire team of auditors with him…"

As the elderly solicitor and his auditors trawled around Kingston's Kingdom, the golf carts carrying Nona and the others had slowly ground to a halt and were now parked outside the entrance to the tunnel network which ran beneath the zoo. Nona stood beside her friends and watched as her teacher unlocked the door before turning to face them all.

"So, everybody knows today's plan and their part in it?" Lawrence Light asked, scanning the group of people now expectantly stood before him.

They all nodded as Mr Light looked directly towards Nona before continuing.

"Today will be different though as it'll be the first time we'll be walking any of the animals out through the tunnel," he explained, "therefore it's vitally important we don't let go any of them as they'll be off and away down these tunnels meaning that it could take forever to find them again - if ever!"

"At least they ought to be able to climb down the ladder on their own accord," Luca said happily, "that will make it a whole lot easier than some of the rescues that we've had to do recently!"

"True, Luca," Mr Light replied, "but let's take no chances anyway…OK, let's go!"

Everyone nodded as Mr Light stepped in through the entrance and into the tunnel, shining his torch ahead of him whilst everyone waited for Nona to follow as always.

But today she hesitated, fearing her next step, somehow certain sure that if she took it, she'd set the ball of fate in motion, it relentlessly rolling towards a conclusion she dreaded yet didn't fully know or understand.

"Nona," her mother asked, placing her hand in the small of her daughter's back, "are you all right?"

"Yeah, I'm fine," Nona nodded. "it's just the fact that I've got a really bad feeling about this."

Mel tried to force a reassuring smile despite her own reservations about their plans that day.

"It'll be OK - we've just got to be as careful and cautious as we usually are and take no silly risks," she replied, "plus, you've got the A team here to back you up today! What could possibly go wrong? Just remember that we're all here for you, especially me."

"Thanks, Mum," Nona replied as she hugged Mel briefly, before breaking away from her to head into the tunnel, shouting, "Come on then - let's do this!"

Spurred on by the sight of their young leader quickly disappearing ahead of them, the others soon followed, leaving Marilyn and Sue following at the rear, closing the bunker door quietly behind them in the process. The journey through the underground network - and the tunnel nicknamed Kong - took longer than any of the other tunnels they'd used previously meaning thirty-five minutes had passed by the time they eventually reached the ladder that brought back them to the surface, its opening directly in the home of the Bonobo Monkeys, the primates' enclosure being directly next to the River Thames itself where the boundary wall of the kingdom ended.

Nona slipped the rucksack she'd carried by hand through the tunnels onto her back and readied herself for the climb. But just as she was about to push herself up onto the first couple of rungs on the ladder, Nona felt someone touch her arm so turned to look into her mother's face, Mel proudly smiling back at her.

"Remember, we're here if you run into any problems up there," she smiled reassuringly, "so don't go taking any chances, you hear?"

"I won't, Mum," Nona replied, "promise…"

"Good - I love you, Nona."

"I know," Nona smiled back…

When Nona reached the top of the ladder, she carefully unscrewed the tunnel hatch and unclasped it, lifting it up to slide it to the side of the exit.

Slowly she peeked her eyes up over the edge of the hatch and scanned the area around her to see two Bonobo Monkeys sat on a log opposite her. Only moments before they'd been lovingly preening one another, picking and eating the bits of dead skin, dirt, ticks, fleas and lice they'd found hidden in their partner's fur. Now they sat motionless, staring at Nona, lips pursed as though they were about to blow her a kiss before the younger monkey suddenly stood on the log and began to jump repeatedly, slapping his palms against the wood as though trying to scare Nona away.

"Shush, I won't hurt you," Nona whispered, putting a finger to her lips, "look – see what I've got here for you...."

Slowly, she took her finger away from her mouth and carefully slid off her rucksack as the two monkeys stared intently at her as Nona slipped her hand into the bag to produce two bananas from it.

"Would you like these?" she asked as she eased herself up to sit on the side of the hatch.

Instantly, the two monkeys cautiously sidled towards her, tentatively reaching out for the two bananas Nona now held in either hand.

"It's OK, I won't bite," Nona whispered as they snatched the bananas from her before running back to sit on the log.

Nona smiled and climbed out of the hatch before slowly walking toward the monkeys, who'd both wasted no time in splitting open the banana skins and were now eagerly licking at the flesh inside.

"There," Nona said as she made her way to the log, carefully sitting down in the space the two primates had left between them on the log, "Now - isn't this lovely?"

The younger monkey turned to look at Nona and bared its mushy banana covered teeth in a huge grin, before continuing to munch away happily as Nona slowly raised her hand to begin to stroke it, relieved to find that it was quite content for her to do so. Nona continued to stroke the youngster before raising her other hand to stroke the second monkey to the other side of her, who again, paid no attention to the gesture.

Relaxing for the first time that day, Nona spied some movement in the bushes to the right of her as three more young and curious Bonobos summoned up the courage to come out and see what was going on in their enclosure.

"Don't worry - there's plenty more where those came from!" Nona smiled, tossing three more bananas over in their direction. As she sat watching the primates happily feeding, Nona caught sight of something else moving outside the enclosure through the bars directly behind the area the three new monkeys had come out from.

Anxiously, she looked at the tunnel hatch which was still open and knew she'd have no time to close it, so immediately rolled back over the log, much to the bemusement of the monkeys next to her.

Shielded by the older monkey now sat in front of her, Nona slowly raised her eyes so that they peeped just above the log to get a clearer view of what was happening outside the enclosure.

Walking the pathway which passed the front of the Bonobos were two smartly dressed men, each carrying a clipboard. Fortunately, they seemed far more interested in them than looking into the monkey enclosure where the tunnel entrance was clearly visible for all to see. Nona listened intently to the conversation the men were having as they purposely marched by...

"Have we any more to do?"

"No, the elephant was the last one in our area of the park."

"Where next then?"

"Back to the entrance to meet with the other teams and to report our findings to Mr Leadbetter I suppose."

"Bit odd though, isn't it?"

"I'll say."

"What do you think he'll do?"

"If the rest of the data he receives is similar to ours, I suspect he'll probably want to launch a full-scale audit of the kingdom to confirm that it's correct..."

Nona watched as the men walked down the hill and waited until they'd shrunk to the size of matchsticks in the distance before standing again.

"Come on," Nona said extending a hand to the young monkey she'd first befriended, "let's go for a little walk, shall we? We can't hang around here for much longer."

The young monkey looked at the hairless hand extended towards it and raised its own to take it. Nona smiled as she felt the bare palm fit snugly in her grasp as the two of them walked happily together towards the tunnel entrance where Clive Tilley's face greeted Nona.

"You all right?" he asked.

"Yes Clive, I'm good, where's Mum?"

"She got a little dizzy climbing up the ladder," Clive smiled, reassuringly, "tiredness, I think, nothing serious though, so I've I volunteered to take her place as I've not been out on that many of these operations meself and I didn't want to leave it too late or else I'd miss out on all the good stuff!"

"That's OK then, we'd best hurry though - there's something going on here today that I don't like," Nona frowned, looking down at the monkey stood beside her, "come on then, little guy, time to go on an adventure together..."

So preoccupied with what was happening in the zoo outside the enclosure, Nona had barely noticed the monkey's pace easing as they'd got closer to the tunnel hatch. Now, the primate had seemed frozen to the spot as it warily peered at the dark hole below its feet.

"Come on," Nona repeated, trying to pull the monkey closer to where Clive was stood on the ladder waiting for them.

But the monkey was having none of it, breaking free from her grasp, hurriedly scuttling back sideways across the enclosure to where its primate mates were waiting for it.

"I don't understand - why doesn't it want to escape?" Nona asked, quizzically looking at Clive.

"Try getting one of the other guys to come over instead," Clive said, "maybe it'll change its mind if it sees one of its brothers or sisters go down there first."

Nona nodded and then turned back towards the older monkey, but it too refused to step foot in the tunnel.

Frustratingly, the same thing happened with the three remaining monkeys when Nona approached each of them, one even refusing to hold her hand before disappearing up into the branches of the tree to the left of their enclosure. Even the prospect of another hand of bananas Clive had then retrieved from the tunnel to hold high above his head had failed to entice any of the monkeys to join him and the others in the dark confines of the tunnel below.

After another fruitless fifteen minutes, Clive sighed deeply and shrugged his shoulders.

"They're never going to come anywhere near this hatch, Nona," he said, "Let's face it - it's time to admit defeat and go home."

"No," came the sharp reply.

"I beg your pardon?"

"I'm not going anywhere without these monkeys," Nona declared, crossing her arms and returning to sit on the log.

"Nona Lancaster, you better come here now!" Clive replied, a much sterner tone now sharpening his words.

"No - here's something funny going on here today, Uncle Clive," Nona replied, "I've a feeling that if we don't get these guys out today then we may never, ever, get the chance to do so again."

Clive rubbed his hand across his forehead and chuckled quietly.

"You're so your mother's daughter!" he laughed, "OK...OK. I've got an idea, but you'll have to wait a little while whilst I try and arrange things. Can you do that for me at least?"

"I can," she whispered, nervously looking back through the bars of the enclosure, "but please hurry - I don't know how much longer we've got to all get safely out of here..."

Chapter 26 – The Heat is On

Despite being someone who considered himself better built for comfort than speed, Clive Tilley was now to running faster than he had ever done since leaving school in what seemed like a lifetime ago...

The last time he'd run any distance of actual note was in a PE lesson where the whole of Year 10 were competing to represent the school in the county finals that year. Clive hated any form of exercise – especially running – at the best of times and was in his customary position of being at the back of the, just in front of Jason Bird who was in last place as they began their second, and final, lung-bursting ascent of the infamous local landmark of Cemetery Hill. Clive's body screamed as he ran in jelly towards the summit, knowing there were a couple of miles still to go after making it to the top before racing through the park which ran alongside his school to reach the finishing line marked out at the school's entrance.

He'd paused momentarily to catch his breath at the top of the climb, allowing 'Birdy' to catch him up. When Birdy had suggested they took a shortcut through the cemetery the hill was nicknamed after, Clive didn't stop to think twice, which he soon regretted as he danced and dodged his way between the crumbling gravestones and tombs that dogged his path as he careered downhill towards the other end of the park.

But this regret turned to one of mighty relief when Clive finally saw the familiar well-walked pathway which led to his school as he burst through the trees, narrowly avoiding being seen by a pack of boys who'd just rounded the corner behind them.

Clive and Birdy continued to run together, knowing that the entrance to the school was now only a couple of hundred metres away around the next bend. He looked at Birdy and smiled broadly as they turned it to see Mr Payne, their insanely fit PE teacher, standing on the gate poised with his clipboard and stopwatch in hand.

Between Mr Payne and the two of them were a couple of other boys, who looked like the final fifty metres or so might be proving too much for their tired and weary young bodies.

"Come on, Birdy," Clive laughed, "it's time for our big finish..."

The two boys immediately began to sprint, their legs eating up the ground beneath them as they started to gain ground on the boys ahead of them. One of the boys casually glanced back and, surprised to see who it was gaining on him, dug deep into his energy reserves, to pick speed as he accelerated for the line. The second boy, however, didn't even flinch or offer any form of resistance as Clive and Birdy easily passed him, gladly accepting defeat as Mr Payne looked up at the three boys who were now conducting their own private and personal race for the finish line. Despite Clive and Birdy's best efforts though, they couldn't quite close the gap on the boy in front of them but as the boy passed by their PE teacher, Clive heard Mr Payne say *"Stokes - 4th..."* before a sudden and quite horrific realisation hit him squarely between the eyes...

Clive worst nightmare was soon confirmed by Mr Payne's next words as he and Birdy crossed the finish line to complete the race. "Fifth place, Master Tilley, closely followed by Master Bird who takes the sixth and the final spot on the cross-country team..." the PE teacher smiles, shaking his head in sheer disbelief at what he'd just witnessed, "Congratulations, you two - you've made it to the county finals! Wel done - I didn't know that either of you had it in you..."

The haunting memory of that day - and the subsequent embarrassment of coming third last with his legendary athletic auntie watching the county finals - now filled Clive's head once again as he hurtled along the tunnels underneath Kingston's Kingdom, back to where Sue and Marilyn were waiting for them all to return. Of course, this time he'd had no choice but to run - he needed to find a mobile phone to urgently use.

Clive had climbed back down the ladder and been staggered to find that between Mel, Lawrence and himself, none of them had even thought of bringing a phone into the tunnels. In desperation, he'd even asked Keeley and Luca, but their negative replies had only confirmed what he already suspected. Mel and Lawrence had done the same too - leaving their phones locked up safely in the back of the minibus, never expecting to have to use them, especially as they would be so deep underground that no signal could reach them even if they wanted one to.

Now, as Clive began to see the light slowly grow at the end of the tunnel, he desperately hoped that either Sue or Marilyn had the good sense and foresight to bring their phones with them that day…

Marilyn and Sue were merrily chattering away as usual when the sound of loud footsteps pounding and heavy breathing gasping began to grow ever louder from the direction of the tunnel behind them as Marilyn grabbed Sue's arm and squeezed it tightly.

"You don't suppose one of the rhinoceroses have escaped the zoo?" she asked nervously.

Sue was about to tell her friend not to be so silly but the deafening noises which were now almost upon them caused her to wonder if her friend was right after all.

The two women slowly began to climb the stairs, backwards as their sweat-stained and soaked friend suddenly burst out of the tunnels causing the women to jump back and shriek in alarm.

"Clive Tilley - don't do that to me!" Marilyn protested, grabbing her chest, "Oh, my aching heart!"

"Need…phone…now…" Clive gasped, holding his hand out in front of him.

"What for?" Marilyn asked, scrabbling about in her pocket.

"No…time…explain…later…phone…please!" Clive heaved, tiredly snapping his fingers in front of him in order to speed her up.

Marilyn finally pulled her phone from her pocket, leant forward and handed it to Clive, who'd now sat on the stairs, desperately trying to catch his breath again. Snatching it from her hand, Clive jabbed at the keypad on the mobile phone, then held it to his ear.

"No…I don't believe this!" Clive screamed as he heard the unobtainable tone shrilly drone away in his ear, "21st Century London and I still can't get a damned phone signal!"

Sue glanced at Marilyn, who shrugged her shoulders.

"It might have something to do with the fact that we are still encased in concrete and thirty feet underground, Clive," Sue reminded him.

Clive rubbed his head, unable to quite believe how stupid he'd been as he looked at the stairs directly in front of him.

"Make way!" he shouted as he stood and forced his legs to run up the unforgiving stone stairwell in front of him…

Although overcast outside, Clive still had to shield his eyes as he burst through the outer door to the bunker, causing him to pause momentarily as his eyes again grew better accustomed to the daylight, allowing him to focus on Marilyn's mobile once more as he hit the redial button and stood waiting as the number he'd first called rang again.

"Come on, come on…" Clive pleaded as he paced back and forth until a welcome and familiar voice finally answered.

"Dis be Doyley, who be dat?"

"Doyley! Thank goodness, it's Clive Tilley here. I really need your help, dude…"

Clive had thought that Doyley wasn't his usual chatty self as he explained the problems he and Nona had encountered with the Bonobo Monkeys but continued to talk rapidly anyway, all too aware that time and circumstance were against them.

It was only after Clive had fully explained everything that had happened and the problems they now faced that Doyley finally spoke.

"Der guys dat she saw are auditors," Doyley solemnly replied, "dey arrived pretty unexpectedly dis morning. She was lucky den as dey were soon all over der park like a bad rash!"

"Why didn't you tell us?" Clive asked impatiently.

"Oi had no chance, dey were wit' me before Oi knew it," Doyley sighed, "dey stuck to me like glue - Oive only just got rid of dem."

Clive bit his lip and paused for a moment. "It changes nothing. Nona's refusing to leave the enclosure without the monkeys."

"So want do yer want from me?" Doyley asked.

"Two long ladders."

"Dat may be a bit of a problem," Doyley replied, "Will one aluminium one and a rope one do yer instead?"

"It's not ideal," Clive replied, "but we've no other choice so it'll have to do, I suppose."

"No worries, Oi! get on it right away," the Irishman said, "it'll take me a few minutes mind - terty tops, as dey are still here and Oive got to be careful not to raise any more alarms dis end."

Clive looked at his watch. "That should be OK, but make sure it's no longer."

"Sure ting. Laters."

Clive waited until he heard the ringtone again before keying in his next number. True to form, it was answered on its third ring.

"Auntie Sheila, it's Clive…I need to ask you a huge favour…"

Whilst Clive was making the return trip back through the tunnels to rejoin the others, Lewis Kingston and John Stafford were welcoming Alistair Leadbetter to Lewis' office. Both wore false, fixed and painted-on smiles, trying to give the solicitor the iimpression they were pleased to see him, which they obviously weren't. But, more importantly, their grins were worn to show him that they'd nothing to fear or hide…

"Can I offer you a drink?" Lewis asked, opening a drinks cabinet, pulling out a crystal drink decanter filled with an amber-coloured liquid.

Leadbetter smiled wanly and shook his head as he adjusted his spectacles.

"No thank you, Mr Kingston, it's a little early in the day for alcohol, even for me," the old solicitor replied before continuing, "however, you may need a stiff drink by the time I've shared my initial findings with you…"

Lewis nodded and perched nonchalantly on the end of his desk. *He's going to ask me about the increase in our animal 'deaths,'* he smugly thought to himself, *damned good job we've covered our tracks so thoroughly and so well…*

Without saying a word, Lewis poured himself a drink and, as he lifted his glass to his lips, looked across at Stafford, a sure sign he wanted the crooked accountant to answer Alistair Leadbetter on his behalf.

"Admittedly, we've been unfortunate to lose so many animals due to the terrible disease which has caused such devastation to our zoo," Stafford began, Lewis sadly nodding his agreement beside him as he continued, "but it's a relatively small number lost compared to the number of creatures we care for in the kingdom."

"Alas," Lewis added, putting his empty glass down, "I'm afraid it's more than likely that we'll see a vast increase in fatalities over the next month or so as the virus really catches hold of the zoo's population. Doctor Au says he's seen nothing like it in all his years."

"I see," said Leadbetter as he moved his spectacles down his nose until they rested on the very tip of it, "that really is most unfortunate, Mr Kingston. However, my most immediate concerns are about the livestock who are still, according to your most recent stock take and reported data, very much alive and kicking…"

Lewis stood and casually walked to the window, as though to say '*whatever*' as he looked out across the zoo.

However, inside his head, his mind was rattling through the possible outcomes the next few sentences exchanged between the three men in his office could have on his future plans.

"What concerns might they be, Alistair?" he asked, watching as Doyley, a huge rucksack slung across his back, and another unknown zoo employee walked along the pathway which led to the very top of Kingston's Kingdom, carrying a large ladder between the two them.

Now what the devil are you two up to? Lewis thought to himself as he took another sip of his drink.

"The missing animals of course, Mr Kingston…."

Leadbetter's unexpected statement caused Lewis to immediately snap back around to stare at the solicitor.

"What do you mean '*missing animals*'?" he asked, "Apart from those who've been lost to this wretched disease, every other still animal is here, safely quarantined or locked up for their own protection."

Leadbetter flicked over a couple of pages the bulldog clip on his clipboard held tightly in place.

"Not according to our initial findings today," he tutted, "based on our audit today, we estimate around 30% of the animal inventory are unaccounted for."

"30%?" Lewis spluttered, "You can't be serious? Your buffoons must have miscounted them.'"

"Yes, I am serious and no, we have not miscounted," Alistair Leadbetter replied firmly, "it appears that many of the smaller species have either vanished or significantly reduced in number since our first inspection after you inherited the kingdom... Penguins, racoons, sloths, snakes, the list goes on."

"Give me that!" Lewis demanded, snatching the clipboard from the solicitor's hands.

Attached to the clipboard was a typed list with the name of every single animal who was listed as being in the kingdom. Alongside these were numbers showing how many there were at the time of Roger Kingston's death. Also against the list were a series of pen marks - ticks, crosses, amended numbers and question marks made by the team of auditors tasked with checking the numbers given by John Stafford when they'd requested their visit.

"Please let me remind you, Mr Kingston, that under the terms of the will, any missing animal who remains unaccounted for will result in you losing your share of the zoo."

Gasping, Lewis felt like he'd been completely blindsided.

"I don't understand," he argued, "the figures you have must be wrong, the staff have been checking the animals constantly, providing me with regular, up to the minute data and details of -"

Suddenly, Lewis stopped talking as a rather large penny finally dropped in his head. He looked back to the window, shook his head and smiled ruefully.

"I knew it…" he chuckled.

"I'm sorry" Leadbetter asked.

"Nothing, just thinking out loud to myself…" Lewis Kingston replied as he rose to his feet, "Grab your coat, Alistair - it's time to have a final chat with my soon-to-be-ex-head zookeeper…"

Nona was now beginning to worry.

What's taking Uncle Clive so long, she thought as she paced up and down the monkey enclosure, taking great care to stay out of sight of the pathway.

Suddenly, Nona heard footsteps fast approaching and ducked down behind the foliage. Her heart was racing as she heard a key in the enclosure lock turn as two separate but distinct sets of footsteps marched in unison into the monkey house.

"Will yer watch where yer going with dat ting!" a familiar voice loudly cried out.

Nona dared to pop her head out from her hiding place to catch the much welcome sight of Doyley and another zoo worker struggling with a long, silver ladder as they entered the enclosure.

"Let's set it up against der wall over dere. Dat OK wit' yer, Nona?" the Irishman asked, without turning from where he was standing.

Nona stepped out from behind the bushes to watch as Doyley's helper struggled to set the ladder against the wall before extending it to its full height.

"Tony's a lovely lad but he's not der sharpest tool in der shed," Doyley laughed before striding forwards to join the young, curly-haired lad he'd brought with him, "Yers got the ting upside down, yer great big eejit!"

Nona smiled as she watched Doyley and Tony's comical attempts to lay the ladder down, before turning it around and lifting it up again to safely rest it against the wall of the enclosure.

"Dere," Doyley said proudly, placing his hands on either side of the ladder before giving it a good shake, "Oil just sort dis out for yer and yer be good to go."

"Sort out what? Good to go where?" Nona urgently asked as Doyley took a long rope ladder which already had two huge hooks attached to it out from the rucksack he'd been carrying before climbing the silver ladder with it, Tony resting a foot on the bottom of it so that it didn't drift away from the wall.

Having failed to get a reply from the Irishman, Nona stepped closer to the ladder he was climbing up and called up at him.

"Sort out what, Doyley?"

"Our escape with the monkeys!" a voice shouted from behind her. Nona spun around to see Clive Tilley climbing out of the tunnel, brushing at the knees of his combat trousers as he did so.

She smiled broadly as he began to walk towards before continuing.

"We're taking them over the wall!" Clive winked as he watched Doyley hook the rope ladder to the top of the wall before unrolling it over the over side, "All good up there?"

"Yer all set," Doyley replied as he climbed back down, "good luck, Oi hopes it all goes well. Me and Tony here will head off now to run interference whilst yer two get up to some monkey business of yer own!"

Doyley ruffled Nona's hair as he walked past her before gathering up his now empty rucksack, ushering his young helper before him as they quickly made their way out of the enclosure.

"Seriously?" Nona said, looking disbelievingly at Clive, "You and me are taking the monkeys over the wall?"

"Yep," Clive nodded, "got it all figured out...You go up the ladder first, wave some more bananas in the monkeys' direction to get them to follow you, before climbing down the other side of the wall on the rope one Doyley's set up... I'll cover our tracks here before following you.

"But, Clive-" Nona began to reply, looking at the wall in confusion.

"Nona, we don't have much time," he smiled, "can you please just trust me on this?"

Nona nodded and opened her bag, pulling out another hand of bananas from it.

"Here guys, look what I've found more of for you!" she shouted, excitedly waving the fruit at the primates.

The Bonobos, who'd been curiously watching the comings and goings of the *hairless* monkeys in the enclosure whilst safely tucked away in their hidey-holes, suddenly had a new-found bravery as their eyes fixed on the bright yellow skin of the bananas Nona held in her hand. They tilted their heads in unison as she one-handedly began to climb the ladder, her second hand firmly fixed to a rung whilst she rested and readjusted her grip each time she stepped up, allowing her to continue to dangle the bananas from her other hand positioned behind her.

At first, the monkeys continued to watch curiously, repeatedly tilting their heads from side to side before suddenly realising that not only was there free, delicious food on offer to them, but this *hairless* ape climbing the ladder before them was showing them a way to escape their enclosure. Without any further hesitation, the five Bonobos lolloped across the ground and began to scale the ladder, forcing Nona to rapidly increase her speed in order to keep ahead of them.

"Part 1 successfully completed," Clive mumbled as he started to cover their tracks, ready to eventually make his way to the ladder. He paused momentarily as he looked at the wall.

"Now, let's hope Auntie Sheila keeps to her end of the bargain," he whispered to himself, "or else Nona and I are done for…"

Chapter 27 – Argy Bargy

Doyley and his young helper hadn't managed to travel too far away from the monkey enclosure when they were suddenly confronted by Lewis Kingston, John Stafford and Alistair Leadbetter on the main zoo pathway.

"Ah, Mr Kingston, owaya doing?" Doyley smiled cheerily, extending his hand towards his employer.

However, Lewis Kingston just stood there, motionless, except for slowly folding his arms across his chest, ignoring the hand that had been offered to him in greeting. Doyley stood for a moment too, as though frozen in time, before dropping his hand back to his side.

"Been busy I see, Mr Doyle?" Lewis asked, nodding his head towards the rucksack Doyley held in his other hand.

"Ah, well, yer know how it is," the Irishman smiled, "the devil makes work for oidle hands, as me dear old ma always used to say!"

"I've no doubt about that," Lewis sneered, "and I suspect you've been pretty busy with your *idle* hands recently, you old devil you…"

Doyley frowned at the hostile tone of Lewis' voice. "Oim not sure dat Oi follows yer, Mr Kingston?"

"Let me be a little more direct then…" Lewis said, leaning his head forwards a little, "where were you off to earlier today with that ladder of yours?"

"Well, yer see," Doyley began to reply, rubbing the back of his neck with his free hand, "Oi was taking a little stroll early dis morning before dem auditor blokes arrived and Oi noticed dat dere were a few tings which had shifted about a bit in dat bad wind der other night. So, after dey have done wit' me dis morning, Oi fetches me man Tony here–'

"It's Toby, Mr Doyle," Toby-not-Tony interrupted, rolling his eyes and shaking his head dejectedly.

"Po-*ta*-toes, po-*tah*-toes…" Doyley replied before continuing, "Anyways, as Oi was saying, whilst we were doing der odd minor repair here and dere, Oi suddenly comes across a real problem. So Oim tinking to meself *'Do Oi bother yer wit it and get a man wit' a van to comes and fix it or do Oi just go ahead and fix meself?*

So, Oi decides dat we can do it, so we go to get der ladder and no sooner had we got der ladder dere den Oi realises dat Oi forgot to put me tools in me rucksack here! Dat's where we were heading – to go fetch dem! If yers like to wait here, Oi'l be back in a mo, or yers more than welcome to walk wit' me whilst Oi go and-"

"Toby," Lewis barked at the young man who was silently stood beside Doyley, "where's the ladder now?"

The young man who was Toby-not-Tony looked at Lewis, then Doyley and swallowed hard.

"Don't look at him, Toby," Lewis Kingston urged, "if you want to keep your job, you'll tell me exactly where you left that ladder."

"It's in the monkey area, Mr Kingston," Toby-not-Tony reluctantly answered, "in the Bonobos enclosure itself."

"Thank you, Toby," Lewis smiled and began to walk off.

"Oi wouldn't recommend going in dere on yer own - it's not safe at der mo," Doyley said, adding, "now if yer wait just a wee bit whilst Oi collect der tings Oi need to make me repairs, Oi -'

"The only things I want you to go collect are your personal belongings...clear your locker, Mr Doyle - you're fired!" Lewis snapped.

The Irishman just stood there, for once, speechless as his former employer to look at the solicitor stood beside him.

"Please follow me, Alistair - I believe that we're about to find out what has actually happened to my missing animals," Lewis announced as he began to march forwards, followed by John Stafford and the now slightly confused old solicitor before stopping abruptly to look back at Doyley.

"Oh, and by the way," Lewis sniffed, "if you see Miss Maguire on your travels, please tell her that her services are no longer required as she's fired too – it'll save me the time and effort…"

With that, he stormed off, leaving Doyley and Toby-not-Tony to watch in stunned disbelief as the three other men marched away.

"I'm sorry, Mr Doyle, but he gave me no choice," apologised Toby-not-Tony.

"No need, little man - it was only a matter of time before dey found out what Oive been doing anyway," Doyley sadly smiled, "Oi only hope dat Oive stalled dem long enough for Nona and Clive to get dem damned monkeys out over dat wall…"

"Almost there…just don't look down," Clive said to himself, his eyes firmly fixed on the top of the ladder ahead of him.

However, as he stared at the bare bottom of the monkey in front of him, Clive wasn't quite sure which was worse – the height he'd already climbed, or the primate's bare bum in his face!

In their haste to get the monkeys out, Clive had clean forgotten that he'd have to go up the ladder himself. Now, nearly thirty feet above the ground as the ladder gently wobbled beneath him, he'd regretted not taking Mel up on her offer to go that morning, before sending her off with the others, back through the tunnels to the bunker exit instead.

Suddenly, noticing that the monkey in front of him had stopped moving whilst trying to avoid headbutting its bottom, Clive stopped and called above him.

"How are you getting on up there, Nones?"

"Nearly there," Nona replied, "I've checked that the hooks are firmly attached to the top of the wall and I'm just...about...to... look...over...the...edge...now..."

Nona excitedly pulled herself up to peer over the top of the boundary wall of the monkeys' enclosure, frowning instantly as soon as she saw the barren piece of scrubland which was now below her, the murky waters of the Thames lapping against it.

"There's not an awful lot down there, Uncle Clive," she said disappointedly.

"Don't worry about that for now," Clive urged, "just climb down the other side. Hurry!"

Nona, despite her grave misgivings, swung her leg over the side of the wall and carefully stepped onto the nearest rung, feeling the rope give a little before it reassuringly took her full weight. Gingerly, Nona began to climb down the rope ladder, looking back up at the wall which she'd sat on just moments before. Suddenly, a monkey's face appeared above her, Nona instantly recognising it as the older monkey she'd first befriended earlier that day as she waved the hand of bananas she still held at it.

"Here we are.... Come on, just a little bit further to go," Nona whispered gently.

The Bonobo frowned a little and hesitated momentarily but then climbed onto the wall before expertly swinging down after her.

"Yes!" Nona whooped as she continued her descent as a second monkey reached the top and began to follow her by the time she'd reached the midway point on the rope ladder.

By the time Nona had neared the end of it, three Bonobos swung high above her, the weight of the four of them causing the ladder to sway slightly from side to side.

"I'm almost at the bottom but there's a little bit of a jump at the end as the ladder doesn't quite reach the ground," Nona shouted.

"Good, me and the last two monkeys have almost reached the top ourselves," Clive replied as he watched the first Bonobo ahead of him reach the summit, the bald butt ahead of him now moving quicker as it too approached the end of the ladder they were climbing. "We'll be with you soon!"

"No - you won't!" an angry voice shouted out from behind him, "Stop exactly where you are!"

Clive turned and looked back behind as three men stood outside the entrance to the Bonobos enclosure, one of them a thin and weasly looking man who began to urgently rummage around in his trouser pocket.

"I don't think so, mate!" Clive laughed as he quickly reached the top of the wall as the final monkey disappeared over it ahead of him.

"Who was that?" a shocked Alistair Leadbetter asked as Lewis frantically tried to remove his keys from his trousers.

"I've…no…idea," Lewis grunted, angrily ripping the keys out of his pocket, tearing the material in the process, "but I bet you anything you'd like that he's got something to do with that damned sister of mine!"

Lewis finally found the key to the gate and quickly unlocked it, flinging it wide open, just as Clive began to make his way down the rope ladder on the other side of the wall, waving a defiant hand at the three men as Lewis and Stafford ran across the enclosure, Leadbetter puffing as he tried to keep pace with the two much younger men now ahead of him.

"Look out!" Stafford called out, stopping Lewis from plummeting down the tunnel hatch which still lay open on the ground just in front of him.

"Well, I'll be…" Lewis muttered, peering in amazement down into the dark well before remembering where he'd originally been heading.

He quickly composed himself and sped forwards to grab the foot of the silver ladder which was still propped against the outer wall. "Stafford - get on the blower and call the police!" he barked.

John Stafford fumbled in his jacket as Lewis started to gingerly climb the ladder, his lack of athleticism there for all to see as his foot slid between the rungs, causing his leg to slip through the gap, painfully landing against the metal tread.

"Are you all right?" Stafford asked, his phone pressed to his ear. However, by soon judging by the look he saw on Lewis Kingston's face, instantly knew that it was a silly question. Fortunately, before his temperamental boss could hurl any abuse at him, the phone was answered.

"Police please, I'd like to report a break-in," the accountant said before continuing, "or should that be a *break-out*…"

Whilst Stafford continued to give more detail on the phone, Lewis had managed to prise himself out of the gap and was about to start climbing again as Alistair Leadbetter eventually reached the foot of the ladder.

"Lewis, would you please tell me what's going on?" the old solicitor panted.

Lewis sighed and looked at Leadbetter's puzzled and bemused face.

"I firmly believe that my half-sister and her mother, helped by the likes of Mr Doyle and Miss Maguire, have been stealing my animals from me, although I couldn't be absolutely certain until today," Lewis lied, "fortunately, your audit and findings have sadly helped to confirm my suspicions."

"But why would she do that?" Leadbetter asked, "Surely they'd know that Nona would lose her right to Kingston's Kingdom were they to do that?"

"Look, she's just a common little girl from a dodgy council estate," Lewis sneered, "not the brightest of people live in the slums, do they? I think Nona Lancaster and that mother of hers have been spreading rumours and lies about me but when that failed to turn people against me, they came up with the idea to try and discredit me instead so that I lose the zoo and the get the inheritance all to themselves."

"Have you proof of this?" Leadbetter asked as Lewis continued to climb the ladder, causing him to stop abruptly and turn to look down at the solicitor in disbelief.

"Did you honestly not see a man just leg it over the zoo wall with a monkey?" Lewis gasped, "What more proof do you need?"

"I need to see with my own eyes that Miss Lancaster and Nona are actually involved in carrying put these acts themselves," Leadbetter insisted, "that man we saw could be working for anyone - even you, Mr Kingston..."

Lewis stopped on a rung of the ladder and sighed in resignation. "Then you'd better start climbing, old man!"

"I'm not sure that I can!" Leadbetter replied, first looking at the ladder, then up at Lewis, "what with my back and my knees, not to mention the problems I have with my bot..."

"Well, you've a choice to make - believe what I tell you to be or come see for yourself," Lewis interrupted, "either way, I can't hang around whilst you're making your flippin' mind up!"

With that, Lewis began to scurry back up the ladder, leaving the old solicitor to stare at him still blankly.

"Mr Kingston!" Stafford shouted, snapping his phone case shut.

"God - what now?!" Lewis shouted, growing more frustrated by his lack of upward progress.

"I've spoken to the police," the accountant said, adding, "and told them about the monkeys being stolen..."

"So...?" Lewis asked impatiently.

"So, after the operator stopped laughing," Stafford continued, she transferred me to desk sergeant at the Thames River Police."

"Why did she do that?" Lewis frowned.

"Well, the operator reckoned that as the monkeys are already outside the zoo and on the banks of the river, it'll be easier for them to send a river patrol boat here rather than a squad car," Stafford replied, "when I eventually spoke to the desk sergeant, he told me that they'd despatch one here as soon as he could."

"Let's hope they get a shift on then," Lewis grunted as he continued climbing...

Whilst Lewis, Staffor and Leadbetter were arguing, bickering and climbing, on the other side of the wall, Clive stood by Nona on the shoreline as the monkeys happily munched the bananas Nona had finally rewarded them with.

"What now, Uncle Clive?" Nona asked, anxiously scanning the horizon.

Just as Nona had said, the scrubland they stood on was barren and seemed to lead to nowhere, the murky waters of the River Thames lapping at their feet.

In all directions, the land was completely deserted, apart from one small tree, and disappeared from view where both sides of the zoo perimeter wall ended to either side of them.

"We're stranded," Nona moaned as Clive looked at his watch.

"Come on…come on…" he muttered, looking to his left along the length of the bleak and barren shoreline.

"What are you looking for, Uncle Clive?" Nona asked, "there's nothing but water for-"

"There - that!" Clive shrieked, jumping up into the air, scaring the monkeys slightly as he did so.

Nona turned to look to where Clive was now pointing and began to stare as the bow of a large, green riverboat, moving unusually quickly through the choppy waters, made its way around the corner of the furthest zoo wall. Her mouth gaped open as the boat quickly approached where they stood, the sound of its engine causing the monkeys to huddle closer together on the shoreline.

"What the hell's going on, Uncle Clive?" Nona asked as the boat came to a halt about three metres from the shoreline.

"It's our getaway vehicle," Clive replied as the hatch at the back of the boat slid open and an unmistakable mop of unruly grey hair began to appear from below.

"Miss Bridges!" Nona shouted, excitedly waving her hands at her headteacher.

Miss Bridges waved back as she stood on the deck before gathering a long rope in her arms.

"Tie that to the tree to make sure I don't drift off," she shouted, throwing the rope at her nephew.

Clive caught it and quickly secured it to the tree trunk as Miss Bridges made her way to the middle of her boat.

"You took your time, Auntie," Clive smiled.

"Sorry I'm late!" Miss Bridges replied as she unclipped a large box on the top of the riverboat which looked like a bigger version of a car roof box, "I was in the shower when you called. Figured I'd best throw some clothes before getting her, otherwise the animals would flee in a panic if I arrived here in the nuddy!"

Nona looked at Clive and beamed. "I totally forgot that Miss Bridges lived on a riverboat!"

"That she does, Nona…" Clive nodded, "Mind you, it's a good job it's a training day today, else she wouldn't have been on it when I called her!"

"But how did you manage to get here so quickly, Miss Bridges?"

Nona frowned," Aren't riverboats a bit on the slow side?"

"Ordinarily," Miss Bridges grunted as she started to turn a large wheel on the side of the boat, "but I've made a few modifications and enhancements to this old girl over the years…"

Suddenly, a long, extendable gang plank shot out from the box on the river boat, it soon reaching the shore where Nona, Clive and the cowering monkeys were stood.

"Quick, we have to hurry - you go first Nona, I don't think your brother knows you're here and I think it best we keep it that way!" Clive urged as Nona stuck her hand out to one of the monkeys.

"It's OK, you're safe with me," Nona whispered, smiling reassuringly at the Bonobo sat on the ground before her. Instinctively the primate took her hand and began to follow Nona as she ran across the gangplank to where Miss Bridges was stood waiting. Once on the boat, the monkey stopped, turned and began to scream and hoot at the other monkeys on the shore, seeming to tell them that it was OK to follow. Without hesitation they all started to lollop across the gangplank onto the boat, where the first monkey still stood, tightly clutching Nona's hand.

"I think it best you get these little fellas below deck," Miss Bridges said, looking up at the wall as the top of Lewis Kingston's head began to appear.

Nona nodded and dashed to the cabin door, closely followed by the monkeys.

"Fly my pretties, fly!" Miss Bridges laughed as she watched Nona and the Bonobos scurry away into the bowels of the boat...

Lewis Kingston's anger and fury had increased the higher he climbed the ladder, having to stop every time that Leadbetter repeatedly shook it as he followed beneath him.

"For heaven's sake, man, can't you stop it!" Lewis barked, "It's like being on a damned vibration plate up here!"

"I can assure you that I'm not doing it on purpose, Mr Kingston." the solicitor scolded as Leadbetter continued his slow and deliberate ascent.

However, the sight which then greeted Lewis when he eventually reached the top of the wall had incensed him even further as he stood there, open-mouthed, catching a brief glimpse of someone quickly disappearing below deck on a riverboat moored to the shore beneath him – the unseen figure being closely followed by his stolen monkeys.

"Stop!" Lewis again shouted at the man he'd originally seen on the ladder when he first entered the enclosure, "I've called the police!"

"Good for you!" Clive said as he untied the rope and ran to pick up the end of the gangplank before wading out, holding it until he was knee deep in water before jumping up onto the now partially submerged gangplank to run onto the boat.

"You get us underway, Auntie Sheila," Clive said once he'd joined her on deck, replacing her hands on the gangplank wheel with his, "I've got this…"

Lewis felt the veins on the side of his head pulse and bulge as he watched a tall, grey-haired woman sprint back along the boat and down into the cabin as the man turned a large wheel to draw in the gangplank which was fixed to the side of the boat. Quickly coming to his senses again, Lewis spotted the rope ladder and climbed onto the wall before laying on his stomach to swing his legs around, over the edge of the wall. He held the top of it for dear life as he inched his body down the other side until his feet found a rung on the rope ladder to gain a foothold on.

Unexpectedly though, a sharp gust of wind suddenly appeared out of nowhere, violently sweeping at Lewis, almost causing him to fall as he gripped the wall ever tighter whilst the rope ladder swayed back and forth beneath him. But worst was to follow as, somewhat mysteriously, the ends of the rope ladder suddenly and inexplicably severed and frayed from where they'd originally been attached to their mounting hooks as though they'd been sliced clean through by an invisible sword, leaving Lewis precariously hanging there,

"Help!" Lewis cried as he heard the engine of the riverboat loudly rev up behind him before glancing over his shoulder to see the river boat move off at an unusually quick speed.

"*Hermes*…Pah!" Lewis sneered as he caught sight of the boat's name, proudly displayed across the back of its stern.

However, his focus and attention soon returned to his own desperate predicament as he felt his hands begin to lose their grip on the hard, but smooth concrete surface beneath them. Lewis could feel himself falling when, suddenly, an aged and well-weathered hand grabbed his arm, pinching the skin on his forearm as it did so.

"Don't worry young, man, I've got you…" Alistair Leadbetter declared, reaching over to grab Lewis Kingston's other arm.

"Thanks, but who's got you?" Lewis asked anxiously.

The two men struggled for a few moments before Lewis' shoes managed to safely get some purchase on the zoo wall again, allowing him to slowly inch up to the top of it.

Eventually, he sat, one leg on either side of the wall, breathing deeply as Leadbetter mopped his brow with his handkerchief.

"See, I told you it was Nona Lancaster, did you see her too?" Lewis asked after finally catching his breath again.

"All I saw was a green boat sail off and you hanging on for dear life," Leadbetter frowned, "What on Earth happened to the rope?"

"Him!" Lewis growled, pointing at the sky.

"Who, God?" Leadbetter asked.

"No, my dear, departed grandfather…" Lewis muttered, much to Leadbetter's bemusement as Lewis shook his head and swung his leg back over the wall so that both legs now hung over the zoo side of it.

"Anyway, it doesn't matter now," Lewis sighed, "let's go and see where that manhole leads instead, shall we?"

Alistair Leadbetter nodded and slowly started to climb back down the ladder when the sound of an engine grew louder behind them both.

"Stop! Police! Stay exactly where you are!" a gruff voice demanded.

"Typical!" Lewis huffed, turning back to see a Thames River Police boat now rapidly heading towards the shore…

Meanwhile, Nona and Clive Tilley had their work cut out keeping the monkeys below deck, their natural inquisitiveness meaning that they were investigating every nook and cranny on Miss Bridges' riverboat.

One of them repeatedly rolled back and forth across her bed whilst two more monkeys went through her wardrobe, smiling at each other as they tried on different items of clothing, from large, brimmed hats to high heeled shoes.

A fourth monkey had discovered where Miss Bridges kept her breakfast cereals and was happily munching its way through a packet of cornflakes, whilst the fifth and oldest monkey sat next to Miss Bridges who was steering the boat from the front of the cabin.

"I'm so sorry," Nona said apologetically as she chased one of the monkeys who'd grabbed a lipstick off the side and was now wildly smearing it across its face.

"Whatever for?" Miss Bridges laughed, patting her primate co-pilot on the head, "I knew what I was signing up for when I agreed to help you all. Leave them be - they're doing no harm. Let's face it, we've other more pressing matters to contend with..."

"Like what?" Clive asked, sitting down on the bed as the Bonobo monkey who'd previously been rolling on it stopped and sat up, hooking an arm around his shoulder as it swung into his lap grinning wildly.

"Like the river police boat which pulled up to shore not long after we set off," Miss Bridges said, pointing to a black and white television monitor mounted on the roof of the cabin to the left of her head, "that's connected to the CCTV camera on the back of the boat."

Clive and Nona peered at the screen, beyond the waves being caused by their progress, and could just about make out a small boat bobbing about on the water near the zoo wall in the distance.

"What does that mean for us?" Nona asked.

"It depends," Miss Bridges began to reply, "I've no doubt they saw us sail off, so I suspect they may have made note of the boat's name so that they can run checks to see who it's registered to."

"We're done for then," Nona said sadly, slumping on the bed besides Clive and his monkey.

"Not necessarily," Miss Bridges replied without once taking her eyes off the river ahead, "as I've said, I've made a few little upgrades to this old thing - had to during my days as a spy... it's now got a top speed of 50 knots so, depending on what that brother of yours says to the police and how long it takes him to do so, we'll be able to put some distance between us and them."

"But what good is that if they know where we're heading, Miss Bridges?" Nona sighed.

"If we can get to the fortress before they do and get the monkeys off the boat without them seeing us do so, then it'll be his word against ours," the headteacher replied before continuing, "after all, the animals belong to you as well, don't they? They'd then have to go away and get a warrant to legally search my islands. In the meantime, I could then call in a couple of favours from some old friends and get any legal help we might need..."

"Thank you, Miss Bridges," Nona replied, her face now starting to brighten.

"Don't thank me just yet..." Miss Bridges replied, now turning to face her, "police river patrol boats can reach speeds of up to ninety knots, so there's more than enough time for them to catch up with us. Clive, where are the other Zooper Troopers currently?"

"I told them to head back to the minibus and to then meet us at Hoon Island," replied Clive.

"Good – it'll be low tide soon which means that they ought to be able to drive straight across the causeway," Miss Bridges smiled, "call and give them my security codes so that they can let themselves in. Tell them to make their way round to my private jetty at the back of the fortress as we're going to need all the help we can get today..."

Chapter 28 – A Race Against Time

It took Alistair Leadbetter a good fifteen minutes or so to convince the police that they were actually trying to get *into* the zoo again and not *out* of it.

When the police sergeant eventually believed their tall-tale, Lewis Kingston and Alistar Leadbetter, along with John Stafford, who'd been ordered by Lewis to climb the ladder - despite his protests - to join them on the wall, were instructed to crawl along the top of it to the end where the zoo's outer walls met each other nearest the water. On reaching it, the three men found that the police boat had already sent up an extendable rescue ladder for them all to climb down.

"Apologies for the delay, gentlemen, but we had to establish all the facts first," the police sergeant had said when the three men finally joined him on deck as the ladder was retracted back by the constable aboard the police patrol boat.

"Perfectly reasonable and most understandable, Sergeant…?" Leadbetter replied.

"Baxter," Sergeant Baxter replied, adding, "now, you say you believe to know who is responsible for the theft of your animals."

"Yes - their names are Nona and Melanie Lancaster," Lewis ranted, "go send a patrol car to the ramshackle slum they live in Chavsville and arrest the damned lot of them, as well as that mad old Welsh witch of theirs too whilst you're at it…"

"What my client means to say," Leadbetter said softly, placing his hand on Lewis' heaving chest to calm him down, "is that he suspects that Miss Lancaster may have arranged for the removal of some of the zoo's property without his prior knowledge or consent. However, we've no actual, physical proof that she was involved here today though, or at any other time I might add, especially as we only saw a man and a woman lead the monkeys onto the boat and sail off before you eventually arrived today."

"But it's all her doing, I tell you!" Lewis loudly protested.

"That may be the case, sir," Sergeant Baxter said firmly, "but we can only deal with the facts. Now, just to clarify, you say that this man and woman allegedly removed the monkeys, loaded them onto a riverboat and then sailed off with them, is that correct?"

Lewis nodded petulantly as the young police constable rejoined them.

"It must have been the boat which was in the distance just ahead of us as we arrived, Sarge," he said quietly.

"Did you see or note the boat's name or registration number by any chance, Jones?" Sergeant Baxter replied.

"No, Sarge, it was too far ahead to clearly see," PC Jones said, "plus my full attention was on the men on the wall at that point."

"I did – I saw it!" Lewis said excitedly, "The boat's name was Hermes, I saw it written in bold across the back of it as I was hanging from the wall."

"Are you absolutely certain of that?" asked Sergeant Baxter.

"Totally, I remember thinking that it was a stupid name for a boat!" Lewis sniffed.

"Hermes, did you say?" Jones enquired, adding, "I'm pretty sure that's the boat that belongs to Sheila Bridges MBE, the former Olympic athlete and TV celebrity, Sarge."

Sergeant Baxter turned and stared in amazement at the young constable standing beside him.

"How the devil do you know that, Jones?" he asked.

"Well," Jones began to explain, "Hermes was a Greek god, a trickster…on old statues or in artwork he's always shown wearing a pair of winged heeled sandals. Winged heeled…? Runner…? Geddit?"

Sergeant Baxter stood, open-mouthed, shaking his head in complete disbelief.

"That's brilliant deduction, Jones! Truly amazing," he smiled, "we'll make a detective out of you yet, lad!"

"Thank you, Sarge," the young constable grinned.

"You worked out it's Sheila Bridges' boat just from the name of the vessel – remarkable!" said Sergeant Baxter

"Yes, Sarge," Jones proudly nodded, "plus the fact I got called out to her boat earlier this year when one of her dinner parties was getting a little rowdy. She told me why she'd named it Hermes then. I met the Prime Minister there too! She was a bit squiffy and was wearing a pirate's hat - lovely woman though…Shall I radio in to see if Miss Bridges has any other addresses listed other than her river mooring address?"

"Yes, you'd better do that, constable" Sergeant Baxter sighed as Jones disappeared back below deck before turning back to look at Lewis and the others.

"Nice lad - my sister's boy, got him in the force as a favour to his mother..." Sergeant Baxter sighed, "Unfortunately, he's not been blessed with the greatest of criminal minds has our Alan..."

"That's as maybe," Lewis moaned, "but we're wasting precious time here, we should already be after them!"

"How can we chase them if we don't know where they may be heading to, sir?" Sergeant Baxter replied as Jones stuck his head back out of the cabin door.

"Got it, Sarge! Miss Bridges also owns Hoon Island, in the Medway!" Jones said triumphantly.

"There's your answer, sir," Sergeant Baxter said, turning to join the young constable, "You three gentlemen had best come below and buckle yourselves in - it's going to be a pretty bumpy ride if we're to try to catch them up..."

At the exact, same moment that Lewis and the police were setting off to follow Miss Bridges, Nona and the monkeys in the strangest police chase ever, Doyley and Hayley Maguire were desperately trying to negotiate their way through thick traffic across London, the wheels on this particular journey having been set in motion shortly after Lewis Kingston had fired Doyley from the job which had been his life for the previous ten years. The tall Irishman had made his way back to his locker and was emptying the contents of it into a sports holdall when Hayley Maguire had suddenly burst into the room.

"Doyley, I've just seen Toby," she exclaimed, "is it true?"

"It is, doll," he sighed, "Oive been given me marching orders and Oim afraid that he told me to tell yer that yers been fired too."

Maguire smiled and shrugged her shoulders as Doyley continued.

"Oi tought dat yers would be a wee bit more upset than dat, what wit' yer ma an' all?"

"To tell you the truth, I was going to tell him exactly where to stick his job today," Maguire replied, walking over to her own locker, "I had an interview at a small veterinary clinic earlier in the week. They called me this morning to offer me the job, with the chance to eventually become a partner in the practice, if all goes well."

"Well, lookatchew! Oim so happy for yer," Doyley smiled as he cleared out the last of his things before closing and locking the locker door.

"Have you got room in that bag for my things?" Maguire asked.
"Sure ting, doll!" Doyley smiled, "Go get your stuff so dat we can blow dis gaff once an' for all..."

After they'd both said their final goodbyes to all their friends and colleagues at the zoo, Doyley stopped to turn and look back at the kingdom for the last time.
"It's all right," Maguire said, gently stroking his arm, "I feel sad to be leaving too."
"It's not dat," Doyley replied, "it's Elsie - Oive got to say goodbye to the old girl. It ain't right dat Oim leaving her here, der least Oi can do is go and see her one final time. Dat OK wit' yer?"
Maguire nodded and took Doyley's hand.
"Of course it is, Doyley," she smiled, "I'll come with you..."

The two of them found the old elephant wandering around her enclosure sweeping the floor with some brushwood, as though cleaning her bedroom, when they eventually reached the centre of Kingston's Kingdom a few minutes later.
"Dere she is," Doyley smiled as he watched Elsie swing the brushwood, back and forth, "dat's odd though...?"
"What is?" Maguire asked.
"Dat," Doyley answered, pointing at the elephant who was pacing around erratically, "she only ever does dat when she's nervous or upset about sometink."
Upon hearing his voice, Elsie immediately turned to where Doyley and Maguire now stood and began to walk towards them, still holding the brushwood as she raised her trunk high in the air.
"What's wrong, girl?" Doyley called, "What's der matter?"
Elsie continued to move forward, swiftly waving the brushwood from side to side before making a forlorn trumpeting sound as she looked up at Doyley and Hayley, her eyes sad and tear-filled.
"It's as if she somehow already knows that you're leaving her," Maguire said sadly.
"Dat must be it! Oim not wearing me zoo overalls," Doyley replied, looking at the casual clothes he was now wearing, "It's all right, girl, Oil come back and visit yer as often as Oi can."
This failed to pacify the elephant however as she continued to trumpet loudly, adjusting the brushwood in her trunk slightly so that it now pointed directly at Hayley Maguire.

"Looks, she's pointing dat ting at yer now," Doyley said, "she wants yers, to me…"

Maguire looked at the angle of the brushwood held in the elephant's trunk and shook her head.

"No, she doesn't," the young vet replied, "she's pointing it at something above my head…"

Doyley turned and looked in the direction Elsie was indicating and saw that directly behind them, high up on the wall of the zoo restaurant which faced Elsie's enclosure was an old wooden bird box. The Irishman looked at it for a moment before turning back to look at the elephant.

"Is dat what yer pointing at, girl?" he asked.

Elsie trumpeted loudly again and seemed to excitedly bob her head up and down at him.

"Dis day just gets weirder and weirder," Doyley said as he walked towards the wall behind him.

He reached up for the bird box and jumped, but it eluded his grasp, so Doyley looked around and spied a rubbish bin by the pathway. He quickly walked over to the bin, grabbed it and began to drag it over to the wall.

"Doyley - what are you doing?" Maguire asked as the Irishman began to climb up onto the bin.

"For some bizarre reason, Elsie has taken a real dislike to dis ting here…" Doyley said as he carefully balanced on the rounded, plastic rubbish container, "Der least Oi can do before Oi leave is take it down for her if it's bothering her so...'

Behind him, Elsie had quietened again, dropping her trunk to the ground as Doyley gingerly stood on the bin before straightening himself up to peer through the hole in the front of the bird box.

"Just as Oi tought…it's empty, except -" he began to say before stopping.

"Except what?" Maguire asked as Doyley slid the bird box up and off the screws which were firmly holding it in place against the brickwork before carefully turning towards her.

"Will yer take dis a moment whilst Oi gets down, doll?" Doyley asked as he passed the bird box to Maguire before jumping off the bin.

The Irishmen then walked over to his holdall which was resting on the ground by the side of Elsie's enclosure where he'd left it. Maguire peeked through the hole in the front of the bird box. As

Doyley had said, it was empty, save for some old nesting left at the bottom of by its last feathered occupant as well as a small, yellow plastic object with what appeared to be a lens which was attached to the back of it.

"Is that a camera?" Maguire asked, turning to look at Doyley, who was now rummaging around in his bag.

"Yep – looks like a small digital video recorder…ah, der yer are!" Doyley replied, triumphantly producing a screwdriver from his bag before walking back towards her.

"Why does a bird box have a digital recorder in it?" Maguire asked.

"Have yer never noticed dat dere are no birds kept anywhere in der kingdom?" Doyley said, taking the bird box from Maguire, "Mr Kingston loved his feathered friends but refused to put any of dem in cages, preferring dem to fly freely around der park *just as nature intended*' he used to say. Dere's dozens of dese tings scattered all around der zoo, all fitted wit' dese little video recorders inside dem…."

"Why's that?" Maguire asked as she watched Doyley slowly begin to unscrew the back of the bird box, removing one of the badly rusted screws from it as he did so.

"Like Oi said, he loved watching der birds, especially when dey nested and fed dere young," Doyley replied, carefully pulling off the back of the bird box to remove the camera it contained, "every now and den we'd take a random bird box down and watch what had been happening in it over a drop of der good stuff dat he kept in his office…"

The Irishman winked as he pulled open the screen from the side of the video camera and pressed the PLAY button before holding it up to his eyes.

"Well, what can you see?" Maguire asked, standing on tiptoe behind him to try and catch a look.

"Nuttink - it's out of battery," Doyley replied disappointedly before adding, "to be honest wit' yer, Oi haven't given dese tings a second tought since Mr Kingston died as he was the only person who was really interested in looking at dem. Don't feel right lookin' at dem without him being here…"

"I'm sure he'd still want you too," Maguire said, "it would be something to remember him by."

"S'pose yer right," Doyley replied, "it's a shame den dat Oi can't look at dis one though..."

"Were they remotely connected to anywhere else?" Maguire asked.

"Nah, dey ran off batteries...oh yer great dolt, Doyley! Hang on a wee minute..." the Irishman suddenly said, sliding the bottom of the camera off, "Can yer go into me bag and find me torch please."

Maguire searched through the holdall and, upon finding the small flashlight, held it up to show him.

"Unscrew the top of it and pass me der batteries," Doyley said, "are dey AAs?"

"They are."

"Good - pass dem here..."

Doyley took the batteries from Maguire and inserted them into the video camera before sliding the bottom of the battery compartment back into place.

"Here goes nuttink..." he eventually said ad he held the camera back up to his eye.

Slowly, the video recorder whirred into life and went *Ping* as a little green light illuminated on the top of it as Doyley pressed the small *PLAY* button at the side of the screen.

Suddenly, a grainy black and white image appeared, filling the display screen.

"Like you said, Doyley," Maguire sighed, "the bird box hasn't been used for a while by the looks of it. It's a good camera though - look, you can just about make out Elsie walking around her enclosure in the background."

"Well, will yer look at dat..." Doyley smiled, "maybe, it's not been a total waste of time den!"

Smiling broadly, the Irishman pressed the *REWIND* button on the display screen and watched as Elsie moved around again, but this time in reverse and at super-fast speed, day and night rapidly replacing one another, with no sign of any visiting bird being recorded. Occasionally though, images of people walking backwards appeared on screen, as zoo staff and park visitors speedily rewound their way past Elsie's enclosure.

"Stop!" Maguire said suddenly, causing Doyley to instantly hit the *PAUSE* button, "rewind the video a little please, then play it at again normal speed...I think I might've spotted something..."

Silently, Doyley and Maguire watched the short video clip play out before them.

After a minute or two, Doyley pressed the *STOP* button, closed the screen and turned the video recorder off before slipping it into his jacket pocket, swapping it for his mobile phone instead. While Doyley tapped in a number on his phone with his thumb, Maguire sat down on the edge of the pathway, her hand covering her mouth.

As he waited for his call to be answered, the Irishman placed a reassuring hand on Hayley's shoulder, stroking it gently until he heard a woman's voice on the other end of the line.

"Mel? It's Doyley…Where are yer?" Doyley asked, nodding as he listened intently to her reply, "Stay dere – me and Maguire are on our way, we've sometink dat yer all have got to see…."

Behind Doyley and Maguire, Elsie turned and slowly began to move away from the railings, finally dropping the brushwood she'd been carrying for so long that morning.

Eventually, she stopped and closed her eyes as she felt the soft touch of an unseen but familiar hand gently caress her trunk.

Thank you, the wind seemed to quietly whisper in her ear…

Chapter 29 – Landfall

It must have been the motion of the boat swiftly moving through the water that had caused Nona to fall asleep despite the exhilaration she felt in escaping the kingdom.
When she awoke it was with a start sometime later, Nona sitting bolt upright from where she'd dozed off next to Clive on the bed, taking a moment or two to regain her bearings.
"Where are we? What's happened?" she asked, rubbings her eyes so vigorously that they squeaked in their sockets.
"Well, you're still on my boat," Miss Bridges laughed, "however, you'll be pleased to hear that we have now made it to the Thames Estuary."
"How long have I been asleep then?" Nona yawned.
"Oh, for a good half an hour or so - we thought it best to let you and the monkeys rest. Was a bit quieter for the two of us too!" Clive said, winking at Nona.
Sleepily, Nona looked all around her. True enough, the Bonobos were all slumped and snoring in various positions and places around the cabin. She smiled but suddenly caught herself.
"Any sign of Lewis and the police boat?" she asked.
"Oh yes, although it's not fully visible yet, but I know they must be slowly gaining on us," Miss Bridges frowned, "they've also tried to hail me on the radio, but I ignored them."
"How long until we make it to the fortress?" Nona asked urgently.
"About twenty minutes or so – ah, spoke too soon…Look!" Miss Bridges said gesturing up at the monitor.
But Nona had already left her seat and had rushed out through the rear cabin door, Clive giving chase to find her on deck, staring out at the horizon.
"There…" she said, pointing.
Squinting, Clive could just about make out a small blue and white boat in the distance.
"It could be anybody -" he began to say until he saw an occasional blue flash from the top of the patrol boat.
"Yeah, I see it..." he replied, turning back to the hatch to stick his head back through the cabin door, "Can this thing go any faster, Auntie Sheila? We've definitely got company!"
"No," Miss Bridges shouted, adding, "however, with the water

being as choppy as it is currently, the only consolation we have is that whilst they're gradually gaining on us, they won't be able to go at full speed themselves to catch us up - at least that's the hope…"
Nona and Clive turned and made their way back down into the cabin.
"Will we make it back to Hoon Island then before they reach us?" Nona asked anxiously, chewing on her sleeve again.
"I'll do my very best to get us there before they do," Miss Bridges said determinedly, "but it'll be touch and go…"

For his part, Lewis hadn't really had much time to think about the police chase, having spent most of the boat journey with his head hovering over a plastic bucket, his stomach protesting and rebelling against its unexpected 'cruise,' threatening to throw up its entire contents that day.
Will this nightmare never end? Lewis thought to himself as another wave of nausea swept over him, like the waves which were constantly buffeting against the side of the patrol boat.
"I think I can see the Hermes ahead, Sarge," Jones suddenly declared.
Sergeant Baxter pulled a pair of binoculars off the dashboard in front of him and raised them to his eyes.
"Yep, that's it," he nodded, "try hailing them again - see if you can raise them this time."
Baxter turned to look where Lewis, Leadbetter and Stafford sat behind him, all three wearing bright yellow life jackets, causing them to look like a dysfunctional row of minions.
"At least we now know that they're definitely heading to Hoon Island," Sergeant Baxter declared before adding, "Worst case scenario - we detain them there."
Lewis raised his head and wiped a stream of drool from his chin.
"I don't want to wait until they make land," he moaned, "I want you to catch them in the act before they reach the island so put your bloomin' foot down!"
"With all due respect, sir, we're already travelling at over seventy knots. Were you civilians not aboard, then we could, in theory, increase our speed," Sergeant Baxter replied, "However, I have a duty of care to the three of you, so this is the quickest that I am safely prepared to travel at. Rest assured though, we should reach

land when they do though, admittedly, Miss Bridges has caught me a little off-guard with the speed her boat is able to travel at."
"Thank you, Sergeant Baxter, we are most grateful for all your help today," Alistair Leadbetter smiled, before shooting Lewis a look, warning his to say no more.
"I appreciate your understanding, sir," Sergeant Baxter replied being turning back to his young constable, "any luck contacting the Hermes yet?"
"No, Sarge, they are still maintaining radio silence," Jones said, shaking his head.
"Pity…I was hoping this was only going to be a simple family dispute," the sergeant sighed, "maintain our current course and speed, Jones - make sure you don't lose them…"
"Yes, Sarge, I will - I mean, I won't…"

The next twenty minutes proved to be the longest of Nona's young life as she kept ducking in and out of the cabin, desperately checking on the progress of the police boat behind them, hoping, against hope, that it would break off its pursuit of them.
But it hadn't, instead, it was now slowly but surely closing the distance between the two of them, the sight of the patrol boat growing ever larger on the horizon the closer it got to the Hermes. Reluctantly, Nona broke her gaze away from the chasing vessel and looked to the land to the left of her in despair and despondency again. However, hope sprang in her heart as she suddenly realised that there was a large expanse of water between the two land points up ahead of them as she dashed below deck again.
"Is that what I hope it is?" she pleaded.
"Yes dear, we're at the mouth of the Medway," Miss Bridges nodded, "another few minutes and we'll be back on dry land… Clive - phone ahead - make sure they're ready for our arrival when we make landfall. Tell them to also make sure that there's a stiff gin and tonic waiting there for me too…"

"We're gaining on them, Sarge," Jones said as he watched the green boat turn right up ahead of them.
"Indeed, we are though they'll have likely docked by the time we reach them," Sergeant Baxter replied, "still, we'll hopefully arrive not too far behind, meaning that we ought to be close enough to

confirm any illegal cargo they may be carrying with them."
The sergeant then reached down in front of him to produce a loudhailer.
"Let's hope that they don't do anything stupid, mind," he frowned.
"You don't think stealing monkeys and escaping with them by riverboat isn't stupid enough already, Sergeant?" Lewis said sarcastically, still hugging his sick bucket for dear life.
"It's Mr Kingston, isn't it? Sergeant Baxter said as Lewis curtly nodded back at him, "well then, Mr Kingston, let me explain this to you in the simplest of terms - until I am in full possession of the facts, you are not to do anything to hinder nor jeopardise my investigation. Do I make myself perfectly clear?"
"Crystal," Lewis reluctantly replied, lowering his head over the bucket once more...

"Land ahoy!" Miss Bridges shouted as, first, Deadman's Rock then, behind it, Hoon Island clearly came into view.
Nona punched the air in delight at the news but could now see on the monitor above her headteacher's head that the police boat was now close enough for them to see it and its occupants clearly.
"How much further until we reach the jetty?" she asked.
"About a thousand feet," Miss Bridges replied, suddenly cutting the engines of the Hermes.
"Why are we slowing then?" Nona said.
"It's low tide, my dear," Miss Bridges smiles, "must do this last bit slowly and carefully. There's a raft of sandbanks around here I must safely manoeuvre through before we can reach the fortress. One tiny mistake and I could run us aground on any of them..."
"If it's any consolation, Nona," Clive said reassuringly, "if we've had to slow our boat down, they'll have to have done so too..."

"They're slowing!" Lewis shouted, seeing the Hermes reducing its speed ahead of them. "Now's our chance, Sergeant - we can board them before they even reach dry land!"
Sergeant Baxter turned to look at the excitable but unlikeable young man jumping up and down beside him.
"I take it that you don't get out on the water much, Mr Kingston?" the sergeant asked.
"Not if I can help it," Lewis replied, a little colour now returning

to his cheeks.

"These are tidal waters, meaning that we experience tidal fluctuations too," Sergeant Baxter explained, "the Medway is currently at low tide, meaning that whilst we can still travel to Hoon Island, we can only reach it safely by following a small number of tidal water pockets which are trapped here, creating a natural tidal harbour. One mistake though and we could become marooned on any number of those exposed sandbanks. Miss Bridges has the advantage of knowing exactly which way to navigate her boat - all we have to do is patiently follow her."

Lewis opened his mouth to reply but felt a sharp tug on his jacket sleeve.

"Sit down," Leadbetter whispered, "they know what they're doing."

"And what will you do when we get there and discover that I was right about Nona all along?" Lewis sneered.

"If what you say is proven to be true," Leadbetter sighed, "then your sister's share of your grandfather's estate will automatically transfer to you..."

Nona stood close to Miss Bridges as the headteacher carefully steered the Hermes nearer to the island. Through the windscreen at the front of the cabin, Nona could now clearly make out the jetty to the back of the fortress.

"I think our welcome committee is already there waiting to greet us," Miss Bridges said, pointing to a line of people who were excitedly jumping up and down on the jetty, waving their arms high above their heads, "Clive, can you go up top and prepare the mooring ropes for us?"

"Will do," Clive replied, adding, "What do you want me to do about the police in the meantime."

"Nothing – yet…" Miss Bridges replied, "I reckon we'll have a couple of minutes to get the monkeys off the boat before they pull up alongside us. That should give me just enough time to stall them."

"Then what, Miss Bridges?" Nona asked.

"That, my dear, is the sixty-four-million-dollar question…"

As the Hermes drew closer to the jetty, Miss Bridges began to reverse the engines to bring the boat to a stop. Mel, Lawrence and the others waited nervously as Clive, mooring rope in hand, stood at the back of the riverboat.

"Hurry!" Mel cried, now seeing the police patrol boat relentlessly closing in on them.

Clive nodded and threw her the first mooring rope, running to the front of the boat as he did so, Lawrence Light mirroring his run on the jetty, eventually catching the second rope thrown to him.

"Pull us into the side," Clive shouted urgently, "then, when we're next to the jetty, lash the ropes tightly around the mooring posts on either end."

Luca and Marilyn grabbed the rope Mel held, Keeley and Sue doing likewise with Lawrence's as the six of them quickly pulled the boat to shore, it gently bumping against the rubber bumper on the jetty wall as it safely came to rest against it. Clive immediately jumped off the boat and took the rope off Mel to tightly fasten it around the mooring post, before checking that the knot Lawrence had made was as equally secure.

"We're going to need a hand to get all the monkeys off the Hermes before the police arrive," Clive said, running back onto the boat, closely followed by Mel, Luca and Keeley where they met Nona at the cabin door. Mel stopped to give her daughter a brief hug, before following her down into the cabin.

"They're almost here!" Marilyn screamed as first Mel, then Nona emerged from the cabin, both holding a sleepy Bonobo in their arms before running across the deck to jump back onto the jetty.

By now, the police patrol boat was nearly beside the Hermes as Luca, Keeley and Clive quickly followed with the three remaining monkeys they each carried, rapidly chasing after Mel and Nona, who'd started to run up the small, stone steps which led to the fortress courtyard as Sergeant Baxter stepped onto the deck of the patrol boat with his loudhailer in hand.

"Police! Stop!" he shouted, but to no avail as the five monkey-smugglers ahead of them disappeared through the gateway into the safety of the fortress.

Miss Bridges slowly climbed out of the cabin and casually made her way off the boat to join Sue, Marilyn and Lawrence on the jetty as the police boat drifted toward the far end of it.

"What can I do to help you, officer?" Miss Bridges called as Constable Jones jumped onto the jetty - rope in hand – to quickly tie off the patrol boat.

Sergeant Baxter, followed by Lewis, Leadbetter and Stafford,

stepped off the police boat to stand before Miss Bridges.
"Miss Sheila Bridges MBE, I presume?" the sergeant asked.
"The one and only!" Miss Bridges replied, her hands defiantly propped on her hips, "As I said, how may I help you?"
"Don't act the innocent!" Lewis snarled, "I want my damned property back!"
"Mr Leadbetter," Sergeant Baxter said, looking at Lewis, "please can you muzzle your pit-bull and put him back on his leash whilst the grown-ups talk?"
Sighing, Sergeant Baxter turned back to face Miss Bridges.
"As you can see, Miss Bridges," the sergeant said, smiling, "Mr Kingston here is quite upset – he is accusing you of stealing some of his animals from the zoo."
"Stealing animals! How very dare he!" Miss Bridges replied defiantly, "I can assure you, officer, that I've never stolen anything in my life! Is that not so, Mr Light?"
"Yes, Miss Bridges," Lawrence answered, protectively standing beside her, Marilyn and Sue also in close attendance.
"Then perhaps you could please explain to me why your boat was seen outside of Mr Kingston's Zoo earlier today?" Sergeant Baxter asked calmly.
"The last time I looked, officer, it was a free country!" Miss Bridges replied.
"True, but you can't *freely* take monkeys from a zoo without the owner's express permission now, can you?" Sergeant Baxter replied, leaning close to Miss Bridges' ear before whispering, "Look, I know he's a sad specimen of a man, but I saw the monkeys being taken into your property with my own eyes. If he hasn't given you, or the gentleman you were with, authority to do so, I'll have no option but to arrest you both on suspicion of theft."
"But technically, we didn't need his permission, officer..." Miss Bridges sighed, "Look, you seem like a reasonable chap - do I have your word that you'll keep that odious little toad under control whilst we try to sensibly and rationally explain this whole sorry situation to you?"
"You do, ma'am," Sergeant Baxter nodded.
"Then you'd best come with me," Miss Bridges smiled as she turned to walk into the fortress...

Nona, Keeley and Luca were happily playing a makeshift game

of *Tag* with the Bonobo monkeys with Mel and Clive tiredly looking on as the gate to the jetty opened and Miss Bridges purposely walked through it. Clive looked at Mel and smiled broadly before turning back to look at his aunt.

"I take it that the old Sheila Bridges charm work-" he began to say before stopping abruptly on seeing a thick-set uniformed figure enter the courtyard close behind her, followed by three formally dressed men, one of whom he instantly recognised as Lewis Kingston.

"What's going on?" asked Clive as he watched the rest of his friends follow them as another police officer brought up the rear.

"It's all right, dear," Miss Bridges said reassuringly as the children and monkeys all stopped what they were doing and huddled together, "Sergeant Baxter here would like to get to the bottom of all this and is prepared to listen to what we have to say in our defence."

"See - I told you that she was behind all this!" Lewis shouted, jabbing his finger in Nona's direction as he began to walk towards her, only for Mel to step in front of him to block his way.

"You'd better keep away from my daughter if you know what's good for you," Mel snarled, staring up at the taller man.

"Try and stop me..." Lewis growled defiantly.

"If she doesn't stop you, then I will," Lawrence quietly said before quickly moving to stand beside Mel.

Lewis eyeballed Lawrence, trying to intimidate him but the young teacher stood firm, unfazed by the gesture.

"Gentlemen - I suggest you both calm down immediately," Sergeant Baxter said firmly.

Lewis put his hands up to either side of him and stepped back. "As you wish officer, but as you can see, I'm the one who has been wronged here," Lewis said smugly, "they've stolen from me, taken my property from my premises without my consent. That, in my books, is theft at the very least..."

"Property?" Nona screamed, lunging towards Lewis, her angry progress only stopped by Mel's outstretched arm, "They ain't anyone's property, they're living, breathing beings. You don't care about them, only what they're worth to you!"

"That's as maybe, but you still took them without my consent or permission!" Lewis hissed.

"Is that correct, Miss?" Sergeant Baxter asked, stepping forwards to try to defuse the situation.

"Yes, but we had to," Nona replied, "he doesn't care about the animals - he's only interested in making as much money as he can out of them."

"It still doesn't give you the right to take things which don't belong to you, Miss," Sergeant Baxter said.

"But technically, they do," Mel interrupted, "Mr Kingston here is her brother-'

"Half-brother!" Lewis angrily corrected.

"Whatever…" Mel replied, carrying on regardless," their grandfather, Roger Kingston, left each of them half of his zoo when he died earlier this year."

Sergeant Baxter frowned and turned to look at Lewis.

"Well, that does changes matters somewhat," he frowned.

"How does it?" Lewis gasped, "It's not just today that they've stolen from me - animals have been disappearing for weeks!"

"We've only been taking them out of the zoo because you've secretly been selling them off - pretending that they've died naturally!" Nona argued.

"Really?" Lewis scoffed, "And what proof do you have of such a bizarre and preposterous notion?"

"Doyley told me!" Nona replied.

"Oh - would that be the same Mr Doyle who I fired today for gross misconduct? I wouldn't believe a single word that man has to say for himself!" Lewis scoffed, looking at Alistair Leadbetter for his approval, "And as to the death of any of the kingdom's animals, they've all been confirmed and certified by a highly respected and reputable source in Doctor Au. Isn't that correct, Mr Leadbetter?"

All eyes fell on the old solicitor who uneasily shuffled beside him.

"That is indeed correct," Leadbetter replied before adding, "I have conducted an independent audit just this morning and found there to be a satisfactory level of paperwork confirming the deaths of the animals reported to have died recently…"

Lewis Kingston stared smugly at Nona as the solicitor continued.

"However, there also appears to be a rather considerable number of animals who are either missing or unaccounted for…"

"Which my dear *sister* has just confirmed that she and her friends have been removing from the kingdom," Lewis tutted, "without both my prior knowledge or agreement."

"Is that correct, Miss?" Sergeant Baxter asked, now making notes

in his notebook.
Suddenly, Nona realised Lewis had cleverly caught her out and immediately fell silent, Mel wrapping a consoling arm around her.
"Technically, yes," Leadbetter said quietly, "however, there's been no real criminal offence committed here, Sergeant, has there?
"What do you mean, I -" Lewis began to argue before the police officer raised a hand towards him.
"Mr Kingston, I believe the gentleman was speaking to me!" Sergeant Baxter said, more forcibly this time, "No, I'm inclined to agree, sir. What it does appear to be though is an unfortunate family disagreement and a dispute which could and should have been handled a whole lot better without the need for the police to ever become involved in proceedings."
Defiantly, Nona made to reply, but Mel gently squeezed her hand to stop her, knowing that no victory was to come from her saying anything else.
"Yes, please accept my sincerest apologies for the misunderstanding, Sergeant Baxter," Leadbetter replied before turning to look back at Nona, "however, it does pain me to say, Miss Lancaster, that as you've admitted you've been been removing animals without your brother's consent or permission, you have unfortunately broken the terms of your grandfather's will…"
Lewis clapped his hands excitedly and hugged John Stafford, who was shocked by this public show of affection from his employer before Lewis broke away from the accountant to stand smugly glaring at Nona and Mel once again.
"But I was only trying to rescue the animals from *him*!" Nona cried, "It's not fair - you can't let him get away with this!"
"I'm sorry, Miss Lancaster but I've really no choice - it's your word against Mr Kingston's and on the balance of evidence I've seen today supports your brother's version of events more than yours…" Alistair Leadbetter sadly sighed, "Therefore, by the terms of your grandfather's last will and testament, your unauthorised actions means that your share of Kingston's Kingdom will now automatically pass to-"
But the sudden sound of an engine and the continuous honking of its horn prevented Leadbetter from completing his sentence as a motorcycle and sidecar hurtled through the open fortress gates

before speeding towards the group of people who were gathered there, causing the Bonobo monkeys to disperse in panic towards the thick shrubbery at the far side of the courtyard.

"Whatever next...?" Sergeant Baxter sighed in exasperation as the motorcycle screeched sideways before coming to an abrupt halt, kicking up dust and gravel as it did so.

Nona watched in stunned silence as Doyley turned off the engine and stepped off his motorcycle, Hayley Maguire clambering out of the sidecar beside him as raised the visor on his helmet and marched determinedly toward where Nona and the others stood open-mouthed at his dramatic arrival.

"Oh, this day just keeps getting better and better..." Lewis laughed, clapping his hands together, "Mr Leadbetter - please allow me to introduce you to two more members of Nona's band of merry men - Mr Doyle and Miss Maguire, aka Tweedledum and Tweedledumber!"

"Doyley – please tell Mr Leadbetter what Lewis and Doctor Au have been doing with the animals?" Nona pleaded as the former zookeeper and little veterinarian approached her.

"Nona," Leadbetter sighed, "as I've already said, it's your word against that of your brother... Without any physical evidence to back up and support your claims or accusations -"

"Will dis do yer den?" Doyley said, handing the yellow digital video recorder to the solicitor.

"What's this? Leadbetter frowned, turning the small video recorder, he now held over in his hands.

"Just press *PLAY* and watch it..." Doyley said quietly, "it ought to help yer to decide exactly who's telling der truth around here..."

Chapter 30 – The Truth Will Out

For the first very time since stepping foot on the island, Lewis Kingston suddenly appeared to be more than a little unsure of himself.

"Don't listen to him, Alistair - they're just stalling for time," he urged the solicitor who was stood beside him.

"Maybe," Leadbetter replied, "but I owe it to your sister to at least see what this is."

Lewis made a grab for the video recorder, but Sergeant Baxter's long arm prevented him from reaching it.

"Why so jumpy, sir, if you've nothing to hide?" the sergeant coolly asked.

Lewis raised his hands again in mock surrender and stepped away, biting his lip as Leadbetter struggled to open the video recorder's display screen.

"Please, allow me..." Doyley said as he stepped forward and opened the screen, "Are you ready for dis?"

Leadbetter nodded as Sergeant Baxter inched closer to him, quietly intrigued as to what was on the recorder himself as the Irishman pressed the *PLAY* button and then stepped away from the two men.

After a moment or two the screen filled as it had earlier that day with a black and white image of the pathway in front of Elsie's enclosure. There was no sound and the setting was initially devoid of any life or movement, except for the old pygmy elephant walking into her shelter in the far distance of the image displayed.

"What am I looking for?" Leadbetter asked, raising his glasses to rest them on the top of his forehead as he tried to get a better look at the screen.

"Just yer wait and see..." Doyley sombrely replied.

Suddenly, from the left of the display screen, the unmistakeable figure of Roger Kingston appeared as he slowly began to make his way towards the railings. Leadbetter continued to watch as Kingston leant on the top of them and started to cough, rubbing his chest in the process.

"This does appear to confirm that Mr Kingston was experiencing chest pains, as was first suspected at the time of his death..."

Leadbetter said sadly as he continued to watch the scene which continued to unfold before him.

"Please keep watching," Hayley Maguire urged as Doyley slipped an arm around her shoulders.

Now Leadbetter could see a tall man with a wheelbarrow begin to approach Roger Kingston from his right.

"Is that you, Mr Doyle?" the solicitor asked.

"Yep!" Doyley quietly replied.

Leadbetter continued to watch as the two men captured on film happily chatted for a few moments, Roger Kingston appearing to laugh loudly before the Irishman eventually walked away from him. Kingston then turned back towards the railings and appeared to reach into an inside pocket before putting something in his mouth, coughing again as Elsie appeared from her shelter and began to walk towards him.

Behind Leadbetter, Sergeant Baxter watched intently as Kingston stepped up onto one of the railings' crossbars and waved what was in his mouth at the elephant, again rubbing his chest with his free hand.

"This is when he most probably fell into the enclosure the day of his death..." Leadbetter whispered to Sergeant Baxter.

"Pretty dangerous thing to do, standing on the railings like that," Sergeant Baxter remarked as he continued to watch as the scene unfolded once more, Elsie's trunk appearing in view as Kingston continued to talk to her from above.

Suddenly, in the bushes by the bin behind where Roger Kingston stood, there was movement which caused him to abruptly turn towards them.

"That's odd," Leadbetter muttered as Roger Kingston paused to look at the foliage for a few moments before turning back to the enclosure.

As Leadbetter and the police sergeant continued to watch the video, the others stood silently, daring not to speak, fearing the outcomes that the video may be revealing to the two men.

From the corner of his eye, Lawrence suddenly noticed that Lewis Kingston had moved a few paces away from where Leadbetter and the sergeant stood watching the mysterious, secret recording. Back on the screen, Roger Kingston was still standing on the railings, talking to the elephant. Elsie then turned and was walking away from her owner when there appeared to be more movement in the bushes behind him. Kingston turned his head and appeared to mouth something, running a hand across his brow as, suddenly, a figure burst from the bushes and charged towards him planting both hands squarely against Kingston's back before forcing him over the railings…

"Oh my…" Alistair Leadbetter gasped, swallowing hard as the mysterious figure leant over the railings to look down into the elephant enclosure before eventually turning to casually begin to walk back down the pathway, the figure's face clear for the solicitor, the sergeant and all those who'd watch the video to plainly see…

Slowly, Leadbetter and Sergeant Baxter looked at each other wordlessly as Lewis Kingston suddenly decided to run full pelt, for the gates which led out of the fortress.

"Stop him!" the sergeant shouted as Lewis' shoes kicked up the gravel in his desperate attempt to escape, Nona following close behind with Sergeant Baxter and Constable Jones in hot pursuit.

However, Lawrence Light was already one step ahead of everyone else and had flung himself at Lewis Kingston's legs, catching them perfectly in his arms in a rugby tackle, upending the fleeing man so that he fell - face first - into the ground beneath him.

"Gerrrofffff me!" Lewis snarled and kicked as Lawrence lay on top of him, pinning him down until the two police officers came to relieve him, Sergeant Baxter clamping a pair of handcuffs tightly onto Lewis' wrists before hauling him to his feet.

"Lewis Kingston, I'm arresting you on suspicion of murder," Sergeant Baxter said grimly as he and Constable Jones walked Lewis, blood pouring from his split lip and gashed chin, across the courtyard, back in the direction of their police boat, pausing only to take the video camera from Alistair Leadbetter.

As Nona and the others watched the two police officers disappear with Lewis through the gate which led to the jetty, a stunned and eerie silence hung in the air around them - a silence eventually broken by Nona.

"Murder…?" she gasped, "Lewis killed Grandpa?"

Doyley, Maguire and Leadbetter all nodded sadly as Nona threw herself into her mother's arms, Lawrence walking over to join them, causing Mel to smile slightly as she rested her head against his shoulder whilst Nona sobbed into her chest.

"I can assure you I knew nothing about any of this," John Stafford said unconvincingly as he stood next to Leadbetter, "I'm not proud of what I've done but I had no idea about what part Lewis Kingston played in his grandfather's death."
Alistair Leadbetter stroked his chin and thought for a moment before replying.
"Then tell me one thing, Mr Stafford," the solicitor asked, "is there any truth in what Nona was telling us all earlier…?"

Nona had stopped crying by the time Alistair Leadbetter had walked over to join her and the others who were now chatting to each other in stunned disbelief. Only Luca and Keeley were now absent, having been given permission by Miss Bridges to raid the kitchen in order to keep all the Bonobo monkeys amused until they'd time to rehouse them properly later that night.
"Nona," Leadbetter began to say before turning to her mother, "Miss Lancaster – I'm afraid I owe you both a huge apology for not believing you when you first voiced your concerns about your brother to me. Please can you forgive me?"
Nona looked up at her mother, who smiled weakly back at her.
"It's all right, Mr Leadbetter, looking back I can see how farfetched it must have sounded to you," she said quietly, "if only there'd have been some way then to prove what we know now to be true."
"But if we had Nona," Mel added, "we'd have never discovered what really happened to your grandfather and Lewis would have gotten away with his murder."
Nona nodded sadly before turning towards the tall Irishman who was standing just behind her.
"Thank you, Doyley," she said, hugging him.
"Don't mention it," Doyley smiled sadly, patting her gently on the back.
"Yes, thank you, Mr Doyle," Leadbetter repeated before continuing, "anyway, Mr Stafford has just confirmed to me that there may be some truth in what you say about Lewis and Doctor Au, but won't, as yet, go into more detail for fear of further incriminating himself. However, in the meantime, it is my opinion at least that you have not broken the terms set out in your grandfather's will."
"That's good then," Nona sighed.

"You must be happy about that, aren't you?" Mel said, ruffling her daughter's hair.

"Yeah, of course I am…" Nona replied.

"I can sense a *'but'* here," Lawrence smiled.

"But," Nona continued, "Lewis still owns half of the zoo - it could take us years to prove what he and Doctor Au were doing with the animals."

"True," Leadbetter replied, "however, as was clearly stated in your grandfather's will *'any living creature found to have unnaturally died in Kingston's Kingdom by either Lewis or Nona's hand will mean that person loses their share of the inheritance, it automatically reverting to the other…'"*

"I don't understand how this changes anything though," Nona argued, "like I said, it could take years to prove what Lewis did with the animals he sold…"

"That no longer matters as we now have absolute proof of his guilt, Nona," Leadbetter smiled, shaking his head, "the video Mr Doyle found proves Lewis killed your grandfather and as Roger Kingston was a *'living creature found to have unnaturally died in Kingston's Kingdom'* by Lewis Kingston's own hand…"

Nona gasped as it suddenly dawned on her as to what Leadbetter was trying to say as she looked dumbstruck at her mother.

"Does that mean…" she began to ask.

Mel smiled and nodded as the tears began to fill her daughter's eyes.

"Yes, Nona – it means that the whole of Kingston's Kingdom now belongs to you…"

Epilogue

ANIMAL MAGIC!
FIRST VISITORS SET SAIL FOR NEW WILDLIFE SANCTUARY

A new chapter in the long history of one of London's most unique zoos began yesterday with the official opening of the UK's first safari boat tours.

The brainchild of teenager Nona Lancaster and her mother, Mel Light, Lancaster Land welcomed its first guests to its brand-new purpose-built island homes in the Medway Estuary, Kent.

Nona, 13, of Ventham, London, is the granddaughter of the late entrepreneur Roger Kingston, founder and owner of Kingston's Kingdom back in 1967.

After his untimely and unexpected death last year, Nona, her mother and a dedicated group of friends fought a hard and bitter battle with her half-brother Lewis Kingston, 23, over the future of the zoo and its rare and endangered species.

However, when it then came to light that Lewis Kingston was responsible for the murder of their grandfather, Nona and her mother took full ownership of the kingdom and were free to decide what to do to continue Roger Kingston's legacy.

"Whilst I loved to visit Kingston's Kingdom with Grandpa, it never felt right that the animals should be kept behind bars," Nona explained to this reporter.

"So," added Mrs Light, "thanks to the incredible generosity of Sheila Bridges MBE, we moved every animal we possibly could to a new, purpose-built reserve here in the Medway where they can roam freely."

"Each island," Nona continued, "has been carefully designed so that the species on them can co-exist peacefully whilst being cared for and protected by our wonderful staff."

Funding for Lancaster Land has been achieved by the sale of the site the zoo was originally built on with a government-backed business consortium being successful in their bid for the land. The consortium then met with and agreed to the Lancaster family's conditions of sale, with low cost, affordable housing for low-income local families being built on Kingston's Kingdom.

Today, Lancaster Land is unique in the sense that visitors tour the islands from the outside, initially by boat, seeing the animals roam happily on them, free of fencing, cages and steel bars.

Clive Tilley, 35, head of tour operations explains.

"Each tour last 45 minutes, with our visitors watching the animals roam around in their natural environment," he told this reporter, continuing, "then guests can disembark for a guided tour through the islands, getting up close to several different animals and species such as the Bonobo Monkeys, Red Pandas and, of course, the one and only, Elsie the pygmy elephant!"

But what about funding the rest of the costs associated with running the island, especially as school children can visit it completely free of charge on pre-booked trips?

"The money generated from the sale of the original zoo," explained Mrs Light, "plus a massive and anonymous donation we also received means that Lancaster Land can slowly build and develop itself over the next couple of years with no financial concerns whatsoever until it becomes totally self-sufficient, surviving on the income it generates from ticket sales alone."

Friends who helped Nona and her mother in the early days of their plight have all come on board full-time to ensure that the wildlife park is run both ethically and professionally.

Overseeing the day-to-day care and management of the animals is Alan Doyle, 37, the former head zookeeper at Kingston's Kingdom. His fiancée, Hayley Maguire, 28, the zoo's former assistant vet, has taken on the responsibility of looking after all the animals' various medical needs. Head of public relations and visitor satisfaction is Sue Brightside, 42, whilst Marilyn Henderson, 45, runs the educational centre and gift shop, which is based in the Hoon Island Fortress.

When asked as to what her hopes were to the future, Nona looked at her mother and simply told this reporter, "To make my grandfather proud..."

Based on the evidence of the happy animals wandering freely around it and the laughter and excitement to be heard from its visitors, Roger Kingston would be a very proud man indeed.

For further information on Lancaster Land, or to book a tour, visit www.lancasterland.co.uk

Also by Jonas Lane

Slipp In Time
Grammarticus
The Last of the Unicorns
Slipp, Sliding Away
Poppy Copperthwaite: Spellcaster
Locked Down
Another Time, Slipp!
Dragon Chasers: The Knight School
Nona's Ark
Suped and Duped
There's Many a Slipp!
Wilde and Dangerous Things
Poetic Licence
Poppy Copperthwaite: Spelldemic
Sherwood Holmes: The Great Cake Robbery
A Handbook for Young Writers

All book titles available to purchase from
www.JonasLaneAuthor.com
or by ordering from **amazon.co.uk**

Wilde and Dangerous Things

Little did reporter Mason Adams know when answering the newspaper advertisement about working for a detective living in Baker Street how his life would suddenly and dramatically change forever. However, rather than being employed by the world-famous person he was expecting to meet, Mason instead finds himself working with Cordelia Wilde, a brilliant cryptobiologist, haunted by her past, who hunts monsters for a living...

Soon, Wilde and Mason are joined on their adventures by Jullictte, a young French girl escaping her family, hoping to take control of her future. Before long, they find themselves on the trail of a legendary murderer, their hunt taking them from the dark and deadly streets of the East End of London to the mysterious wilds of Dartmoor...

Secretly watched by those seeking to stop the truth from ever being revealed to the world, will the three young and irregular detectives eventually discover the secrets of the wicked and dangerous things that lurk in the shadows of Victorian England...?

Poppy Copperthwaite
Spellcaster

Born into a community of Majeeks, on her 18th birthday - her *Coming of Mage* – Poppy Copperthwaite finally expected to discover the magical powers buried deep within her in order to claim her birthright and eventually rule her parents' kingdom. Instead, her hopes and dreams are left in tatters when the cruel, fickle finger of fate conspires against her, leaving Poppy desperately hoping to find a way to unlock and unleash her true Majeek potential.

Sent to a magical and mystical foundation, Poppy faces a frantic race against time, whilst taking part in a series of tests and experiments to discover what type of spellcaster she is, under the watchful eye of the spellcialist, Doctor Leopold Harryhausen.

But with the clock ticking and her enemies plotting and conspiring against her, can Poppy and her group of weird and dysfunctional friends - a rude and grumpy boggart, a legendary witch and another teenage Majeek, lost somewhere between time - find a way to let loose the dormant powers trapped within her so that Poppy Copperthwaite can truly become the spellcaster she was always destined to be...?

Grammarticus

'Words - so innocent and powerless as they are...how potent for good and evil they become in the hands of one who knows how to combine them...' – Nathaniel Hawthorne.

When a group of young friends, faced with the very real prospect of failing their impending SATs tests, stumble across a strange old textbook hidden away in the banned section of their school library, they think that they have finally found the answer to all of their problems.

However, soon the mysterious and mischievous tome *Grammarticus* poses more questions than answers, causing chaos when many a word – often spoken in jest - have deadly and dramatic repercussions for the six of them and those who inadvertently cross their paths.

Desperate to right the wrongs that they have unwittingly created, Zach, Shannon, Chelsea-May, Dev, Kadija and Antonio soon find themselves in the ultimate war of words with their evil and dragonesque English teacher, who is hellbent on using the legendary book and its secrets for herself, no matter how grave the consequences may be...

Praise from the readers of Jonas Lane's books

"As an avid reader, I know when I've found something special when I can't pull myself away from a book. I read Slipp In Time in only a few hours and loved every minute of it!"

"Loved it! Great to read a kids' book that has pace adventure and humour…What's not to like about time travel on a sofa! Watch out for *'Hamster Ragu'* and *'pomegranate shootout'*!"

"As an English teacher, this is one I will definitely be reading with my students. Looking forward to the next one…. did I mention the tantalising cliffhanger at the end?"

"A really good adventure of two young children on a journey, including history and good humour. Kids will definitely enjoy this book and with a cliffhanger like that will be eagerly awaiting the next episode and adventure!"

"I bought this book for my 10-year-old daughter. Despite being an avid reader, she always chooses very similar reading styles (cute puppies, girls having sleepovers, blah blah!) Therefore, I wanted to help widen her reading world. Boy did this book fit the brief! Engaging characters and a writing style that made her want a second book immediately! Can't wait for the sequel!!"

"Excellent read from start to finish. Could not stop turning the pages once I started."

"… brilliant for children and teenagers that love an adventure."

"Fantastic book! Bought this for my 11-year-old son to encourage him to read… he loved it and can't wait for more!"

"I bought this for my 9-year-old daughter who loves anything to do with science and time travel! She absolutely loved it and read it in a couple of days. Well written and easy to comprehend and fitting with today's society. Bring on the next one!"

"Bought this book for myself...loved the imagination of the author...would recommend it to anyone who loves to read and put themselves into the story. Look forward to his and my next journey!"

"Fantastic...loved the story and the references to history. Can't wait for the next book to see what's happened. What a cliffhanger!"

"A fantastic read, suited for all ages, with relatable characters and an interesting plot. The book has a brilliant ending that has left me wanting the second instalment already!"

"Amazing and clever storyline that kept my 8-year-old daughter (and us!) hooked!! What a cliffhanger at the end! Cannot wait to read the next one and really hope there will be more."

"Bought this book for my seven-year-old son. He really enjoyed it, as did I! Believable characters, funny situations with good links to real events in history. We are both looking forward to the next Slipp story!"

"A lovely story, cleverly written. Once you start to read it you can't put it down."

"Brilliant...This should be rated six stars!"

"Really enjoyed this, suitable for all ages, needs to be a film!"

"...most writers write in a similar way, but Jonas Lane doesn't...that's what makes his books unlike any others."

"My 13-year-old is dyslexic and has read very few books from cover to cover but he read all this one, so thank you for this book being accessible for all, looking forward to the next one."
"A fantastic read, suited for all ages, with relatable characters and an interesting plot. The book has a brilliant ending that has left me wanting the second instalment already!

"Captivating...Just finished reading this novel with my 6-year-old. We loved it and it had her gripped throughout. Loved how the ending left us wanting more. Fortunately, we have the second novel to hand ready to start straight away!

"A very good read for children and adults. Includes time travel, humour and history. I will recommend this book and I think it'll encourage more children to read."

"I would recommend this book to all teachers as I was able to help develop and then read stories that my class were very proud of writing."

"Fantastic easy read story for all ages, adventure and history all in one. Ends with a great cliffhanger can't wait for the next adventure."

"Once again Jonas Lane hasn't disappointed with his well-balanced mix of humour and history. The easy-to-read style of these brilliant books means that my youngest daughter now is wanting to join in. Hopefully, the next one is in the pipeline, so we can all have one each!!!!"

"A heartwarming story full of humour, excitement and morality. Written in a dynamic rhythm that keeps you willfully entranced!"

Thanks to all those that have left such wonderful comments.

Authors and writers live or die by the reviews given by their readers. Please take a moment to share your opinions and leave a review by visiting the site that you purchased this book from.

Alternatively, visit Jonas at his website as he would welcome your feedback.

Printed in Great Britain
by Amazon